From the Ground Up

From the Ground Up

A JOURNEY
TO REIMAGINE
THE PROMISE
OF AMERICA

HOWARD
SCHULTZ

with Joanne Gordon

RANDOM HOUSE | NEW YORK

From the Ground Up is a work of nonfiction.
Some names and identifying details have been changed.

Published in the United States by Random House,
an imprint and division of Penguin Random House LLC, New York.

RANDOM HOUSE and the HOUSE colophon are registered trademarks of
Penguin Random House LLC.

Hardback ISBN 9780525509448
International edition ISBN 9781984854841
Ebook ISBN 9780525509455

Printed in the United States of America on acid-free paper

randomhousebooks.com

2 4 6 8 9 7 5 3 1

First Edition

Book design by Susan Turner

To my wife, Sheri, who taught me what it truly means
to live with compassion and love.

CONTENTS

PREFACE   ix

Part One   Beginnings

CHAPTER 1   Conflicted   3

CHAPTER 2   Connection   10

CHAPTER 3   A Different Kind of Company   18

CHAPTER 4   In the Mud   36

CHAPTER 5   Powerless   49

CHAPTER 6   Dysfunction   56

Part Two   Intention and Reinvention

CHAPTER 7   The Dignity of Work   75

CHAPTER 8   Better Angels   88

CHAPTER 9   Duty   101

CHAPTER 10   This Is Not Charity   115

CHAPTER 11   Unintended Consequences   125

CHAPTER 12   Role and Responsibility   142

CHAPTER 13   For Love of Country   157

CHAPTER 14   A Promise Made   163

CHAPTER 15   A Promise Kept 170

Part Three   Bridging Divides

CHAPTER 16   Discuss   189

CHAPTER 17   The Third Rail in the Third Place   204

CHAPTER 18   Rethink the Possible   218

CHAPTER 19   Start Somewhere   235

CHAPTER 20   Share Your Blanket   246

CHAPTER 21   Gumption   262

CHAPTER 22   Filial Piety   269

CHAPTER 23   Welcoming Places   286

CHAPTER 24   Accountable   301

CHAPTER 25   A Better Version of Us   316

EPILOGUE: OUR CLIMB   331

ACKNOWLEDGMENTS   337

PHOTOGRAPH CREDITS   341

INDEX   345

PREFACE

The stairwell was where I went to escape.

Most people in the apartment building used the elevator, unless it broke down. Even when it did, no one walked up the steps that led to the roof. So that's where I sat.

On some days Billy, my best friend, joined me. But mostly I sat alone when things got too chaotic at home. My bedroom, which overlooked a parking lot, wasn't an option—I shared it with my younger sister and brother—and our apartment was so small and my parents' voices so loud that even under my bedsheets I couldn't escape. But sitting on those steps, I felt safe. That place was my refuge. An urban nest.

The stairwell wasn't quiet. I could still hear people arguing, or heavy doors slamming shut, or the thunder of other kids pounding up or down the steps on lower floors. Noise bounced off the hollow hallways' concrete walls and echoed in my ears. But in that stairwell I found some peace. And while sometimes I cried, I mostly thought about playing basketball, or the Yankees—and the possibility of my becoming a switch hitter like Mickey Mantle. As I got older I sat on those steps and fantasized about leaving home, trying to picture life beyond the borders of childhood. Images were hard to summon but I knew what I wanted to feel. I wanted to shed the anxiety that could ripple through me when I turned the doorknob to apartment 7G.

I was three years old when we moved into the cramped two-bedroom apartment in the Bayview housing projects in Canarsie, located on a swath of former swampland on the southeastern edge of Brooklyn. In 1956, my family was one of more than one thousand low-income households that qualified to live in the freshly baked brick buildings constructed by the New York City Housing Authority. It was a new alternative to the decaying city slums. Projects like Bayview were not designed to be dead ends, but to jump-start lives. I wasn't so sure what that meant for me. Over the years, my mom tried to instill in me the notion that there was something better beyond Canarsie and within my reach, but it was hard to see. What I did see, every day, was my dad, who spent so much time lying on our couch that my mother nicknamed him Mr. Horizontal. The scent of his malaise and frustration—with himself, with us, with bosses I never met, with a system I didn't understand—seeped into the fabric of our family's life.

In the stairwell, I created a little distance between me and the suffocating air of home. Sitting on the cold, hard steps shrouded in dim light, I felt some peace. But I struggled to see past the concrete walls around me.

Canarsie, Brooklyn, was, and still is, the last stop on the L train from New York City. As I sat in the stairwell, the idea of what might lie beyond my small world began to take shape in my imagination.

Throughout my life I have been haunted, and fueled, by childhood memories. From my father, I saw what can happen to a life when a person's dignity is stripped away. From my mother, I was imprinted with the belief that the last stop on the train was not going to be the last stop in my life—that I could work and learn and plan and dream my way out of the place I was born into.

The juxtaposing forces of a father who had less than he wanted and a mother who wanted more for her son spurred me, eventually, to imagine a different future for myself. To see my world not as it was, but as it could be. This became a lifetime habit. And in some ways, that's the story I've tried to tell in this book: how we can all reimagine a better future by learning from the past with as much clarity and wisdom as we can muster, and by summoning the will and doing the work to bring that future into being. This has been my life's journey.

The stairwell was the first place where my imagination took flight, but not the last. When I began my own business in the mid-1980s, I was inspired by old, even ancient, influences: coffee, which has been consumed for centuries, as well as the human need for connection and community, which is embedded in our DNA. I envisioned a different way to bring those things together: Starbucks stores. When I opened my first espresso bars, I wanted to create places where people could escape the chaos of the day and feel a sense of belonging. More than forty years later, going to Starbucks has become routine and respite for millions of people across more than seventy-seven countries. Not home, not work, Starbucks stores have become known as a "third place."

For me, the idea of a "third place" is not just something that exists between four walls. It is a mind-set. A way to exist in the world. That's why I set out to build a profitable business that also expressed a core ethos: that people of all kinds can come together and uplift one another.

In that respect, aspects of the Starbucks journey reflect aspects of the American journey. Not because the country is a business, but because the business of the country has always been a constant struggle to balance the seemingly competing priorities of humanity and prosperity. I fiercely believe that Starbucks attempts to be a different kind of company—one that my own father, a working class laborer, never had a chance to work for—are worth sharing at this fragile yet auspicious moment in our country's history, when truth and dignity need to make a thunderous comeback.

In a sense, these pages are less about Starbucks and my childhood than about the place in which we were both born: the United States of America. The intertwined narratives of my youth and my final years at Starbucks tell a bigger story. It's a story about reinvention and renewal. About possibilities. About the power of people to change the lives of others as well as their own. It's a story about what we can do for our-selves and for each other, as well as the responsibility we all have to reimagine our shared future. And reimagine we must.

Ideals that our nation was founded on, including equality and lib-erty for all, have yet to be fully realized. In some corners, their very existence is being threatened. The continuation of American democ-racy also is not a foregone conclusion. In fact, the American Dream that I have lived and still believe in—the notion that everyone should have an equal opportunity to rise from the ground up—is at a cross-roads. More people need to have a fair chance at their dreams, however humble or ambitious those dreams may be, and now is the time to talk about what those chances might look like for everyone. Together, we have the potential to reimagine and deliver on the promise of our country, as I hope this book reveals.

Ultimately, I wrote *From the Ground Up* because I am optimistic about the future and I wanted to share what I've learned from the past. While not a memoir, it is an honest reflection about how my earliest experiences—some of which I've never made public until now—pervaded and informed the life I led once I got out of the stairwell and headed west, beyond everything I knew, in search of what I imagined was possible. And while this is also not a business book, it is a behind-the-scenes exploration of one business's journey to try to answer a vital question of our time: What can we do to effect meaningful change and create the just, fair, and secure future we all desire?

I hope *From the Ground Up* will spark something in you, perhaps even inspire a movement, to embrace all that is right with our country, face what needs to be fixed, and discover how we might use our vast resources and individual assets in new ways to lift ourselves and one another to greater heights. Not just by deploying our money, time, and voices, but by unleashing expertise, ingenuity, influence, empathy, so-cial networks, collaborative spirit, courage, technologies, as well as transforming our common physical and virtual spaces into places where people can connect with civility and respect. None of us exists in isolation. Healthy, happy communities rely on the interdependence of their members. We are in this together.

Sometimes it's hard to see beyond what's in front of us, especially when chaos clouds the view. The will and ability to reimagine the future is at the heart of this country's beginning, as well as a concept that crept into my consciousness when I was just a boy. Why I grabbed hold of this idea, and how it manifested itself over the years, are parallel stories I'm finally ready to tell.

PART
ONE

Beginnings

CHAPTER 1

Conflicted

Our memories of our parents are incomplete scrapbooks. As children, we're only privy to slices of the lives that our mothers and fathers lead. What happens out of earshot or beyond view is as invisible as air, so the person behind the parent often remains a mystery.

And yet their full effect as human beings is potent. Our parents imprint upon us values and ideas, desires and behaviors. As I've looked back on my own youth to connect the dots between past and present, the scenes that stand out chill and comfort. I can see how my own decisions—for myself, for my loved ones, and for Starbucks—have been shaped by two people I never really knew.

When I was a grade-school kid, my heart would beat faster whenever I opened the door to our apartment. If I saw the kitchen table covered with a sheet and more than the usual five chairs crowded around it, I knew our already-cramped home would soon be taken over by Nana's bossy voice, the pungent smell of borscht, and the boisterous laughter of strangers.

On those evenings, my father, Fred, would come home from whatever job he had at the time and lie on the couch while my mother fed my younger sister, my baby brother, and me an early dinner. Then she would send us off to bed—the three of us shared one room—and remind us to be quiet and to keep the door shut. In her voice and eyes, I could hear and see a calm resignation. She wanted the night to end as much as I did.

After we were put to bed, I'd sometimes get up and poke my head out of our bedroom door, or sneak a peek into the kitchen to take in the unfolding scene. At around 8 P.M. the cast of characters would begin invading our home. They arrived in packs of two and three, shedding worn coats onto the plastic-covered living room couch if it was winter, and shuffled to our kitchen, where they plunked into chairs and lit up the first of the night's cigarettes. For hours this motley crew grumbled, gambled, cackled, and, on some nights, slurped the chicken soup that Nana would make from a freshly butchered bird.

These raucous poker games could happen several nights a week. During Brooklyn's humid summers, the men sat around in their worn-out undershirts, bits of hard-boiled egg collecting in their stubble. The ladies, some of whom showed up with rollers tucked under headscarves, would shrug right out of their housedresses and sit in their girdles and cotton bras, fanning themselves against the heat with their playing cards. Hard-edged chatter filled the apartment as the players yelled over and at each other. I would stare in frozen, wide-eyed wonder at how our family's kitchen had been turned into a backdrop for this rough-and-tumble Brooklyn crew. The hum of their unfiltered banter now filled our small apartment, a shift from the more common in-stances of icy silences and adult arguing. For me the effect was disori-enting. Clearly these adults were having some kind of raucous fun. For them, it was a cheery night out, a break from workaday lives, a change in scenery from their own homes, a chance to win some cash. But their brand of fun coated me in discomfort. Sensing that my parents were not eager hosts, but subservient to the chief, my nana, I felt diminished in my own home, driven to the margins as I retreated back to my room. But even then the fast patter of a fresh shuffle would reach me under the sheets that I pulled over my head, letting me know the night was far from over.

"Ante up, suckers!"

The volume rose by the hour and by the drink.

"Full house beats three of a kind."

"You gonna call, Breshafski?"

"Kiss my ass, ya shiksa!"

"Hey, get me another rum and Coke."

Someone on a losing streak would curse the deck for their bad luck, and I might hear a metal chair slide across the linoleum and hit the stove and then a storm of footsteps moving toward our bathroom, where players relieved themselves next to the sink where I brushed my teeth.

The pack sat in our kitchen as if it was their private club, and in a way it was. Each person had to pay to play. The fee included a chair at the table and a meal. Once hunkered down, they followed their own rules and rituals.

My mom and dad served as the party's hired hands, and if the games got contentious the players could take out their frustrations on them. Some directed obscenities at my mom as she delivered heaps of food on our family's plates and refilled our milk glasses with liquor. My parents took it. They were subordinate to the paying customers—and to Nana. My grandmother was, unequivocally, the boss. She could be nasty and abusive, barking at my father and hurling insults at my mother that no daughter, or grandson, should ever have to hear. But I heard it all.

Eventually I would fall into a restless sleep and at some point the house would fall quiet again. When I wandered into the kitchen the morning after, I'd find empty chairs askew and a room that reeked of smoke. I'd eat my cornflakes next to ashtrays filled with cigarette butts. My mother was always awake, too, and she'd pack me a lunch, which I carried as I groggily joined the streams of kids who, I assumed, had slept soundly in apartments more peaceful than my own. I never knew when the poker players would return—at least not until the next time I opened the door to our apartment and saw the kitchen furniture rearranged.

My maternal grandmother, Lillian, started hosting the illegal card games after she and my Poppy, Woolf, divorced. For years Nana made a living running the games out of her modest house in East New York and eventually from our apartment, too, where she gathered a revolving cabal of players. Once assembled, they would gamble their meager paychecks, government subsidies, or the cash my grandmother lent to them, for which she charged high interest.

Nana was bank and hostess. She arranged for her customers to be picked up by a driver, who was often my father. While bets were placed, a hired waitress—or, more often, my mother—served the drinks and home-cooked food. Sometimes Nana sat in on the games, but even if she didn't she walked away the biggest winner because she took a cut of each pot. At the end of the night, my father would chauffeur the players, who were almost certainly drunk, back home.

On nights the card games were held at my nana's house, my parents left my sister, Ronnie, baby brother, Michael, and me alone for hours while they performed their duties.

Nana's customers were not rich, but the gathering was worth the price each paid to be part of it. For them, the card games were serious entertainment. For my grandmother, they were business. For me, they were traumatic.

When the games were at our apartment, I never felt in physical danger, but I also didn't feel safe. I was a skinny boy with brown hair and a wide smile who relied on manners more than muscle to get by. In the projects, I realized early on that my best defense was a good offense: being well behaved and well liked, and trying to keep control. I was like many kids, especially those from volatile circumstances: because of my feelings of vulnerability and powerlessness, I was drawn to order and stability. I gravitated to things that seemed to be missing at home, like predictability and transparency and kindness, especially from adults. That was the way I wanted life to be, the normal way I thought it should be. The card games violated that ideal. The experience overwhelmed me with anxiety and shame. I only hoped no one else would find out about our abnormal home.

Trying to keep it hidden from other people, including my friend Billy, who lived across the hall, was exhausting. If anyone asked me about the late-night hoots and howls coming out of our apartment, or the strangers who spilled into the hallway at odd hours, I was stricken with embarrassment.

In my later years, I found out that my parents hosted Nana's card games to make money. Nana paid them to be her waitress and chauffeur. But I didn't know all that then. My parents never explained anything to me. *Just go to your room, Howard, shut the door, be quiet.*

My father never completed high school and spent his working life ricocheting between odd, low-paying jobs. He had few if any employable skills aside from driving. And while there is dignity in a day's labor, no matter how simple or technical, my father didn't derive any sense of pride or purpose from his work. "Daddy's tired, let him sleep," my mother cautioned if we approached when he was lying on the couch. But even when he was awake, he was closed off and unapproachable, masked by fatigue. At some point in his past, the man my nana called "a bum" had been stripped of ambition and will. It was as if life itself seemed to tire him out.

My father also spent more money than he had. Even though we lived in subsidized public housing where the rent was less than one hundred dollars a month, my dad was always short. He'd buy used tires for his car at the junkyard, but then treat himself to a manicure and pricey haircut. Arguing over money at the kitchen table while counting the leftover cash from his slim paychecks, sketchy loans, and assorted off-the-book income sources, including the card games, was a contentious ritual for my parents that I tried to avoid. Luckily, I had my stairwell retreat.

I also tried to avoid my father's temper. He was quick to yell at Ronnie, Michael, and me, and it wasn't uncommon for him to whack me or, occasionally, improvise other forms of physical punishment. One night at dinner he shoved my face into a plate of steaming spaghetti.

The ringing telephone was another source of anxiety. The sound of the clanging rotary box hanging on the wall could stiffen my wiry frame. My mother often had me answer the phone for her, in case it was a bill collector. "Sorry, my parents aren't home," I'd say as one or both of them looked at me. I'd hang up, ashamed of the lie. Later, when my parents sent me to borrow money from people we knew, I did so with my head lowered, ashamed of the truth.

I feared my father and at times I loathed him because of how his behavior made me feel. But there were also moments when, even as a kid, I could sense his pain.

I was seven years old on a cold winter day in 1961, in the middle of a snowball fight behind our building, when my mother leaned out the window of our seventh-floor apartment and waved wildly for me to come home.

"Dad had an accident," my mother told me when I came running into our apartment. "I have to go to the hospital."

My father's job at the time had been driving a truck, delivering clean cloth diapers to people's homes—and picking up the dirty ones. For months he'd been coming home from work complaining about the odor and the mess. Sometimes I'd get a whiff of what he was talking about from his clothes. He said it was the worst job in the world and I believed him.

On that wet, slippery winter day, he was making deliveries when he fell on a sheet of ice. The fall broke his hip and his ankle. For the next month, every time I opened the door to our apartment I saw my father sprawled on our couch, his five-foot, eight-inch frame immobile, imprisoned in a cast. His fingers clung to a Marlboro cigarette, and his handsome face was fixed in a pained grimace.

In America in the 1960s, an uneducated, unskilled worker like my dad who got hurt on the job was typically dismissed without notice. The accident left my father with no income, no health insurance, no workers' compensation, and because my parents had no savings, they had nothing to fall back on. My mother couldn't get a job; at the time of the accident she was seven months pregnant with Michael. If not for a local charitable organization, Jewish Family Services, my family would have run out of food.

In years since, I've tried to imagine the situation from my father's point of view. How did being trapped inside the cast, the victim of an accident, shift his view of life? He had enough sense of responsibility for his growing family to take on the "worst job in the world" to support us. But what did he get for it? Abandonment by the company whose work broke him. Maybe that incident tipped the scale, and a man who thought he had a sliver of a chance to make something of his life discovered, during a long, cold winter, that one slip-up can lead to purgatory. I'll never know what was going through his mind and heart at that moment. But the sight of my helpless father slumped on the couch wedged itself into my consciousness forever.

In the years following his accident, my home life became even less inviting. The stairwell wasn't my only sanctuary. My other refuge was the playfield of the projects. On its concrete grounds, I discovered a hard-edged paradise of possibilities and belonging.

CHAPTER 2

Connection

My apartment was shrouded in a fog of anxiety and shame, but I had a wholly different experience outside. The playgrounds and ball fields of the projects were where I found myself.

On summer days and weekends, or in the marvelously empty hours between school and dinner, hundreds of kids living in Bayview would push through the metal-and-glass front doors of our buildings and spill out into our thirty-three-acre backyard, where we came together in unsupervised packs for rounds of stickball, spitball, punchball, slap ball, or ring-a-levio. But skelly may have been my favorite.

Under the hot summer sun—Bayview's young trees weren't yet tall enough to cast the shade they were planted to provide—we'd crouch on bony knees and, with crinkled foreheads and squinting eyes, try to calculate the ideal force required to flick a flattened bottle cap into one of the thirteen painted boxes of skelly's asphalt game board. The player with the most on-target flicks won. For an edge, I'd use my mother's oven to melt crayons into our dented bottle caps. Wax gave the caps more weight so they were easier to control, and the wins we racked up were worth my mother's anger when she found stains of color in her oven.

For hours my friends and I huddled together, our sticky arms touching, oblivious to the onion scent of our kid sweat. With each flick we called each other out. When someone was declared the winner, we played again or peeled off to play a different game. Sometimes a dad, even mine, joined in. Games were serious business. We all felt the need to prove ourselves. At the very least, we wanted to avoid losing. And yet, we also felt connected. As we sat so close, our minds pinned to the same goal, a kind of intimacy emerged. A web of camaraderie bound us together.

The playgrounds weren't the only place we found connection. My family came to the Bayview housing projects in 1956. Our building was among twenty-three identical apartment towers. In ours alone were twenty boys about my age. We grew up together, running up and down long hallways and venturing in and out of each other's apartments with ease. Most doors were left unlocked. Because each maroon door looked the same, it was common to accidentally walk into the wrong apartment, assuming it was your own. And when you realized your mistake—*Hey, when did we get new furniture? Why do I smell cabbage?*—you laughed it off, and so did the apartment's occupants. No one worried about intruders.

Fights in Bayview didn't typically escalate to deadly violence, but they were tough in their own way. Years later, my friend Billy talked about the projects where we grew up as a place where kids who weren't strong, fast, or funny didn't last long. That might be true—for all our connection, we were still piled on top of each other in a space that was separate from other Brooklyn neighborhoods. When I told people outside Bayview where I lived, I felt branded as one of the poorer kids. Living in government-funded housing defined me. Inside Bayview's perimeters, where we were all poor, another kind of status had to be earned, especially among boys and young men. Through games, sports, hurled insults, jokes, and fistfights, we proved our worth to one another. But even with that, the urban outdoors where I grew up felt more than safe. It was the first community I ever knew.

In retrospect, I can see the projects themselves as a sort of sprawling third place. Not home, not work or school. These outdoor spaces were without much obligation. They were places we chose to be. Places where our lives could intersect with the lives of others who became

friends, or at least familiar faces. The grounds—with their benches
and play areas—invited engagement among neighbors. In turn, they
served up a kind of social sustenance.

In junior high and high school, my passion switched from games
like skelly to more intense team sports. The ratio of kids to courts in
the projects was so unbalanced that it bred a competitive culture with
real stakes. Anyone who wanted to join a pickup game of basketball or
touch football just had to show up, but the price to stay on the field or
court was you had to win. It was a ruthless meritocracy. If your team
lost, you got kicked off the court to take your place in the line of bystanders waiting their next turn. Hours might pass until you made it
back in. Standing on the sidelines, feeling useless and bored, or returning to my apartment, feeling anxious and bored, were unacceptable
outcomes for me. If winning required diving on the unforgiving concrete and scraping off a layer of skin, then that's what I did. I rarely
went home before dusk. When I got hungry around lunchtime, I stood
under our apartment window and hollered up to my mom, who dropped
a tuna sandwich seven stories into my waiting hands. I'd eat it in four
bites as I ran back to rejoin a game.

In spring and summer, the basketball court was where I would try
to prove my worth. I'd jump out of bed, knock on Billy's door, and
within seconds we'd be out of the building and on the court. I was
hypnotized by the flow of banter, grunts, high-fives, and methodical
thumps of a dribbling ball. And when a player broke away, a swarm of
cheap-soled sneakers chased him up or down the court like our futures
depended on blocking or making the next basket. To win, you had to
play tough. Calling foul was a sign of weakness, and sometimes fights
broke out. I loved it all. But mostly I loved being among other kids on
the center court, constantly competing for the right to stay and play.

In the chill of fall, the boys turned to football, and because there
were no large fields nearby we played on the asphalt basketball courts.
It wasn't tackle, but touch football with Brooklyn rules can still take a
kid down hard, especially the quarterback, which was my usual position. When I played tackle football in high school, my nose broke and
I had a few concussions. I also suffered a hairline fracture in my neck,

which would not be discovered until many years later. But the intensity of sports did not diminish my desire to play, and year after year, pass after pass, block after block, I endured bruises and skinned flesh from crashing down on the cold hard ground. The projects I grew up in may have been safe from crime, but there were no soft landings.

Sometimes I organized pickup games, going door to door to recruit players or shouting an invite to a potential point guard or wide receiver I saw walking across the yard. I'd easily corral enough kids for a defense and an offense. All willing players were eligible. They just had to prove themselves once they had the ball.

Every time I played sports, I stood a little taller, partly because I was inches above most kids my age, but also because I felt more confident as an athlete than I did as a student or as a son. I had some natural athletic ability, but the real reason I held my own on the court or field was because with a ball in my hands I always felt good enough.

I didn't have to exchange a lot of words with fellow players to feel connected. When we came together in a huddle, or if someone cocked a chin in approval after I threw for a touchdown or made a basket from outside the key, I felt a bulletproof sense of belonging, something I rarely experienced among family. These moments seemed to last forever in my childhood. But they disappeared from my life much too soon, and with them went my sense of community. It was years before I found it again.

"Buon giorno!"

A thin older man behind a counter greeted me like I was a neighbor who had opened the door to his home, unannounced but welcome. Savoring the aroma of freshly ground coffee, I returned his smile and walked up to the counter. It was early morning in Milan, Italy, and I was in the city for the first time to attend a trade show for work. I had popped into this espresso bar on my way to the show.

It was 1983, the year I turned thirty.

Sidling up to the counter, I couldn't take my eyes off the man behind it. With an athletic precision, he ground coffee beans, measured the dark grounds, and then packed them into a short-handled basket that he inserted into a gleaming chrome machine, which gurgled before he pulled a lever. Streams of amber liquid dripped into a tiny white porcelain cup. Throughout the dance, he chatted in quick bursts of Italian with three other customers who stood side by side at his coffee bar. Peering into his workspace, I thought, *Who is this person?* On some invisible cue, he placed one of his beverages before me. Holding the dainty cup in my hands, I felt as if I had been given a precious gift. I sipped the punch of flavor.

"*Grazie!*" I said.

The way he prepared and served coffee was unlike anything I'd seen in American restaurants, where coffee sat in reheated pots before being unceremoniously dumped into dingy mugs. But this! This was theater!

What is this place? I was utterly enthralled at what was clearly an ordinary occasion to the locals at the bar. I wanted to stay.

I was working at the time as the director of marketing for a small coffee roaster and retailer in Seattle with a rather risqué mermaid as its logo. The company was named after a character in Herman Melville's novel *Moby-Dick,* Ahab's first mate, Starbuck. Starbucks Coffee Company specialized in roasting and selling whole-bean coffee from all over the world. At Starbucks, I had already learned that coffee wasn't just an efficient caffeine delivery system; it was a nuanced and flavorful beverage to be savored and appreciated.

The company had been founded in 1971 by Gerald Baldwin, Gordon Bowker, and Zev Siegl. After I first met Jerry and Gordon in 1981, they taught me that the coffee most Americans consumed came from beans called *Robusta,* which were cheaper and inferior in flavor compared to the finer *Arabica* beans that Starbucks purchased. Starbucks roasted their coffee beans "dark," a European tradition that many aficionados believed brought out more of a bean's flavor. Most Americans, myself included, were accustomed to beans that were more lightly roasted, which was why, when I had my first taste of Starbucks coffee, I was overwhelmed by its flavor. My parents only drank instant coffee, or ground coffee from a can, which my mom made in a tin electric percolator when we had people over. The stuff I guzzled to perk me up during college, or during my morning commutes, was swill compared to my first sip of Starbucks' bold dark roast.

One year into working at Starbucks, I figured that I had discovered all there was to know about coffee. Then I walked into that espresso bar in Milan.

After drinking my espresso, I was excited to taste more and to know more, so I thanked the gentleman behind the counter and paid the cashier. As I made my way to the trade show, I couldn't walk a block without passing another coffee bar. I spent the next week exploring more throughout the city. Many were stripped of ornament—espresso pit stops. In their narrow, smoky interiors, customers, mostly men, stood at counters and lingered over their drinks, bantering in Italian. Other coffee places were more elegant, stylish, and spacious, destinations for a diverse clientele: women with or without children in tow, kids in school uniforms, students with books, retired folks. Friends just hanging out. Customers also sat alone reading, writing, gazing. There was a pulse of energy even when a shop was quiet. In many establishments, chatter mixed with a soundtrack of Italian opera. The environment was also nothing like those clanky, fluorescent New York diners I was familiar with.

The workers making the espresso, I learned, were called *baristas*. Sitting at the espresso bars, I discovered that many of them spoke English, so I asked a lot of questions. I found out that "pulling" shots of espresso requires just the right combination of water flow, temperature, pressure, and time to extract the fullest, strongest flavor from just the right amount of finely ground coffee beans. This complicated maneuver involves pouring, grinding, weighing, tamping, waiting, dripping, and then cleaning the equipment so the next shot has a chance of being as good as the last. The performance—as choreographed as a dance, as energetic as a football play, as sacred as a ritual—takes place just inches from discerning customers, one small cup, or demitasse, at a time. I was told that the dense foam that forms the top layer of espresso is called *crema,* and when espresso is infused into warm, frothy, steamed milk, it creates a drink that Italians call a *caffè latte.*

My first sip filled my mouth with a symphony of sweetness and silk. I'd never tasted anything like it.

Of the many coffee experts I had met since moving to Seattle and joining Starbucks, none had introduced me to the theater and romance of espresso.

Italians understood the emotional relationship that people could have with coffee and had built a vibrant culture around it, elevating a commodity into an art and creating warm, welcoming spaces where baristas and others knew your name. Coffee could bring people together in a place. Like wine, it was a social beverage, but unlike wine it was a stimulant. Consumed while in conversation or when people were alone, coffee could become fuel for conversation or powerful introspection. These gathering places were part of people's routines—spaces for simple, improvised, familiar comfort and community.

The cafés and espresso bars I visited could not have been further from the playgrounds and sport courts I grew up in, but they drew out of me old feelings I'd left behind in my youth: the sense of belonging.

The thrill that met this epiphany was visceral. My body felt electric and my mind swam with ideas. Nothing on par with Italy's cafés existed in the America I knew, but I intuitively believed that people would respond to the espresso bar experience just as I had, with curiosity and delight. I became convinced that translating that experience in America was the next step for Starbucks.

At the time, Starbucks was not serving beverages. We just bagged our roasted beans in our five stores and sent loyal customers on their way. Our little company—with its reputation for exceptional coffee—was in an ideal position to introduce the United States to the theater and the convivial community of the espresso bar.

I could not let this idea go. On the flight back to Seattle, I jotted down plans. I even drew designs for how to integrate an espresso bar into our existing stores. I arrived back at Starbucks' offices exuberant.

Starbucks founders did not share my enthusiasm. They wanted to stay true to their vision of selling whole-bean coffee, period. I respected their singleness of purpose, but my heart was pulling me in another direction. Eventually, I convinced Jerry to let me open a tiny espresso bar inside a new Starbucks store at the intersection of Fourth and Spring streets in Seattle. Despite being tucked away in a corner of the store, it attracted a lot of customers, many of whom tasted their first *caffè latte* and came back each day for another. *Success,* I thought. But Jerry and Gordon weren't interested in expanding the concept.

I was heartbroken. "Starbucks can be a great experience, not just a great coffee roaster and retail store," I argued. I was relentless but their faces never lit up. They didn't see what I saw. To their credit, Jerry and Gordon respected my passion even though it was not theirs. These two men had risked so much to build their business, and so they understood what it felt like to love an idea so much that you can't let it go.

I stayed with Starbucks for one more year before leaving to start my own company—and to control my own destiny.

CHAPTER 3

A Different Kind of Company

H oward, let's take a walk."

My father-in-law tapped my shoulder and motioned me toward the front door of our house. It was barely 5 P.M. but already dark, a typical December day in Seattle, where sunlight makes brief, dingy appearances.

It was 1985. Ronald Reagan was in his second term as president, Microsoft was ten years old, Live Aid concerts were raising money to help feed people in Africa, and the Dow Jones average was on the verge of passing 1,500 for the first time. I was thirty-two years old. I pulled on a windbreaker, put our dog, Jonas, on a leash, and the three of us left my wife, Sheri, and her mom, Rae, at home.

Sheri and I had met seven years earlier, when we both lived and worked in Manhattan. In 1978, I'd done what lots of young people living in New York City still do: I'd rented a house with a group of friends in the cluster of beach towns at the east end of Long Island known as the Hamptons, where we could gather on weekends to escape the city's hot, smelly streets. I was making good money, but not enough to afford an equal portion of the rent, so my friends agreed to give me a reduced rate if I ran the house, which meant I put my name on the lease, collected everyone's portion of the security deposit, and got our rent paid on time. We all shared the cooking and grocery shopping, and as much cleaning as a group of guys living together is willing to do.

One weekend in early July, a bunch of us were playing football on the beach. Near us, a group of young women was hanging out in the sun. I was drawn to one of them in particular—a woman with a striking shock of wavy blond hair and a warm, wide smile. I walked up to her and we started chatting. Aside from being beautiful, she was easy to talk to and made me laugh. But there was something more. I called her that night. When we spoke the next day, I asked if she would have dinner with me when we got back to the city.

I wanted to know everything about Sheri Kersch. I soon learned that she had grown up in the small, middle-class city of Lima, Ohio, had studied political science and psychology at the University of Denver, and had gotten into law school but had chosen to study interior design in New York City instead. I wasn't surprised. She had great style.

From our first date we both felt a magnetic connection. We just wanted to be around each other, and I quickly discovered that Sheri possessed attributes I'd hoped to find in a life partner, including a broad view of the world, intelligence, and strong family values. She was also adventurous yet grounded, and had an ease and energy that felt comfortable and exciting at the same time. Sheri was ambitious but had no sense of entitlement, and I was especially smitten by her confidence; she had strong opinions and stood up for what she thought was right. She was also more mature than other women our age whom I'd met, yet didn't take herself too seriously. And like me, she dreamed of a bigger life for herself, even if she didn't know what that life would look like.

Not long after we met, I invited Sheri to a birthday party at my apartment in Greenwich Village. At some point during the evening, my mother phoned me, upset about a family matter. Her calls for support, emotional and financial, were frequent, and I went into my bedroom to get away from the noise so I could try to calm her. I didn't know it at the time, but Sheri overheard a snippet of the conversation. Much later, she told me that my promises to help my mother had made a positive impression upon her.

In me, Sheri said she saw a responsible young man. I was definitely serious, probably too serious for a twenty-five-year-old, but I was working hard to make a living and had a mother who routinely called me in emotional disarray. Being her ballast was a role I had assumed in childhood and never shed. Meeting Sheri brought a welcome levity into my life, a lightness of spirit that became among the many, many reasons I fell in love with her.

We married in 1982, in a small ceremony in the Hamptons with only our families in attendance, followed by a party with friends and relatives. The affair was simple and inexpensive; Sheri's touch made it elegant. For me, it was also magical. I could not believe that the stunning, bright, kind woman I had met on a beach was now my wife.

By the time we were married, I had also come to love and respect Sheri's parents. The Kersch family, with their modest Midwest ranch house and warm family dinners, felt "normal" compared to my own. But of course they had their own stories.

Sheri's mom, Rae, was one of six children orphaned at a young age, after their mother died in childbirth and their father was later killed in an auto accident. When Rae and her siblings were separated, she moved in with a great-aunt who made her drop out of school to cook and clean. Eventually, Rae moved out and got a job to support herself in Detroit. That's where she met and married Harry Kersch.

Harry was born in Canada, one of five kids, and came to the United States as a teenager after high school. For many years he worked in a factory that cleaned uniforms. Then, in his midthirties, when Rae was pregnant with one of Sheri's older brothers, Harry spied a tiny ad in a newspaper. A retail laundry business in a small Ohio town was for sale. Harry found two investors and bought the modest company. For one year, he slept in the laundry facility during the week and took the train back to Detroit on weekends to see Rae and their two sons.

In 1954, the year Sheri was born, Harry and Rae bought their first home, a one-story ranch house, in Lima. He spent the next thirty years building his business, expanding it into a commercial enterprise. New

Method Laundry and Ohio Coverall Service rented uniforms to many of the plants and factories in the area, picking up the dirty clothes and delivering clean ones. The industrial laundry business was not glamorous. The plant was hot and sticky, and Harry often took the wheel of his own delivery truck and drove more than a hundred miles to pick up the oil- and chemical-streaked coveralls worn by workers at the region's big car and steel manufacturers.

Growing up, Sheri and her brothers worked at the company. When she was twelve, Sheri began manning the cash register for the dry-cleaning side of the business.

The company's success allowed Harry and Rae to raise Sheri and her two older brothers in a simple and comfortable lifestyle. They put all three children through college, and sold New Method when they were in their midsixties. I was struck by the energy and focus Harry brought to his endeavors; he offered a model of hard work, responsibility, and entrepreneurship that my own father hadn't given me.

These days Harry was in good humor and enjoying the fruits of his labors.

As we walked in silence I could sense that my father-in-law was not about to deliver a genial pep talk.

I had left Starbucks to pursue the espresso bar idea that had enchanted me in Italy, and for eight months I'd been trying to raise nearly $1.7 million to fund a capital-intensive retail start-up. I'd named the company Il Giornale, which means "newspaper" in Italian, and can also mean "daily." My business model was based on the premise that Il Giornale cafés and espresso bars would become a daily ritual for people in Seattle, and eventually in other cities.

I wasn't taking a salary, we barely had any savings, and our first child was due in less than a month. As planned, we were living off Sheri's income as an interior designer until Il Giornale raised enough money and could afford to pay me a salary.

At first, raising money had been deceptively easy. My former bosses Jerry and Gordon, despite their lack of interest in building espresso bars for Starbucks, said they believed in me enough to invest $150,000. They even let me work out of Starbucks' offices and provided helpful advice. I was grateful for their money and their mentoring. My second investors were originally friends of Sheri's. Carol Bobo also was an interior designer, and her husband, Ron Margolis, was an obstetrician who invested in new businesses. Carol had told Ron about us, and they invited us for dinner to hear more about my plans. I didn't know Ron as well as Sheri knew Carol, but our families had a lot in common. Carol and Ron were new parents and had a gentle giant of a dog, an Irish wolfhound that liked to romp with Jonas on the path around a local lake.

Seated at their dining room table, I was ready to make my pitch. I'd brought architectural drawings, and the stack of papers next to my plate documented a rigorous business plan that accounted for how I would spend every dollar people invested to build one hundred stores. First, however, I spoke to Carol and Ron about my trip to Italy and how I had been captivated by the espresso bars, and my belief that the coffeehouse experience had a place in American culture. I got more enthusiastic with every word.

As I began to unfurl my papers, Ron stopped me. "Howard, our ability is reading people," he said. "How much do you need?" That evening Carol and Ron wrote Il Giornale a check for $100,000. They were not investing in my idea; they were investing in Sheri and me. I left their house elated, but also conscious that I had new friends' money in my pocket. I did not want to lose their money—or their friendship.

Foolishly, I assumed that raising the remaining $1.4 million from individual investors would be just as easy as the first $250,000. I was not prepared for the steep climb.

I knew nothing about raising money from venture capital firms, which in the late eighties were not as abundant or accessible as they would become during the next decade.

A bank loan was not an option I wanted to consider. Memories of my parents arguing about how to pay their bills, and the shame I felt when they put me on the phone to talk to debt collectors or ask friends for money, still tasted bitter. My exposure to their financial trials had instilled in me an aversion to debt, even though I had learned, as a businessperson, that debt was not dangerous if managed well and that credit is essential to jump-starting a small business. Access to capital allows companies to buy equipment, pay rent, and employ people. But because the mere idea of debt still stung, I didn't think I could sleep at night if I funded Il Giornale with a bank loan.

Behind my suit, tie, and friendliness, I was a young businessman haunted by the anxiety of a childhood steeped in financial insecurity.

So instead of trying to get a bank loan, I was asking individuals to invest their own money in exchange for a percentage of ownership in the company. Having investors would dilute my personal stake, but that was a sacrifice I preferred to taking on debt.

In the months after Jerry, Gordon, Carol, and Ron said yes, more than one hundred potential investors said no—in various ways. People didn't return my calls. They hung up on me. They regarded me with skepticism or suspicion when we met, then said they'd get back to me but never did. Some lectured me that they knew more about retail than I did, and implied, not subtly, that my idea to build espresso bars and sell odd-sounding drinks in paper cups was silly and stupid—and by association so was I. Some of Seattle's more successful business leaders mocked the idea while condescending to explain why I would fail. The rejections took a toll. Sometimes, before meeting with potential investors, I'd walk around the block a few times to calm my nerves.

Many nights I came home to Sheri feeling dejected. But because she was pregnant, I tried not to saddle her with my stress. I'd wake up the next morning, walk Jonas, and knot my tie again. *This will be a good day,* I'd tell myself, and off I'd go. I met with potential investors for breakfast and lunch. I sat at the lonely end of long conference tables in office towers with pricey views of Seattle's magnificent waterfront. Repeating my pitch over and over and over, I'd summon once again the enthusiasm that had come over me in the cafés of Milan, and try to convey my deep belief in my ambitious business plan.

The rejection was daunting. It would be so easy to believe the critics. But I would not relent. Just because others cannot see your vision doesn't mean that vision isn't achievable. Still, the line between forging ahead and giving up can be so thin for an entrepreneur that it's easy to cross over, especially when your father-in-law suggests, on a chilly December evening, that it's time for you to quit.

"Howard," Harry said, halting my thoughts, "I respect what you've been trying to do over the last year, but let's look at the facts. Sheri is working and has a salary. You have a hobby and no salary. And my daughter is going to give birth in a month." He stopped walking and faced me with the love of a father. "Son, you need to get a job."

He said this with great respect, and the empathy of a fellow entrepreneur. I felt embarrassed. I had so much respect for Harry, and for Sheri, and of course the same thoughts had run through my mind. But hearing someone voice my fear—that I was creating a family life that in any way resembled the financial desperation and irresponsibility of my childhood—was devastating. *Had he talked to Sheri? Did she agree?* The part of me that sought stability knew Harry was right. I felt as though I were watching a bright, beautiful bubble burst. Standing in front of my father-in-law, whom I loved, I nodded, and then I cried. He put his hand on my shoulder.

I didn't mention anything to Sheri about our conversation until later that night.

"I had an interesting talk with your father," I said when we were alone. I told her everything he had said, knowing that if Sheri told me she wanted me to stop raising money and to get a job, even to work at Starbucks again, I would do it.

"Howard," she said, "there's no way we're giving this up."

In January 1986, our son, Jordan, was born.

By the end of the summer, about 30 of the now 242 people I had asked to invest in Il Giornale had said yes. Among them was an angel of a man named Jack Rodgers, who gave me money even after his own investment group turned me down; another angel named Arnie Prentice not only invested, but introduced me to clients of his financial services firm who would also go on to invest. Two of the largest checks I received were from a man named Harold Gorelick, who was in the muffler business, and his nephew, the famous saxophonist Kenny G. People such as Jack and Arnie put their reputations on the line to support me, and because they were willing to, I was able to raise $1.65 million, enough to move ahead with my plans.

I started to staff up, looking for people whose competence and friendliness reminded me of the baristas I had seen in Italy. The people I hired wanted to work at a job they would enjoy and for a company they could feel good about. Part of my business plan, I had explained to every investor, was being known as a great place to work. We would be a company that tried to ensure employees could be their best selves and had a chance to live their best lives. In fact, the first mission statement I ever wrote as the head of my new company, in 1986, included these words: "We expect our coffee bars to enhance the environment in which people work. We recognize that rewards must be psychological as well as financial, and strive for an atmosphere where each individual can share in the growth. . . ."

If we were going to build a business around the core ideas of community in our stores, then a sense of human connection had to exist in our offices. I was surrounding myself with people who felt passionate about the products we sold, who were ambitious and kindhearted.

By now, I also had met so many people whose working lives were nothing like my father's. From Sheri to Starbucks' cofounders to my coworkers, I knew men and women whose work nourished them in ways that my dad's jobs never did. I wanted Starbucks to be such a place. From the inside out, I was trying to build the kind of company that my father never got a chance to work for. Or, as I would phrase it in later years, to try to balance profitability with a social conscience. Our values were human values. Ethics, integrity, sharing, support, teamwork, caring, respect, and loyalty were all ideals I included in that first mission statement. I also wanted to instill a sense of ambitious camaraderie: "We will set aggressive goals and drive ourselves to achieve them," the mission statement said. "It's an adventure, and we're in it together."

Given the company's size today, it can be hard to imagine that Starbucks was once a small retailer with a handful of locations that many people did not believe would grow beyond Seattle. I wrote about the company's earlier years in my first book, *Pour Your Heart Into It*.

It was a time of exhausting twelve-hour days, of laughter-filled meetings, and of heated debates over pizza in my house. It was a time spent finding more investors, hiring staff, and meeting people who would become lifelong friends and mentors. Every day, I was learning how to lead, and maturing, through trial and error.

It was also the period when Il Giornale bought Starbucks. The Starbucks Corporation of today is actually Il Giornale, which I founded in 1985. In an unexpected twist, Il Giornale acquired Starbucks Coffee Company in 1987 and renamed the new company the Starbucks Corporation. The new entity built off many of Starbucks' original assets, including its roasting facilities, its name, its logo, its existing locations, and its people. The espresso bar concept, growth aspirations, and values were my own, baked into how I envisioned Il Giornale from its conception.

But as the company grew, we never took our eyes off our initial mission. The first place for us to show our values was, of course, with our own workers. From the beginning, I wanted to create a business model that was different from the command-and-control relationship between employers and employees during my dad's working years. I never shook off the indelible image of my father immobile on the couch after he slipped on the ice, helpless and abandoned by the company he was working for when the accident occurred. Workers deserved a different relationship to the companies they helped to build, one based on trust, mutual care, and honesty. This belief informed two of our earliest decisions at Starbucks.

The first was that I wanted to extend healthcare benefits to employees who worked part-time. Few companies, especially in retail, provided it, and those that did tended to restrict it to people who worked no fewer than thirty hours a week. But two-thirds of Starbucks employees worked about twenty hours a week. Extending healthcare insurance to part-time employees went against the trend: in the late eighties, companies began trying to significantly reduce healthcare costs, not increase them.

Most of our investors pushed back. Starbucks wasn't yet profitable.

I argued that it was the right thing to do, and it was a smart business decision. Giving healthcare benefits to part-timers could engender loyalty, reducing the costs of turnover. If a barista quit, finding and training a replacement cost about $3,000. Providing a barista with full benefits for one year cost half as much, about $1,500. Plus, some customers were such regulars that baristas knew their favorite drinks. If those baristas quit, customer connections would break—and those connections were essential to our business model.

In 1988, Starbucks became among the first private companies in the U.S. to provide comprehensive health insurance to part-time employees working twenty or more hours a week. It was one of the best decisions we ever made.

Over time we would broaden the coverage to reflect people's needs.

In 1991, one of Starbucks' longest and most devoted employees, Jim Kerrigan, came into my office and told me he had AIDS. I had no idea Jim was sick, and I was devastated when he told me his disease had entered a new phase and he had to stop working. As we cried together in my office, I searched for words to console him.

At the time, Starbucks' health insurance did not cover people with a terminal illness. Our early workforce tended to be young and healthy. Because of Jim, we created a new policy. For employees who had terminal illnesses, healthcare coverage extended from the time they could no longer work until they were able to access government insurance programs, which then was about twenty-nine months.

Jim passed away within the year. I spoke to him often and visited him at hospice during his final months and weeks. After he died, his family sent a letter expressing their gratitude, explaining that Jim would not have had the money to care for himself if it hadn't been for Starbucks' insurance. I still miss him.

In September 1991, I made the next big decision about the relationship between the company and its workers. Starbucks became the only privately owned company we knew of to issue equity in the form of stock options, not just to full-time employees, but to part-time employees, too. This was the second-best decision we made during our early years. We called the program Bean Stock, and because it gave each employee part ownership of the company, we began referring to our employees as "partners."

There's a fuzzy videotape of the day I announced Bean Stock in our Kent, Washington, roasting plant. I stood at a black podium and explained to the folks who had gathered what we were doing.

"No matter where you are in the company—the roasting plant, the stores, the office—every person will have a stake in the success of the company." The plan had taken more than a year to put together, because no model of a public or private company giving stock options to all its employees existed. It had never been done before. For a start-up that was not yet making money to do it was rarer still. Once again, I had to convince skeptical investors that sharing our success with our own people was core to our business. Like providing healthcare coverage, it was not only the right thing to do, but it would induce levels of loyalty and respect for the business that would enhance the company's financial performance for years to come.

For me, giving ownership to people regardless of their job description also felt quite personal. My parents had never owned anything. Not a house, and certainly not a piece of a company. Bean Stock was a chance to elevate people's lives. As the company's value grew, so did the value of our shares and partners' sense of security, as well as the choices and options they had for themselves and their families.

At first people did not understand how owning Bean Stock had the potential to make a noticeable difference in their lives. The first stock options were granted at $6 a share. Since then, Bean Stock has generated $1.5 billion in pre-tax gains for baristas and shift supervisors, as well as for store managers and managers in the field, augmenting base salaries and hourly paychecks. The stock's increasing market value has helped people build retirement savings as well as put down payments on houses, afford college, pay off debt, take vacations, or start their own businesses. From June 1992 to November 2018, Starbucks total shareholder return was 21,826 percent. In other words, $10,000 invested at the IPO was worth $2,182,620.

To this day, when I meet partners in our stores for the first time, I often ask if they have a Bean Stock story. Many also post their stories online. Sarah Swanson used her stock to pay for her wedding, buy a new car, and put money toward a down payment on her first home. A part-time barista and nurse chose to use her stock to pay for kidney dialysis treatments for patients in Nepal. Just recently, I was at an event and the woman who owned the catering company came up to me. "I used to work at Starbucks," she said. "Bean Stock bought my business."

One of my favorite Bean Stock stories is about Kenny Kraning, who joined Starbucks in 1990 at the age of twenty-seven. Kenny has Down syndrome, and his first job at Starbucks was putting labels on packages of coffee as they came off the conveyor belt at our roasting plant. When the plant moved to a city too far for Kenny to commute to, I assured him and his family that Kenny would always have a job with Starbucks. For the past twenty years, Kenny has helped restock the many kitchens and coffee rooms throughout the company's headquarters. He and his roving cart of glasses, coffee beans, and teas are beloved fixtures in the hallways, and Kenny has always done his work with pride. Those who know Kenny have great affection for him.

He and I would have lunch together a few times a year in the company cafeteria or in my office, and often on his birthday. Kenny was born in Indiana, on the same day that John F. Kennedy was assassinated. He especially liked talking about wrestling, so I would ask him about his favorite wrestlers and his face would light up. Kenny was, for me, a perpetually uplifting spirit. Sometimes when I was in a bad mood, I'd walk the halls looking for him. Three or four minutes chatting with Kenny could change the rhythm of my day.

The value of Kenny's Bean Stock grew so much over the years that he could afford to buy a two-bedroom condo in the 1990s, which is where he still lives on his own. Now fifty-five, Kenny also has a very, very healthy nest egg. In fact, each day at 2 P.M. he stops in to see the team at Starbucks that oversees Bean Stock. There, Kenny checks the company's current stock price—not to compute the value of his portfolio, but because he truly loves the company and wants it to do well.

Being entrepreneurial is not just about inventing new products or creating fresh experiences for customers. Innovation must happen behind the scenes, too, for people who work for the company. For innovations to be sustainable, they must reflect and advance our values, not just serve our business interests. We have not always succeeded the first time around, and we rely on our partners to tell us when we need to improve. Helping our store managers schedule work shifts for baristas, for example, is a complicated process that has to meet each store's business needs and the needs of our diverse partner population, especially part-time workers who have to balance work with outside obligations. We have definitely struggled to get scheduling right. For a while, software and policies we put in place to make the process more efficient for our store managers had the unintended effect of making daily life more difficult for some partners, especially single parents who couldn't find flexible child care or ended up working too many hours without rest. It took a while, but we revamped the software and our policies to ensure more predictability, consistency, and flexibility. Being entrepreneurial means you will fail. You just have to be willing to listen to people who tell you something is broken, and then fix it.

Envisioning policies like Bean Stock and healthcare insurance for all employees was no less creative than the process of coming up with some of the customized beverages we served in our stores. And like our products, these benefits were not things we offered at the expense of the company. Although to some, they seemed overly generous or at least at odds with maximizing profit, they were in fact engines that made our business model work. The success of Starbucks was rooted in our primary products: our coffee and the customer experience in our stores. That meant sourcing and serving high-quality coffee in a retail environment that was inviting, warm, and sociable. To achieve that, we needed people who were invested in and proud of their work, happy to be there, excited to learn about coffee, and eager to serve customers. Investing in our partners and giving them a stake in the success of the business turned them into deeply invested collaborators in the mission of the company.

In a larger sense, healthcare and Bean Stock were also my way of paying forward the support that I'd received from the few people who had my back when I was starting the company. I wanted to provide that kind of support to the people who joined me in this work, and show them the same spirit of trust and belief. By transforming employee benefits from something minimal to something genuinely fair, even unexpected, I hoped to show our partners that the company had the backs of its people.

The year Starbucks went public, in 1992, we had 165 stores and a market value of $250 million. In the decade that followed, Starbucks stores expanded to more cities and initiated new rituals for Americans, like the midday coffee break. People began to swap their daily drip coffee for *caffè lattes* and cappuccinos. We also were introducing Americans to a new language around coffee. Our drink sizes were not small, medium, and large, but short, tall, and grande. Customizing your coffee beverage to suit your tastes was also unique, and it became a competitive advantage for us. At Starbucks, you could order a drink whose flavor wasn't available anywhere else. Over time, there would be more than 170,000 variations of Starbucks beverages.

One store, one beverage at a time, Starbucks was changing America socially and culturally—in ways that I'd dreamed, and in ways I never imagined, during those magical days in Italy.

In cities as well as small towns, our stores became places where senior citizens gathered in the morning and where students hung out after school. Mothers rolled in with strollers throughout the day. During nights and weekends, singles came in and struck up conversations with strangers; some couples got engaged or married in the Starbucks store where they met. People in the suburbs came to Starbucks for the same reasons as people in urban areas. To converse. To read. To create. To work. To debate. To be out and about, to people-watch, to see friends in a familiar, safe, and welcoming place.

When I began Il Giornale, I had a sense that the experience we wanted to cultivate in our stores—one that fostered human connection over great coffee—would appeal to a wide range of people. Our success in so many disparate corners of the country, however, incited us to think more critically about what, specifically, our customers were responding to.

Starbucks stores were providing an experience that did not exist in many American neighborhoods: a common, accessible gathering place that felt uncommonly welcoming. Our store interiors were designed to help people escape the chaos and stress of their daily lives—for five minutes or a few hours. The muted colors and soft lighting. The calm, uplifting music. The hum of conversation. The soothing aroma of freshly ground coffee. The sweet, unexpected taste of Italian-inspired beverages, each custom-prepared by a professional barista. Whether you ordered a cup of black coffee or a complex espresso drink, it was served fresh and with a friendly word and kind smile, and by someone who might even know your name. All these sensations came together to provide a moment of tranquility and sociability.

Our popularity was nourished by coinciding trends. In the nineties, the rise of the Internet and the remote workforce had more people self-employed or holding jobs that involved working from home, which meant they didn't go to an office. At a Starbucks, they could sit alone and still feel part of a community. And unlike fast-food chains, our stores weren't designed for quick consumption. Unlike restaurants, our core products were not full meals; we served customers at all hours of the day and let them linger long after they'd finished.

Our coffee could cost more than what you could get at a donut shop or at a McDonald's or from a cart on a city corner. But the quality of our beans was higher, our beverages were unique and customized, and the coffee came wrapped in an emotional experience.

In the press, I've heard people refer to Starbucks coffee as an affordable luxury. Other people I've met over the years have described our stores as a democratizing force, making special moments and clean, comfortable spaces available to more people.

In addition to opening more stores, we explored other ways to grow revenue. We opened our first drive-thru location. We invented a new product, the Frappuccino® blended beverage, which we bottled and sold in supermarkets as well as in stores. Starbucks also bought a tea company.

The ideals that Starbucks has tried to bring to life in its stores were not only embraced in America. In 1996, Starbucks opened its first store outside North America, in Japan. The day we launched, we had a line of customers around the block. Next we went to Singapore, the Philippines, and on to New Zealand, Malaysia, and the United Kingdom. And in 1999, to China.

No one thing or one person propelled our success. Every day was a team effort. My intent was to surround myself with people who had expertise and experience beyond my own. I could fill another book with the names of those who contributed to Starbucks' growth over the years. Three people in particular, however, helped shape the culture from its earliest days.

Dave Olsen, a man who personified a passion for coffee, was our first chief coffee buyer. His knowledge bred respect that bordered on awe, and his humility and humor set a joyful tone inside the company for the twenty-seven years he spent with us. Dave had run a small café in Seattle before joining me and Il Giornale in 1986, and he, more than anyone, understood my vision of creating community around coffee.

Howard Behar was a force from the moment he joined us in 1989 to run store operations. He was nearly ten years older than me, had a retail background, and his influences were many. Howard put in place systems and processes we needed to operate more fluidly. But just as valuable, he imprinted upon the company the power of candor and the value of truth telling. He taught me—a kid who grew up trying to keep peace in my own home—that disagreement was not a sign of disrespect, and that heated conflict was not something to avoid. Just the opposite. If Howard had an opinion, he voiced it, and he encouraged others to do so, too. He didn't hesitate to argue with people, especially me. Through his leadership style, I saw that honest communication, even when it stings emotionally, is the root of productive problem solving.

It was Howard who initiated the practice of holding "open forums" inside the company. Every quarter, senior managers met with all interested employees who wanted to talk about the company's performance, offer ideas, or air grievances. Howard wanted people to feel free to challenge each other without fear of ridicule or how someone might react. Talking openly was awkward for a lot of people at first, but with time I personally got more comfortable with direct conflict. If people are upset about something and not discussing it, the most productive solution is to broach the problem head on. Open forums, and the expectation for honesty that they bred, became a signature ritual inside the company.

In 2000, I stepped down as chief executive to focus less on day-to-day operations and more on international expansion as chairman and chief global strategist. Starbucks was performing exceptionally well. With 2,800 stores in fifteen countries, our revenue was just shy of $2 billion.

In the eight years since our 1992 IPO, we had achieved a compounded annual growth rate of 49 percent.

The individual who became CEO was Orin Smith, Starbucks' beloved and widely respected chief operating officer. Orin was eleven years my senior and, like Howard Behar, both my mentor and my peer. The three of us ran the company side by side for ten years with such collaborative energy that those we worked with referred to us—the two Howards and Orin—as H2O.

I thought of Orin as a big brother, and was grateful when he agreed to become CEO for five years before retiring himself. As chief, Orin imbued the company with greater operational discipline, but also reinforced our culture of caring. My original mission statement had included this aspiration: "We wish to be an economic, intellectual, and social asset in communities where we operate." Orin's leadership further brought that aspiration to life. During his tenure, Starbucks ramped up its commitment to social issues. Between 2000 and 2005, the company gave more than $47 million to youth and literacy programs, as well as to victims of natural disasters. We took steps to reduce our stores' environmental impact by purchasing renewable energy and setting goals to reduce water consumption and conserve energy. We also created sourcing guidelines to ensure that the coffee we bought was ethically grown and responsibly traded.

In 2005, as planned, Orin left the company. He was replaced by Jim Donald. Jim had been heading our North American operations since 2002 and had come to Starbucks with a background in retail and with values that mirrored the company's. He had a personable leadership style, and people enjoyed working for him. Under Jim's leadership, the company continued to set high bars for growth, which Wall Street held us accountable to meeting. We opened in smaller cities throughout the United States and in places like Dublin, Cairo, and Bucharest. We also began selling our coffee in grocery stores and serving Starbucks coffee in restaurants and hotels. And we expanded our brand into non-coffee markets like entertainment, selling CDs, books, and games in our stores. By the end of 2007, Starbucks' market valuation had soared to $14.9 billion. We had seventeen thousand stores in forty-nine countries, and our U.S. store count had grown to more than eleven thousand.

The twenty-year journey the company had been on felt like a magical carpet ride—until it didn't.

Growth has a way of covering up mistakes.

CHAPTER 4

In the Mud

My father absolutely loved baseball. He was a student of the game. He always knew the stats and starting lineups and could be quite critical of Casey Stengel or Ralph Houk, the Yankees' managers when I was young.

Three or four times each season, the two of us took the subway from Canarsie to the Bronx and sat in the original Yankee Stadium. Settled in the middle of the right-field bleachers—*Look, Roger Maris!*—my dad would watch the field but also keep meticulous track of each play on fill-in-the-blank scorecards that were distributed with the day's program. Hunching over his card, he documented each player's performance, penciling a delicate "K" in the empty box when an umpire called a strikeout, or an "SB" if someone stole a base. He took great pride in his penmanship, which to my astonishment was impeccable. He kept all his filled-out scorecards stashed in a shoebox. Other than vinyl records, those scorecards were the only things I knew my dad collected.

I adopted his reverence, and vividly remember walking into the long, dark tunnel that led into the ballpark and seeing the grandness of the old Yankee Stadium when I emerged at the other end. It was a cathedral. I couldn't believe I was there, where for the next four hours everything would be perfect because I was sitting next to my dad, eating hot dogs and watching the game in the era of our hero, Mickey

Mantle. For eighteen years, the record-setting center fielder's boyish grin, his humble head-down, elbows-out run, and his booming homers sent thousands of us to our feet. People loved Mickey like we knew him off the field, and because he came from a place that wasn't special. Yet here he was, rounding third again. The number 7 was written on almost everything I owned.

My dad and I attended two Mickey Mantle Days at Yankee Stadium. The first was on September 18, 1965, a date I easily pluck from memory, and the second was when the number 7 jersey was officially retired in front of more than sixty thousand fans in 1969. When the forty-minute ceremony began, even the Coca-Cola vendors stopped selling to watch the historic event.

After a chorus of "We want Mickey," the man of honor, dressed in a dark gray suit and striped blue tie, walked out of the dugout. For nine whole minutes, tens of thousands of fans lucky enough to get tickets stood and cheered like crazy, ignoring the announcer's calls for quiet.

A salty-haired Joe DiMaggio presented Mickey with a plaque that listed what seemed like inhuman accomplishments for a kid who grew up in poverty and played ball in a sandlot. Mickey had 536 career home runs, 2,415 career hits, a .300 or higher batting record in each of ten years, three Most Valuable Player league titles, and held world records for homers, runs, RBIs, extra base hits, and total bases during World Series games. In 1956, he also won baseball's elusive Triple Crown by leading the league in batting average, home runs, and runs batted in during a single season.

When Mickey finally spoke into the microphones, his Oklahoma drawl filled the stadium. "Baseball was real good to me. And playing eighteen years in Yankee Stadium for you folks is the best thing that could ever happen to a ballplayer."

It was one week before Father's Day, and I knew in my heart, if not in my head, that baseball was the best thing that happened to my dad and me. The Mick was a big reason why. When he retired, it was the end of an era.

———

No one bad decision, tactic, or person was to blame for Starbucks' fall in 2008. Like a single loose thread that unravels a sweater inch by inch, the damage to the company had been slow. Even though I was no longer overseeing daily operations, I was complicit in the incremental decline of the business.

By 2007, the company's slide had become obvious to me, especially when I walked into stores. The rich aroma of freshly ground coffee from Sumatra or Costa Rica had become weak to undetectable. Sometimes when I walked into a store, all I could smell was burnt cheese from the new breakfast sandwiches we were selling. New espresso machines that we had installed to increase efficiency were so tall they prevented customers from watching baristas create their beverages and kept baristas from easily engaging with customers in the same manner that had enchanted me back in Milan.

Operationally, the company had made a lot of poor decisions about store locations, what products besides coffee to sell in our stores, how we trained our baristas, and how we packaged and stored our roasted coffee beans. Many of the choices probably seemed right at the time, and on their own merits would not have been a problem, but their sum led to a watering down of the in-store experience and our brand.

On Valentine's Day of that year, I expressed my concerns in a confidential email to our senior leaders: "We desperately need to make the changes necessary to evoke the heritage, the tradition, and the passion that we all have for the true Starbucks Experience," I wrote. "Let's get back to the core. Push for innovation and do the things necessary to once again differentiate Starbucks from all others."

Someone, I still don't know who, leaked my memo to the media, and what should have been a private admission of failure spiraled into a humiliating public news story. My critiques were posted online, and clichéd headlines declared trouble was brewing at Starbucks.

In the months that followed, our financial performance revealed there was truth to my concerns. One metric of a retail company's health is comparable store sales, or "comps"—the year-to-year rate of revenue growth or loss in existing stores. Every morning for almost twenty years,

I had woken up early and, after making my coffee, gone to my computer and looked at the same-store sales data from the prior day. The numbers usually told an upbeat story. For most of my career, comps had been cause for celebration. For the past sixteen years, Starbucks had posted 5 percent or better comps, an impressive track record in retail.

In the fall of 2007, however, I began to sit at the screen and shake my head in disappointment. Comps were slipping, and the implications made me restless. Slowing sales were more than data on a screen. They could affect people's lives. As Starbucks CEO, I had lived with this responsibility every day. Now, as chairman, I felt like the former captain of a ship whose boat was sinking but who had little power to save it.

By the end of the year, our quarterly comp had sunk to one percent, our worst performance since 1992.

I never planned to return as CEO, but my love of the company and the responsibility I felt for our people and their families prompted me to do so in January 2008. Back in the driver's seat, I confronted the full scope of the company's challenges.

In addition to our self-inflicted problems, we also faced seismic shifts in consumer behavior, increased competition from fast-food chains and independent coffee shops, and an economy hurtling toward the financial crisis that would destroy trillions of dollars in personal wealth and spur a credit crunch, a housing bust, and high unemployment as it mushroomed into a full-blown global recession, resulting in a cycle of uncertainty that would grip the country for years to come.

Starbucks leaders and I would have to navigate the blustery economy while cleaning up our own mess.

Growing up, I had learned the game of chess from an eclectic assortment of men who regularly played it outside on benches scattered throughout the sprawling housing project and in nearby parks.

I can't recall what originally attracted me to the clusters of rumpled players of various ages and backgrounds; most of my friends had no interest. But once I began to observe the chess players, I found their quiet intensity, their internal strategizing, and their competitive cama-raderie as engaging as skelly and baseball.

My father didn't like chess. I think he was put off by its headiness. Despite his studied approach to baseball, he was not a contemplative person. Perhaps the fact that his son liked something so alien to his own nature made him uncomfortable, or threatened. Whatever his rea-sons, he disliked chess so much that he forbade me to play in the park or at home. I enjoyed it too much to follow his order. I also didn't want to get whacked, so I snuck off to patches of park that were a walkable distance from our apartment building but far enough away so the chance of someone I knew spotting me was slim.

For me, playing chess was as much about winning as it was about figuring out how to get better. I marveled at the foresight and intricacy the game demanded, and I absorbed the rules by watching and asking questions. *Why'd you move your rook to that square? How'd you take out his queen?* My teachers were the men who frequented the parks with such consistency that I assumed none of them had jobs. Their intelli-gence, however, was undeniable. They answered my queries with pa-tience and knowledge. I drank in their guidance. A few even gave me tattered pamphlets and dog-eared books about the game, which I hid from my dad under my bed and read when he wasn't home.

One day I was seated across from one of the regular players when I made a move that clearly disappointed him. He crinkled his scraggly eyebrows, leaned over the board, and whispered, "Kid, great chess players know how to play the opponent *and* the board."

"What do you mean?" I asked.

"The opponent is one-dimensional," he said, "but the board has all these angles, and great players know how to play all the angles to ef-fectively move around the chessboard." His advice to view the board through a wider, multidimensional lens improved my chess game dra-matically.

In retrospect, it also helped me lead Starbucks, especially when I returned as CEO. There were so many angles to consider.

———

Just as no single misstep had brought Starbucks down, transforming the company back to health required a combination of moves. Inside the company, we referred to this period in Starbucks' history as "the transformation," and it was a tense, exciting time that I wrote about in my second book, *Onward*.

The steps we took shaped the kind of company we would go on to be.

I have always said that Starbucks is at its best when we are fostering personal connections—in our stores, in communities, in our offices. Achieving such an amorphous goal is the sum of myriad details: a friendly barista who prepares your drink with expertise, store décor that feels fresh but familiar, products that reflect consumers' changing lifestyles, store managers skilled at leading teams and overseeing budgets, workers who are cared for and compensated fairly. Few of these things directly flow to the revenue or earnings of the business, but they combine to create what we have referred to internally as the *Starbucks Experience* for customers.

Forsaking these elements, as we had done over time, was taking a subtle toll. We had lost sight of what made Starbucks special. We had also lost sight of the details.

As soon as I returned as CEO, I convened a team of new and long-time partners for a brainstorming summit. It was orchestrated by a creative agency, SYPartners, who designed the meeting to be experiential, like our stores. The SYP team took us through exercises that evoked talk of music, art, and commerce and sparked personal conversations. We reflected on our dreams as individuals. And we were honest about the state of the company. *What had we lost? How could we see the market differently? How could we reimagine Starbucks but stay true to our values and heritage?*

The summit was a jolt of inspiration and ideas. Not long after, we crafted a one-page memo that articulated a new vision and steps to achieve it. We titled it "Transformational Agenda," and sent it to every partner in our offices and to every store manager.

Our aspiration, the memo stated, was to become "one of the most recognized and respected brands in the world, known for inspiring and nurturing the human spirit."

Next, the memo summarized seven priorities: be recognized as the undisputed coffee authority; engage and inspire our partners with better training and new benefits; reignite customers' emotional attachment to our brand; expand our stores around the world, but try to make each one feel like the heart of the local neighborhood; be a leader in ethical sourcing and environmental impact efforts; create new, relevant products to help grow revenue; operate a more efficient and profitable business model.

Partners posted the memo by their desks and in stores. The mission gave many of them a sense of renewed purpose; once again, Starbucks was about more than coffee and profit. We had a reason for being that was bigger than ourselves. The seven steps also instilled a sense of security because they were a map to guide how people spent their time and the company's money.

During the next two years, Starbucks introduced new products, like Starbucks VIA instant coffee. We updated our stores' interiors to showcase coffee and enhance the feeling of community; on the walls were hung stunning photographs of coffee farms or paintings by local artists. Many stores also installed long tables for communal seating. We upgraded our in-store technology so it was easier to ring up customers' orders. We replaced our espresso machines with shorter, more attractive models. We began communicating with our customers on social media. We increased our support for coffee farmers around the world. Once again, the aroma of freshly roasted coffee filled stores.

One day in February 2008, we closed 7,100 stores in the United States at the same time to retrain our baristas in the art of making espresso. Shutting stores simultaneously achieved two ends. It efficiently taught 135,000 baristas how to correctly pour espresso and steam milk, which improved the quality of millions of beverages immediately. The mass closing also made a public statement: Starbucks was serious about being better.

Of all the moves, the most valuable was one that focused on our own people, in our stores.

———

When you start a business, you do not operate from a lofty place. You can't afford to. You think about every detail.

During this precarious period in Starbucks' history, we needed to ground ourselves in details. Starbucks' leaders, including myself, had to stop approaching our $10 billion business from a thirty-thousand-foot view and think more like a single merchant.

"It is so vitally important that we get back to the roots of the business, that we get back in the mud," I declared during a meeting. "Let's get our hands in the mud!" I literally pleaded, holding my hands out in front of me. *Get in the mud* became a mantra I repeated. In fact, one day when I was walking through the offices of Starbucks' store architects and designers, I stopped in my tracks when a poster caught my eye. A pair of dirt-smudged hands, palms up, framed the words "The world belongs to the few people who are not afraid to get their hands dirty." I asked to borrow the poster and marched it to the eighth floor, where I placed it on the wall of our boardroom so Starbucks' executive team would see it every time we met.

Being in the mud also meant realizing where so much of the power of our business's success resided. Not in the boardroom, but on the ground, in the stores, with our store managers and baristas.

Each manager of a Starbucks store is, in effect, an entrepreneur overseeing a $1 million business. Improving the company's financial performance required our almost ten thousand U.S. store managers to increase their individual store's sales and profits. I needed each manager to feel personally accountable for his or her store's performance. Everyone needed to understand what was required of them, and that the company's survival was at stake. They also needed to be together, physically, in the same space. Sitting side by side and among each other around tables, store managers could talk about what they were hearing, swap stories, learn from one another, and feel the camaraderie of fellow partners. I needed to be among them.

My idea of bringing thousands of store managers to one city, at a cost of $30 million at a time when the company was trying to reduce expenses, met with resistance. A four-day leadership conference seemed like a boondoggle. I urged our board of directors to understand that the conference was a worthwhile investment. After some heated discussions, I was able to persuade them to see that investing in our people at this time was the most important thing we could do.

Many cities wanted to host us, but we chose New Orleans, which in 2008 was still recovering from the devastations of 2005's Hurricane Katrina. The conference itself was held at the convention center. We outfitted the two-story-high pavilion to immerse our store managers in the story of coffee. There were nearly one thousand coffee trees representing countries where we sourced our beans. Partners walked through the replicas of coffee farms, raking green coffee beans spread out on long patios as if drying in the sun. They toured a mock roasting plant, complete with a huge coffee roaster that had been assembled on-site. They attended coffee tastings to refresh their knowledge.

The focus was on basics like coffee education, as well as improving customer service and enhancing management skills. But I also wanted the conference to reinforce our values, to ensure our people saw Starbucks as more than a moneymaking business.

Before we had a single meeting about coffee, we began to rekindle the values of the company. Every attendee spent a day volunteering in the New Orleans neighborhoods most devastated by Katrina, including the Ninth Ward with its decimated homes and businesses. Three years after the hurricane, the area still looked fresh from the flood's damage. Many homes were still uninhabitable. Public parks were overgrown with weeds, their benches and swing sets broken, rusted, abandoned. Toppled buildings had not been resurrected. Shuttered stores had never reopened.

Busloads of Starbucks partners descended on parks and neighborhoods to paint, clean, plant, and build at the direction of local nonprofits we had contacted before our arrival. These groups had no precedent for hosting thousands of volunteers all at once. They didn't have enough supervisors or enough shovels. So we bought our supplies, $1 million worth, enough to fill two rental trucks. Each day of the conference, our partners spent five hours doing whatever needed doing in New Orleans. In one public park, we planted 6,500 plugs of coastal grasses, installed ten picnic tables, and laid four dump trucks' worth of mulch.

At a stadium where high school football games were played, our partners scraped and painted 1,296 steps, twelve entrance ramps, hundreds of yards of railing, and a half-mile-long fence.

I spent my volunteer hours helping paint one of the eighty-six
homes we repaired that week so families could move back in. Many of
us spent time talking with the men and women who had lived through
Katrina. We heard stories not only of individual sacrifice and loss, but
also of neighbors taking care of neighbors. The power of community,
and resilience, was so evident in New Orleans.

"When you give up," said a slim older man whose home we worked
on, "you might as well lay down and die." We weren't just giving people
back their homes, but also helping to restore a sense of dignity.

Our approximately fifty thousand hours of volunteer efforts were a
small boost for the city, but also reminded our store managers of the
positive effects they could have in their own neighborhoods.

On the last day, we gathered everyone together at the massive New
Orleans Arena. I wanted to be honest about the extent of our company's
problems and what we had to do to fix them—but also exert optimism
about our potential to do so. Before I stepped onstage without a script,
a few of my colleagues urged me not to scare people by revealing just
how low our sales were trending, or just how vulnerable the company
had become to outside influences. If managers knew how bad things
were, they might leave the company or lose confidence in its leaders.

I thought back to what I had learned from mentors like Howard Behar,
about the power of truth to tackle challenges. I could not forgo honesty
with the very people who had the power to turn the company around.
They needed knowledge to do their jobs. The truth, I also believed, would
cement their trust in us, and their commitment. In turn, I trusted that they
would rally to the cause with hope versus run away in fear.

"We are here to celebrate our heritage and traditions, and also to
have an honest and direct conversation about what we are responsible
to do as leaders," I said, once onstage. "We are not a perfect company.
We make mistakes every single day." I explained that we were facing
perhaps the most difficult economic situation since the Great Depression. "It's real. It is serious." I explained that people did not have as

much money as they once did, and that Starbucks more often than not was a discretionary purchase.

Our managers needed to see how they could be part of a solution. "What does it mean to take it personally?" I asked everyone at the arena. "What does it mean when you know for a fact that the beverage you just handed over to the customer was not made to the standard of espresso excellence? We each have to take accountability and responsibility for the things that we observe, the things that we experience. And the things that we learn."

If the latte wasn't perfect, I gave them permission to pour it out and remake it.

By asking them to choose to do what was right for the customer, I was giving them license to be leaders. I also was asking them to take their jobs personally, and to recognize the responsibility they had to themselves as well as one another, their families, and to all the people who came before them who were relying on us to preserve and enhance the *Starbucks Experience*.

The success we had enjoyed in the past, I emphasized, was not an entitlement. We had to earn it every day—one cup at a time.

Ultimately, I was asking them to do much more than just increase sales. If Starbucks was not a profitable business we would cease to exist, and if we ceased to exist we could not continue to create human connections and thus pursue our core purpose, which was and continues to be to achieve that fragile balance between profitability and social responsibility.

Each customer deserved the perfect beverage and to be treated as a human being in a world that could feel dehumanizing. Reminding our partners about this dual role was the intent of the experience in New Orleans.

"The power of the Starbucks brand is not some external force," I said in closing. "It is you."

After the conference, thousands of managers returned to their stores across the country with more than new expertise. Many believed that they had the potential to help turn the company around. They also had the desire to do so.

The outcome of the multimillion-dollar conference could not be quantified, but without coming together as we did, I know without question that Starbucks would not have recovered from its bleakest days.

There was a day during the transformation that Starbucks' stock price dipped below seven dollars a share, down more than 80 percent from the 2006 high. Around that time, I took a phone call from an anxious shareholder who managed money for a large financial institution.

"Howard, we've owned this stock for a long while. We know you're under tremendous pressure and we feel very strongly that this is the time to cut the healthcare benefit." For years, Starbucks had been spending more money on healthcare coverage for our partners than we spent on coffee. Between 2000 and 2009, healthcare costs were up almost 50 percent per partner. "Everyone will understand you had no choice," he told me. It was a short phone call.

Of course we had a choice. Yes, eliminating or reducing healthcare for our partners could immediately boost profits. Wall Street would cheer. But it would be utterly unfair to thousands of people and their families, and verge on inhumane. It would also sap spirits and breach trust. I knew we'd never recover.

Being a public company comes with fiduciary responsibilities to investors. To achieve the long-term value for them, it's always been my belief that a company must first create value for its employees as well as its customers. Unfortunately, Wall Street does not always see it the same way and too often treats investments such as healthcare coverage or, say, the New Orleans conference, as dilutive. Such a short-term perspective can bring down the company's value.

Wall Street's failure to recognize future benefits of current expenditures, as well as its push to see growth every single quarter, is part of the short-term mentality that's become a systematic problem of modern-day capitalism. There's little patience or tolerance for the necessary investments, risk-taking, and inevitable mistakes that keep companies successful. Companies that become complicit with Wall Street, and fear the short-term costs of reinvention and change, even failures, don't stand the test of time.

I also understood, however, that not every decision Starbucks made would feel good. There are times when the survival of an organization requires choices that result in sacrifice and losses for individuals, as well as for the organization itself.

Turning Starbucks around demanded undoing mistakes, and that caused pain. For example, because we opened too many stores, we had to close some six hundred poorly performing ones. Because our operations in Seattle had gotten bloated, we had to lay people off at our headquarters. These moves were necessary to return us to profitability and sustain the business. The emotional toll they took on me was nothing compared to the effects on people who lost their jobs or watched colleagues pack up their desks or hand in green aprons. I got emails from partners who felt betrayed and questioned whether we were honoring our values. Read one curt note: "To provide an uplifting experience that enriches people's lives every day. Do you remember when that used to mean something? I do." Never had I felt more accountable for ensuring that the company's success was sustainable.

That's why eliminating healthcare coverage was not an option I would consider when the shareholder called me. Despite the immediate financial gains, not every decision we made could be economic.

In 2011, Starbucks began a run of thirty consecutive fiscal quarters of record revenue and earnings. The transformation that unofficially began with a leaked memo in 2007 became part of Starbucks' history as we transitioned from turnaround to growth mode.

For me, that transformation period was a revelation: I'd witnessed what was possible when individuals come together to achieve a shared goal. We had defied predictions of our demise, and were thriving.

I emerged from this time feeling empowered and wondering if perhaps Starbucks wasn't built for something bigger than I originally envisioned. Going forward, maybe we could use our success and scale for good in ways we had yet to imagine. It was just an idea, until it became an imperative.

CHAPTER 5

Powerless

My mother walked at a breakneck pace for what seemed like hundreds of blocks to my wiry, seven-year-old legs. We passed my elementary school, P.S. 272, crossed the busiest avenue, and walked by the retailers of my youth: Waldbaum's, Grabstein's Deli, and Ruby the knish man, who served steaming ten-cent potato knishes from his dented rolling wagon. Then we boarded a public bus that trundled north.

Some of the Brooklyn neighborhoods we rode through were different from Canarsie. Their aging tenements were built decades before the sterile 1950s towers of our public housing complex. But I also saw familiar sights. Women pushed strollers or pulled metal baskets full of groceries. Men gathered on corners and in front of restaurants, in collegial packs. More than one movie theater marquee announced that *The Alamo,* starring John Wayne, was "COMING SOON," and signs in luncheonette windows declared allegiance to Coca-Cola or Pepsi-Cola.

After my mother and I stepped off the bus, we walked a bit farther to join a crowd of people spilling off the sidewalks and into the streets, standing shoulder to shoulder. For an hour, all of us waited. Finally, there was applause. Surrounded by adults twice my height, I could not see the person that people seemed so excited about, but I could hear the voice, full of charm and certainty, that would soon become familiar.

"My name is John Kennedy, and I come here as the Democratic

candidate for the presidency of the United States." Given the distance I recall traveling with my mother and the length of time I recall listening, I believe that we were standing at the corner of Fulton Street and Nostrand Avenue, about five miles from Canarsie, on October 20, 1960. And although I cannot recall the exact words John F. Kennedy delivered to us—Kennedy gave nine speeches in Brooklyn that month, five of them in one day—I have searched archives and found copies of those speeches, and I can easily imagine which of his words must have resonated with my mother and left a mark on my own consciousness.

"I don't say that all people have equal talent," Kennedy told his crowd of supporters. "But what I do say is that everyone should have their chance to develop their talent equally." My mother and I were far from where he stood, but I can remember my mom craning her neck to see her candidate, and smiling, which she didn't do all that often. My mother was five foot four inches tall, had a slight frame and dark hair, and dressed plainly. That day, she glowed.

"I want it said at the end of our administration, if we are successful, that every American had an equal chance, every American had a fair chance to develop his talents, and that is all we ask and that is all that any American asks." I can still feel my mother's hand gripping mine tighter with each word. Only when Kennedy stopped speaking did she release my hand, so she could clap.

Nothing matched my mother's deep affection for JFK. My father seemed indifferent; I don't remember him talking much about the charismatic politician. But my mother listened to Kennedy as if he were speaking directly to her, Elaine Schultz.

She did not have to bring me along that day. It was such a haul. But I like to think that doing so was her way of showing me just how much she longed to believe in the yet unfulfilled promise of the country, and in the possibilities it held for her son.

I opened the door to a dark apartment and the sound of wailing. My fifth-grade teacher had told us all to leave school before the final bell, and when I arrived home I saw my mom paralyzed on the couch. She stared at the television through tears as the Magnavox's rabbit-ear antennas and black-and-white lines delivered what may have been the worst news she'd ever heard.

In the past hour, her favorite newscaster, the stately Walter Cronkite, had appeared on live TV in shirtsleeves and a skinny tie. Seated behind a desk in a bustling CBS newsroom, he held up a photograph of a long black Lincoln Continental driving down a city street, and pointed out the backseat of the four-door convertible where John F. Kennedy and his wife, Jackie, had been sitting when the president had been shot. That was all Cronkite knew until he was handed a piece of paper. Peering through his black-rimmed glasses, he read what was written on live TV.

"From Dallas, Texas, the flash apparently official." Cronkite removed his glasses and looked into the camera. "President Kennedy died at one P.M. Central Standard Time." He looked at a clock on the wall. "Two o'clock Eastern Standard Time, some thirty-eight minutes ago."

For a few empty seconds, he didn't speak.

This clip replayed during the incessant news coverage that followed the assassination of our president. I watched it over and over with my mom, reliving the moment, each time hoping, foolishly, that the words Cronkite read would be different. Instead, the most trusted man in America blinked back tears.

For the next three days, my mother cried and smoked as she watched TV, devastated. Her attention didn't deviate from the screen. She didn't eat, she barely slept, she didn't dress for the day. Her grief was visceral and thorough and deep enough to drown in. Those tears that didn't soak into Kleenex or get wiped on her sleeve dripped onto the clear plastic cover that protected our couch from us.

My father was moved by Kennedy's death, too, I think, but not enough to join her vigil. I must have understood that it was up to me to fill the empty space next to her. Also, I wanted to be there. So together we sat in a haze of cigarette smoke, staring at the TV screen. Amid scenes of orchestrated moments of a wife and a country in mourning, newscasters would ad-lib eulogies with phrases like "a promise unfulfilled." They were trying to make sense of his murder for themselves, and for us.

No one close to our family had died during my short life, except Billy's dad, who had a heart attack. That was my first experience with death. Kennedy's assassination was my second, and I absorbed the tragedy through my mother, because when you're ten, your mother matters more than a president.

She experienced her hero's death in phases. In my memory, she was inconsolable at first, then grim and eventually inaccessible, even to a son sitting so close. The two of us never talked to each other about what we were witnessing or experiencing. Compatriots in emotional isolation, I watched as the loss that struck her like a thunderbolt on Friday afternoon settled over her like a lead blanket.

On Sunday, before the president's funeral procession left for the Capitol, the TV cameras took us to the basement of the Dallas police station where, voices of newsmen told us, any minute now the president's accused assassin, Lee Harvey Oswald, would be ushered from the jail to an armored vehicle that would take him to a maximum-security prison. Then Oswald appeared. He looked quite ordinary in a collared shirt and sweater as he was swiftly marshaled through a frenzy of plainclothes detectives and reporters. Suddenly, a scuffle. Another man burst through the cluster and ran up to Oswald. The sound of a gunshot followed. Oswald crumpled forward as a pack of suited men descended on him and a voice yelled, "He's been shot. He's been shot. . . . There's no doubt about it, Lee Harvey Oswald has been shot!" My mother screamed.

It was some years later when my mother was wheeled out of our apartment on a stretcher and into the small elevator of our building. As she was driven away in an ambulance for reasons I never knew, I looked on from our seventh-story window. I can still feel my skin prickle.

Did I understand at the time—I was maybe eleven or twelve—that my mother was ill with a disease I could not see? That something other than her bones was broken? Did I understand why her condition had to be whispered about? Perhaps I did, which is why as a boy I felt helpless and ashamed. When she returned from the hospital, the reason she went in was never discussed in front of me. And my parents' silence on the matter implied that the shame I felt was warranted.

I am not sure when I came to know that my mother suffered from depression. In the 1950s and 1960s, depression was not widely understood or considered a common, socially acceptable condition. It was not treatable with the antidepressant medications that exist now. Day to day, my mother did not come off to me as a person in distress.

Her own life circumstances were not easy. From girlhood, she received the brunt of her mother's verbal brutality. As a young married woman and mother, she was saddled with financial pressures, the stress of raising three children in a tiny apartment, and a tense marriage to a man who hopscotched from job to job and had a fiery temper.

I was aware that she was sad at times, but in the days and weeks after President Kennedy's death she was as dark as I'd ever known her. She became emotionally erratic and unpredictable. One night, with the whole family in the car, my father drove through a stop sign. A policeman pulled us over and asked my father to get out of the car. From the backseat, I could see the policeman write my father a ticket, and my eyes widened as my father ripped the ticket to pieces right in front of the cop. Scraps of paper fluttered to the ground like snow in the glare of our car's beaming headlights. I'd never even conceived that such an act of disrespect to a police officer was possible. My dad had broken the law! I unloaded my astonishment from the backseat. "Dad, I can't believe you did that!" I said, or something to that effect. Whatever words flew from my mouth prompted my mother, in a flash of emotion, to whip around in her seat, reach her arm into the back of the car, and whack me across the face with a cold hard hand.

As she aged, her darkness increasingly showed up as anger and even cruelty. The mother-in-law Sheri knew, and the grandmother my kids knew, was a broken woman.

The extent of her depression was revealed to me in later years. She had initially been treated with electroshock therapy, which was administered more crudely than it is today. I do not know how long or how often my mother got those treatments, or how they were paid for, or what other side effects they may have had. I also found out that my mother suffered at least one nervous breakdown, which may have been the reason she was taken to the hospital that day in my memory.

There was also the time that she may have tried to take her own life.

One day, Billy's mother told his older brother, Marty, that my mom had taken too many sleeping pills and needed to be driven to the hospital quickly. How Billy's mother knew this I don't know. What I do know is that Marty, who was just fifteen or sixteen at the time and had his junior driver's license, somehow got to my mom and gathered her in his arms, set on taking her to the hospital in his uncle's car. As Marty carried my mother to the elevator, my father showed up, took over, and brought her to the hospital himself.

The idea that my mother would try to take her life is almost too painful a scenario to imagine, or accept. But I also knew a lot was not right with my mom.

There were times during my childhood when I felt helpless. The murder of a president and an assassination that played out on TV come to mind. But I struggled even more with having no control at home, especially when I witnessed what I perceived as my parents' emotional traumas, whether or not they were self-induced. The image of my dad in a cast, unable to work. The internal reel of my mother being lifted into an ambulance, lost even to herself. The calls from bill collectors whose demands my family could not meet. These memories evoke feelings of powerlessness that sit with me still. How I wanted to reshape the status quo, for my parents and for myself. But I was a kid. I had no idea what to do. Paralyzed in my skin, I didn't have the words, the authority, or the know-how to change what seemed like fate. I had the impetus, but not the means.

Only on the playgrounds, the sport courts, or on chessboards could I affect an outcome.

At home, all I could do was try not to further upset my father or make my mom's low moods worse. So instead of injecting myself into chaos, I peeled away by hiding under the bed covers during the uncomfortable card games, retreating to the stairwell, or sitting next to my mother in silence.

My attempts at self-restraint made childhood easier as a boy. But as I grew older and began to exert control over my own life and, eventually, lead a company, I was no longer able or willing to tolerate feelings of powerlessness.

I believe most of us are uncomfortable being bystanders when we see something broken, or when we experience someone suffering. But for a lot of us, it's hard to know what to do once our awareness is awakened and our empathy is piqued. This has definitely been true of me, and in a way this book is about my journey to understand how to activate the power we all have to make meaningful differences in people's lives.

My mother tried, despite her demons, to bring stability, even hope, to our family life. She kept a spotless home. She packed school lunches, tossed me sandwiches to fuel my schoolyard games, hushed us so we wouldn't rile a sleeping father, cooked delicious dinners, made us feel loved. During elementary school, she often picked me up after school and we'd walk hand in hand to a windowless little truck with LIBRARY ON WHEELS painted on its sides. Through a door behind the back wheel of the vehicle, I would enter a mobile library whose packed shelves gave me access to worlds beyond my own. My mom helped me get my first library card.

She believed America was a country where a kid from the projects had a chance to rise above his station in life. She got me to believe it, too, by exposing me to the words of JFK, leading me to books, and encouraging me to become the first in my family to get a college degree. It was my mother who imprinted upon me the belief that anything is possible in America. I love her for it. I also love America, because, for me, the promise was real.

The instinct to step in and help when someone or something I loved was hurting served me well leading Starbucks, a company I love almost as much as my family. After turning around Starbucks, my impulse to try to heal was directed at another object of my affection that was suffering.

CHAPTER 6

Dysfunction

I have come to believe that people must not stand by in the face of human distress and broken systems. And if these two predicaments are intertwined—if human suffering is the result of others abdicating their responsibilities, or showing a lack of respect for another person—it becomes what can only be described as an injustice.

In me, injustice sparks a restlessness I have tried to combat with the tools and resources I have at the time. As a kid, I could sit with my mother when no one else did. As a young man, I could give half my paycheck to my parents. As a young entrepreneur, I could provide healthcare benefits to workers who might not have them otherwise. As I've gotten older, my responses to my restlessness over injustice have become increasingly focused. I credit this shift to my maturing understanding of human nature and complex issues, and to the influence of those around me, especially my wife, Sheri, and daughter, Addison.

When Addy was a little girl and lost her first tooth, Sheri and I left her a letter from the tooth fairy. "I am so proud to be your Tooth Fairy!" it began. "You are a wonderful little lady with such a big heart and special soul, growing up to be such a good person. If I can provide such a special girl with a little advice, I'd say: Try your best in school, be a good listener, show respect to your teacher and your fellow classmates."

Respect has always been important to Addy, who has blossomed into a caring, strong woman. She is especially attuned to people who treat others meanly or with disregard. During summers in high school, she worked at a deli and sometimes came home talking about how rude customers could be. When she started dating, Addy would assess a young man's character by how well or poorly he treated the waitstaff at a restaurant. She continues to believe you can learn a lot about people by how they treat others.

My kids were fortunate. They grew up in a comfortable home, went to good schools, enjoyed family vacations. Still, Addy was keenly attuned to the world beyond ours, and she wanted to be part of it. In high school, she volunteered at food banks and shelters. As a social worker, she's held jobs in underfunded, understaffed elementary schools where many of the kids are being raised by single parents, relatives, or in foster families, and come from dangerous neighborhoods. She's counseled young people in the LGBTQ community, and provided guidance for men and women with addictions. Most recently, she has served as a postgraduate fellow at the Robin Hood Foundation, a nonprofit that fights poverty in New York City.

For years, Addy and I have made a little ritual out of occasionally sitting and talking on a bench outside a Starbucks store near our home. When she was younger, I tried to impart some wisdom during those treasured father-daughter moments. These days, it's my daughter who enlightens me, teaching me patience and encouraging me to be more forgiving of human nature. Showing me how change can come, albeit slowly. I'm still learning.

My sense of right and wrong can at times be black and white, which leads me to be judgmental of those who I feel have, for example, violated a trust, a loyalty, or even a moral imperative. There have been times when I found it hard to forgive someone, even a family member or longtime friend or colleague, for a transgression, or to see past the inevitable foibles of human nature. I also tend to hold people in charge to especially high standards, myself included.

Sheri and Addy have helped me better understand my restlessness, curb my impatience, and focus my intentions. My experiences trying to address dysfunction around me, at work, and in the world, would also teach me to pair emotion with reason.

My upper body was trapped in a thick metal brace.

It was July 2011. With Starbucks back to financial health, I finally had time for an overdue operation. Doctors had fused a hairline fracture that I had sustained playing football as a teenager, and they ordered me to rest for at least a month.

Lying on the couch was not a natural state for me. I couldn't use a computer. Standing up was a painful chore. When I wasn't talking to coworkers on my phone about Starbucks business, I was distracting myself by watching television. And that month, cable news was playing up events unfolding in Washington, D.C.

Unless new budget legislation was passed by August 2, lawmakers and pundits were warning that the government would not be able to pay its bills.

I usually did not get sucked into play-by-play headlines. Stuck at home, however, immobile on the couch, I found myself fixated on the events. The most immediate, unresolved issue was whether or not the federal government should increase the so-called debt ceiling, the amount of money the country could borrow to pay its bills. Republicans said they wouldn't even vote on raising the ceiling unless a new bill included massive cuts to spending; their underlying tactic, however, was to obstruct the agenda of President Barack Obama. Democrats, meanwhile, said they wouldn't consider raising the debt ceiling that summer without also raising taxes.

Politicians postured in front of cameras, insisting they were doing everything they could to prevent the deadline from passing without causing harm to the American people, blaming their counterparts across the aisle for the gridlock. Day after day, leaders from both parties would disappear behind closed doors to ostensibly work out a deal, then emerge shaking their heads. When a bipartisan budget proposal surfaced, calling for stiff compromises, it never made it out of committee. Congressional votes were called, then canceled. Filibusters were threatened. Blame was abundant.

Two things in particular plagued me. First, missing the deadline, or hitting the ceiling, meant that some of the country's most vulnerable and deserving citizens—people on Medicare, veterans, Social Security recipients, government employees, and federal pensioners—would have late, partial, or missed payments. People would immediately feel the painful effects of political gamesmanship.

Second, raising the debt ceiling was a false goal. What the nation needed was not more debt but a comprehensive, balanced budget, coupled with a bipartisan economic plan that spurred long-term economic growth, increased jobs, and helped more citizens help themselves by lifting stagnant wages for the dwindling middle class, getting more young people through college, putting entrepreneurs back in business, and assisting the most vulnerable with basic needs, like healthcare.

In other words, not only was the fight itself poorly handled, they were fighting over the wrong thing in the first place. Instead of coming together to address these very real needs of the American people, politicians were arguing about whether to accumulate more debt and whether to raise or lower taxes. These are important macro decisions, but they are not growth strategies.

Our elected officials were putting the interests of their respective parties over the interests of the country, and not doing their jobs. Watching such reckless leadership from my perch on the couch, trapped in a neck brace, made me feel as upset and powerless as I once did as a kid listening to my parents fight about money.

With hours to go on August 2, 2011, Congress passed—and President Obama signed—the Budget Control Act of 2011, raising the debt ceiling by $400 billion. It was a short-term fix, and the political dysfunction that led to it did not go unnoticed.

Days later, Standard & Poor's downgraded the U.S. credit rating for the first time ever. The rating went from a sterling AAA status to the less impressive AA+. The reason for the downgrade was not financial: S&P cited "political brinksmanship" for making America's governance "less stable, effective and predictable." This third-party indictment of elected leaders further stoked my ire.

I was witnessing these events in D.C. through an unusual lens:

I was a CEO coming off two years steering a company back to sustained profitability and growth mode, and I was feeling relief as well as confidence. I had seen what was possible when committed people come together to solve problems with creativity and judiciousness.

Also, that July, for the first time in years, I was in a position— physically, because I was relegated to the couch, and mentally, because Starbucks was stable—to contemplate issues beyond our own business.

And I was a steward of a company whose founding mission was to be an economic, intellectual, and social asset in communities. I never forgot that.

Finally, I loved my country.

That summer, a thick exasperation washed over me. Our elected officials were failing to honor a core principle of democracy, which is a willingness to compromise for the good of the whole. Instead, too many were being driven by self-preservation. By failing to work together to find common ground and budge from their party's ideology, they hoped to ensure their own reelection. Worse than partisanship and self-interest, we were witnessing a collapse of the democratic spirit, and that, more than anything, distressed me.

Like many citizens I spoke with, I wondered what I could or should do.

Sitting at home in 2011, I also pondered what, if any, role Starbucks might play given the news of the day, while keeping in mind my fiduciary responsibilities to the company. Starbucks had dipped its toe into a sort of grassroots activism before. In 2008, we offered a free brewed coffee on Election Day to anyone who said they voted, and again to people who pledged to volunteer in their communities as part of a call for national service.

I thought about a passage of our recently updated mission statement, which we had written during the transformation: "Every store is part of a community, and we take our responsibility to be good neighbors seriously."

I asked myself, *What does it mean for a company to be a good neighbor?*

The Sunday before I was scheduled to return to work in early August, I wrote a memo to Starbucks partners asking them to recognize that our customers might be feeling stressed about political events. We could try to ease their anxiety, I suggested, by continuing to make our stores a friendly local respite.

I received enough emails from partners who appreciated the sentiment that it made me want to do more. *Could we get the attention of elected officials who had stopped working for the people?* A few weeks later, I sent another letter, this one to 150 business leaders. I respectfully asked each CEO to make two pledges. First, to boycott political contributions to all incumbent politicians until Congress and the president reached a bipartisan, long-term deal on debt, revenue, and spending.

"We aim to push our elected leaders to face the nation's long-term fiscal challenges with civility, honesty, and a willingness to sacrifice their own re-election," I wrote.

The second pledge I asked of my fellow CEOs was to commit to creating more jobs.

"The only way to get the country's economic circulatory system flowing again is to start pumping lifeblood through it. We are not going to wait for government to create an incentive program or a stimulus. We are hiring more people now. We do this because we want to set in motion an upward spiral of confidence."

Now that I was voicing my opinions beyond the walls of Starbucks, the letter invited outside criticism. "Sorry, Howard, we need fewer not more businesspeople involved in the political process," wrote one prominent former CEO in a blog criticizing the boycott idea. Fox News called it "risky business." Others simply disagreed with my approach.

One chief executive declined to make the pledges because, he argued, the roots of America's fractured political system went beyond money and special interests to include unfair election practices like gerrymandering. In other words, my focus was misplaced.

There were also backers. "What I particularly like about Schultz's idea," wrote columnist Joe Nocera in *The New York Times*, "is that it is not just another plea for compromise and civility, which does nothing to affect political behavior." Nocera called the pledges hardheaded and practical.

Encouraged, I wrote a third letter, this one addressed to the American people. It was intended to express not just my voice, but the voices of many. It appeared as a full-page ad in national newspapers:

> I love our country. And I am a beneficiary of the promise of America. But today, I am very concerned that at times I do not recognize the America that I love. Like so many of you, I am deeply disappointed by the pervasive failure of leadership in Washington. . . . While our Founding Fathers recognized the constructive value of political debate, we must send a message to today's elected officials in a civil, respectful voice they hear and understand, that the time to put citizenship ahead of partisanship is now.

The letter invited "fellow concerned citizens" to join me on a call-in town hall meeting streamed online. On September 6, as Congress and the president returned from their summer breaks, I sat in front of cameras with a panel that included a Harvard Business School professor, a federal budget expert, and the cofounder of a bipartisan group whose mission was to fix government by focusing on issues, not ideologies.

"We're here to change the hyper-partisanship in Washington!" said our enthusiastic moderator, kicking off the call, and for ninety minutes the panelists and I shared our opinions while people called in to express anguish and ideas with refreshing civility.

Yet something about the whole broadcast felt off. Unproductive. The people who called in were a narrow sliver of the populace. We were talking to ourselves. The other panelists, who were much more experienced with government than I was, seemed to lack a sense of urgency.

Restless in my seat, I asked myself how sitting on a panel would help the country.

In the end, airing my voice made me feel less powerless, as did withholding my own political contributions. But feeling better is not the same as doing better.

Speaking out is a necessary beginning, but not the same as real change.

My frenzy of expression that summer was the start of a longer journey. As the country's slide into antagonistic, partisan paralysis continued, my frustration flared and I grappled with more questions: When was it right to speak out as citizen Howard Schultz? When was it right to speak out as Starbucks' chief executive officer? Should Starbucks speak out as a company, through words and actions? What words were worthwhile? Which actions would have meaning? More broadly, what did it mean to be a good corporate citizen, and what roles should companies play in helping the societies in which they flourish? Did I have a responsibility, as a citizen and as a CEO, to try to help the country in which I had achieved my own dreams?

A year after the so-called debt ceiling debacle, elected officials in both parties were back at it, spreading false fears, provoking uncertainty, once again using the nation's budget to try to score points for political self-interest rather than steer the country toward shared prosperity.

On January 1, 2013, two laws were scheduled to take effect: previously enacted tax cuts would expire, raising taxes for most Americans, and $500 billion in government spending would immediately stop.

An angst-ridden message being sent by politicians and ginned up by the media was that a simultaneous tax hike and spending cut would cause financial pain for ordinary people, depleting families' take-home income while eliminating government jobs, contracts, and programs that millions counted on for income.

This was not true. The immediacy of the effects was being distorted: the majority of Americans would not suffer some cataclysmic drop in financial security on New Year's Day if a new law wasn't passed. Politicians were imposing unnecessary anxiety on the American people, who were still worrying about their wallets and panicking that the value of their nest eggs would drop suddenly, as they had during the financial crisis of 2008.

I read the morning headlines and listened to the news as I drove to work. So much more was at stake than quickly passing a budget. The great hope and challenge of American history has been to widen opportunity. As a beneficiary of that opportunity, I was becoming increasingly dismayed that the political antics in D.C. were putting access to opportunities like education and jobs out of reach for more people. Another fiscal crisis had been manufactured and now the country was holding its breath to see if politicians' failure to reach a practical compromise through collaborative debate would push us over what was being called "the fiscal cliff" on January 1.

I did not want to stand idly by as fearmongering replaced collaborative governing, leaving a nation in the lurch. Writing letters as I had done a year earlier seemed pointless. If anything, disrespectful discourse had increased, political divides had widened.

Just before the Christmas holiday, I convened a group of people at Starbucks to discuss what the company might do. I did not think we'd dramatically shift the behavior of elected officials. But staying quiet was unacceptable to me and, I believed, to a lot of people at the company who expected us to stay engaged now that we had already spoken out. We just had to act in a way that reflected our authentic voice and values as a company.

We came up with an idea. Rather than add to the country's angst, we would try to inject a positive message into the fray via an unexpected messenger.

On December 26, 2012, we asked baristas in our 120 Washington, D.C.–area stores to write "Come Together" on customers' cups. We chose those two words because they reflected what we believed to be a widespread hope that Republicans and Democrats would come together to avoid the cliff and enact a long-term budget.

This was the first time that we used the cup to deliver a message. For years, we'd rejected requests to advertise on Starbucks' white and green cup. It was a sacred space that carried our core product and became personal the moment a barista handed the cup to a customer. The closest we ever came to using the cups to make a statement was printing inspiring quotations on its sides.

Of course, I knew that the chances of a senator seeing "Come Together" scribbled on a cup and having a moral awakening were slim. But I viewed writing "Come Together" on cups an act of civic engagement, no less American than holding up a picket sign or writing to your congressperson.

How the company expressed its intentions going forward would continue to be an ongoing experiment.

The country avoided falling off the manufactured cliff when the U.S. House of Representatives approved a Senate bill that temporarily staved off the widespread tax increases and spending cuts. It was another short-term fix. No long-term budget was yet in place.

Ten months later, in October 2013, the federal government shut down. It felt like a massive slap in the face to the country.

On the second day of the shutdown, I was walking through our Seattle headquarters. Starbucks operations are housed in a long, nine-story brick building that was once a warehouse and distribution center for the catalog division of Sears, Roebuck and Company. Floors that once housed all manner of goods had been gutted and redesigned into a colorful maze of intersecting hallways, open stairways, clusters of comfy chairs for impromptu conversations, and meeting rooms named after our coffees. Each floor has a unique layout, and walking around the building can be a fun or infuriating experience. It's quite easy to get lost.

At the center of the building's eighth floor, four divergent hallways merge in a bright, communal space that includes a fully functioning Starbucks store. Several times a week, I stood in line for a beverage. Depending on the time, I drank either a doppio espresso macchiato—

two shots of espresso with a dollup of steamed milk—or a fresh-brewed cup of dark roast coffee.

Walking by the espresso bar that day, I saw a new hire, John A. C. Kelly, waiting in line. John is hard to miss and easy to approach. Tall and affable, he often looks as if he's about to break out in a smile. John had been hired to proactively represent Starbucks with governments and other civic stakeholders, in the United States and around the world.

Starbucks has never maintained a Washington, D.C., lobbying office. Compared to major companies in industries that are far more regulated than coffee, our presence in the nation's capital, aside from our stores, has been limited. Over the years, we have lobbied the government on issues related to climate change, food safety, higher education, veterans, youth hiring, taxes, international trade, and workplace policies.

In the nineties, I'd been invited to the White House and Capitol Hill to talk about Starbucks' unique healthcare benefits. During the last decade, however, we were not proactively sharing our company's full story with lawmakers, missing a chance to provide a deeper understanding of our business philosophy, as well as advocate for the ways that companies can show up in society. John was hired to help steward a more proactive approach.

His knowledge of D.C. was paired with a passion for a good cause. I was curious about John's opinion on the shutdown. He told me it was an embarrassment and a travesty for the country. "What do you think we should be doing about it?" My question caught him off guard. What CEO steers into a political quagmire? "John, what would *you* do about it?" I was trying to encourage John to think differently, and give him permission to shed any preconceived limits about how corporations addressed social and political issues.

Enthused by our conversation, John headed to the office of Vivek Varma, the company's head of public affairs, and the brainstorming began. It was fueled by questions. How does a company go beyond rhetoric without veering into heavy-handed activism? How could we minimize being perceived as opportunist when we were not looking to profit from the shutdown, but show up as a responsible corporate citizen? Could we do something to unite people on both sides of the fiscal debate without being divisive and becoming part of the problem? What, exactly, did we expect to accomplish?

A week into the shutdown, a headline pulled at my heart and incited in me a new sense of fury and urgency: "Shutdown Denies Death and Burial Benefits to Families of 4 Dead Soldiers." Four of America's troops who had been deployed to Kandahar province in southern Afghanistan were killed when they knowingly entered a minefield to rescue wounded comrades.

Sergeant Patrick C. Hawkins and First Lieutenant Jennifer M. Moreno were twenty-five years old.

Private Cody J. Patterson and Sergeant Joseph M. Peters were twenty-four.

These young soldiers' bodies were scheduled to arrive at Dover Air Force Base the next day, according to articles, but if their families wanted to be present when the flag-draped coffins of their loved ones arrived, they now had to pay their own way to Delaware.

Under the terms of the shutdown, the Department of Defense was withholding the usual travel funds as well as death benefits, including $100,000 for each family, a twelve-month allowance for housing, and money to pay for each fallen warrior's funeral.

In business, how companies spend money reveals their values. Had I cut healthcare benefits for Starbucks partners when pressured, the move would have been unethical and communicated a lack of respect for our people. Running a business was different than running a government, but denying death benefits, even if temporarily, telegraphed profound disrespect for the Gold Star families of these four fallen young soldiers. I tried to put myself in the shoes of the parents, and imagined their pain had been compounded.

The treatment of these families was more than undignified. It was unconscionable. It also was indicative of a bigger issue: our government's failure to allocate resources to address the needs of Americans in distress, including, but beyond, veterans and their families. This latest transgression was undeniable proof that the dysfunction among our political class had reached a new low.

We decided to implement one idea the brainstorming had wrought. A longtime Starbucks partner suggested that Starbucks start a petition urging the government to reopen. I liked it because I saw a petition as another form of civic engagement, one that Starbucks was uniquely suited to execute. Through our stores, we could reach citizens around the country who also felt appalled, frustrated, powerless. With the clock ticking, the idea had to be simple to execute. All we had to do was email the petition to store managers with instructions to print and display it, and provide them with context.

A few people at the company tried to nix it, calling a petition a campy exercise with an unrealistic goal. I explained the beauty was not the outcome, but the intention, and what that intent could mean to our own partners and customers. Here was a chance to use our scale for good, and authentically demonstrate our values. It was a chance not to amplify my voice alone, but to create a direct, democratic forum and give more people a voice.

On Friday, October 11, customers who entered Starbucks stores in the U.S. came across something a little different: a small table with some pens, a clipboard securing papers, and a self-explanatory invitation:

To our leaders in Washington, D.C., now's the time to come together to: (1) Reopen our government to serve the people, (2) Pay our debts on time to avoid another financial crisis, (3) Pass a bipartisan, long-term budget deal by the end of the year.

A corresponding digital petition resided online, but for me the power of the initiative was in creating a sense of engagement in the physical space of the store. There was something personal about walking into your local coffee shop and gathering around a table with neighbors to express your voice. At a time when government seemed remote, a pen and paper offered a tactile way to reach out. To be heard. John, who knew the partisan ways of Washington, D.C., was especially proud that the petition had found common ground by being written in a way that brought people together intellectually and emotionally, without dividing them politically.

The following Monday, the government shutdown entered its third week.

On Tuesday, thousands of FedEx envelopes, bags, and boxes arrived at our Seattle headquarters. The packages were heaped into huge bins and wheeled to a windowless fourth-floor conference room where more than one hundred volunteers from throughout the building showed up with an enthused, public-minded spirit and a professional intensity. At long tables, partners from every department of the company spread out stacks of petitions and began to sort and tally the signatures collected. They reviewed each petition page twice for accuracy and checked for duplicate names. They logged ZIP codes. It was not glamorous work, but those in the room radiated a sense of purpose. They felt like they were doing something. They had so much pride that the company was trying to give people a voice.

At one moment, amid the rustle of shuffling papers and whispered counting of signatures, I stood in the middle of the room and took in the hum of camaraderie. It was a sensation that did not emanate from the seat of government. The people in this room believed what they were doing was worthwhile. Their pride was real. Their intentions pure.

I got a little choked up.

"The work you are doing right now, it probably was not what you came into Starbucks to do today," I said as the buzz quieted. "But I just want to say a few things. In your hands is a physical manifestation of our values and guiding principles." Never did I doubt, I told them, that we should do this. "We all know that America is better than this and we all know that something is wrong, and if we just sit here as a company or as citizens and do nothing and allow this to continue, then we literally become part of the problem."

By midday, the signature tally was nearing 1.5 million, with more than one thousand stores' petitions yet to be counted.

On Wednesday, sixteen cardboard boxes packed with petitions

arrived at a Starbucks store on Pennsylvania Avenue in Washington, D.C. About twenty partners wearing their green aprons proudly delivered just shy of 2 million signatures to the Capitol and to the White House.

On Thursday, one of our partners who climbed the steps of the Capitol emailed his team. "Yesterday in D.C. was extraordinary—My favorite day as a partner in four years at Starbucks."

On Friday, the federal government reopened.

The petition had nothing to do with it. The timing was coincidental. Did anyone in government even open the boxes? We never knew. Did it matter?

Many of us felt part of something bigger.

The number of signatures we collected and the feedback from customers and partners reflected a worn-out public that wanted to be heard. Next to some signatures, the words "thank you" had been written in the petition's margins. Customers told us it was a good idea to put pressure on Congress. That the petition's message was important, because the government was supposed to take care of its people. One person expressed hope that someone in Washington would listen to those they were elected to serve.

The petition was also criticized. Starbucks was accused of injecting a political agenda into commerce and, on the other hand, for not going far enough. Critics laughed, called us gadflies. John Kelly got an earful from his former colleagues in D.C. How could he be involved in something so superficial? John held his ground: "Remember why you went to Washington in the first place?" he countered. "Remember how you wanted to make a difference because you believed in government and that the people needed a voice?" This would not be the last time John's practical idealism influenced our actions.

In the days that followed, the emotions around the shutdown receded. The petition became a memory. I began to come to terms with a reality.

Yes, collecting and counting signatures had given many of our partners and our customers something more to do than watch the news and complain—which is sometimes as far as democratic engagement goes these days, which is not far enough.

But like the three letters I had written, and like our baristas writing "Come Together" on cups, the petition, too, was mostly symbolic. None of the outcomes were substantial enough to help people who were hurting. We had acted, yes, but not all actions are equal in value. Once again, feeling good is not the same as doing good. These were lessons only experience could teach me.

There is a place for protests and petitions and loud voices in a democracy. Symbols and speech are hugely meaningful—galvanizing and cathartic. The aspirational words of John F. Kennedy on that long-ago Brooklyn day, to give every American "an equal chance" at success, had moved my mother to push me toward bigger things. Ambitious words are a place where dreams begin. But one decade into the twenty-first century, the United States, a country founded on the most ambitious of words, was facing profound, complex challenges. The promise of America—which I define as having a chance to rise above your station in life in part because you have access to opportunities like education and employment—was becoming more elusive for more people. Every citizen should be able to attend good schools, and be in a position to obtain, hold down, and excel at a good job. If I really wanted Starbucks to try to make a difference in people's lives, going about it by calling out our elected officials was a fruitless route.

Flying across the country on Starbucks business had become a routine part of my job, but I never tired of the view. On clear days, during take-offs and landings, or between spotty cloud cover, I could look out the window and see pieces of America. Her office parks and skyscrapers. Her great lakes, brown rivers, and streaming highways. I've seen countless pool-spotted backyards and white-dotted graveyards and always, on the outskirts of big cities, rows and rows of identical houses lined up like obedient children waiting their turn. There are junkyards not far from gardens, and grain silos hours from smoky industry. On the shore of Lake Michigan, the Chicago skyline rises from the flat Midwest canvas like the page of a pop-up book. In San Francisco, bay bridges connect the dots of hilly environs. Whole mountaintops are missing in Appalachian coal country, while on Texas landscapes wind turbines dance in place. From coast to coast, I can spy unruly forests and mall parking lots and high school rooftops and sometimes even a steeple. Tiny towns sprout up along endless fields. Traveling at night, sometimes all I see is a single light.

From above, I watched America unfold like a majestic tapestry. But what I see from up high is a beautiful illusion. Truth is on the ground, in the miraculous, mundane, and messy details of people's lives. Truth is in the mud.

Starbucks is in every state. Whether people like the company or not, we are an undeniable presence in communities, on the ground across America. I always tried to spend as much time as I could on that ground and in our stores, talking to partners and customers—and listening more than I spoke. Among the things I've learned is that the cliché is true: most people do share the same desires—to be valued, to be understood, to be loved, to have a chance to go after our dreams, however humble or audacious those dreams may be. Beyond that, I've come to believe that the majority of people have potential that is easy to overlook, but that when tapped is boundless. Most people I have met in America want to be in control of their own fate. They just need a chance.

My colleagues and I were contemplating whether Starbucks had a bigger role to play in America, beyond creating a sense of human connection and community in our stores. A role in addressing the economic and social problems that had little or nothing to do with selling coffee. Could we, should we, apply the same creative muscle and rigor that we applied to our products and operations to help address problems facing the country? Was doing so part of our mission? Did we have a responsibility, as a corporate citizen, to wade into such choppy waters? And if so, how far could we go? How far should we go?

As a CEO and as a U.S. citizen, I was asking myself a larger question: *What does it mean not to be a bystander?*

PART
TWO

Intention and Reinvention

CHAPTER 7

The Dignity of Work

I saw the same man at the same Starbucks store almost daily. This wasn't unusual. We all have our daily routines. But each time I walked into the store near my home in 2011, I was, for some reason, struck by the sight of this middle-aged, neatly dressed gentleman. One day I walked up to him.

"I noticed that you're here every day. Thank you for coming to Starbucks." I extended my hand. Rather than just shake it, he took me aside. He knew who I was.

"Sir, I come here every day because I have nowhere else to go."

He was not homeless. He told me he had a family. But he had been out of work a long time. There were no jobs, he said, and after a few minutes, he started to cry. I put my hand on his shoulder. In his face, I saw shadows of my father.

Lack of work, I know, can be a destabilizing force, and not just financially. When we work, we bring home more than paychecks. Our jobs and places of employment are potential sources of joy, self-worth, or disgrace. And while a job well done can deliver pride and a sense of purpose, a bad job, or no job, can sap a soul.

In 2011, about 14 million Americans were waiting on the sidelines, unemployed. The vast majority, I would argue, were eager to be back in the game. Work demands a lot, but it also fulfills, and with no new jobs being created and our elected leaders failing to drive economic growth, I believed that the United States was facing a deficit that wasn't just economic. We had a deficit of dignity. And that was a problem.

I'd spent a lot of my life confronted with and contemplating the importance of dignity in our lives. Its tenets—self-respect and the sense that we are worthy of others' respect—were things I believed that my father lacked, and that I wanted for myself and others. Upholding human dignity is at the core of Starbucks' intentions, embedded in our mission.

But dignity, I have come to learn, is not something easily bestowed. It also must be earned. A job in and of itself does not endow us with self-respect. Rather, respect comes from having a choice of job. It comes from how we perform—our effort, our accountability, our results. And from how we are treated—when we are treated with compassion, with attention to our needs, and with gratitude for our contributions, our sense of self-worth is enhanced. Options, effort, achievement, respect—these are all sources of dignity. On the contrary, a bad boss, chronic unemployment, and poor performance chip away at our confidence. A lack of good job options, or access to them, can yield a collective malaise.

And while dignity is neither a right nor a privilege, it is essential to the good health of an individual, an organization, even a country.

"How are we going to get America back to work?"

It was Friday, August 26, 2011, and I was sitting among a dozen Starbucks people I'd called together from various parts of the company—coffee, digital, marketing, store operations, logistics. I'd assembled the group with Vivek Varma, our public affairs head. Vivek had become one of my most trusted colleagues since coming to Starbucks in 2008. He'd previously been at Microsoft, advising on communications and policy initiatives, and spent time on Capitol Hill after law school. Vivek brought a unique perspective to our work together. Raised in the small town of Chickasha, Oklahoma, by parents who had immigrated from India, Vivek was a nationally ranked tennis player and, as of that summer, a proud new dad. I valued his ability to stay calm under pressure and to ground big ideas in practical thinking.

My new intention, I explained, was to spur job growth in the country, beyond the people Starbucks was able to hire. Doing so could help rev the economy, making a difference in the lives of people like the gentleman I'd met in our store.

Of all the problems facing the nation, employment was an area in which Starbucks had the most credibility. Creating jobs was what we did. That year, the company was on track to hire twelve thousand more new partners globally. But we could only afford to employ so many people. If we wanted Starbucks to help make a dent in the country's high unemployment situation, we had to look beyond our own ability to hire.

I asked for ideas and provided a few guidelines. "We must do something soon." Analysts at Morgan Stanley had just lowered their economic forecast for the United States, warning that both the U.S. and Europe were close to yet another recession. Also, we had to produce measurable results, not just good feelings.

People began to offer thoughts. We could donate money to job-training programs, or use our stores as places for job seekers to get help with résumés and career counseling.

Adam Brotman spoke up. "I've been doing some of my own homework."

Adam was a Seattle-born entrepreneur who had founded the digital music company PlayNetwork, which had provided the music inside Starbucks stores since 1998. Now he worked for us, helping build our digital and mobile network for customers. Adam was smart, curious, and kindhearted and often volunteered for creative projects outside his job description. He continued, "My research keeps leading me to small businesses and the obstacles they're up against."

Small businesses can be the job engines of local economies. But they weren't growing. The Great Recession had slammed small companies especially hard, in part because they relied on capital from banks to fund their initial growth. But since 2008, many banks across the country had either closed or merged with bigger institutions, and most were only lending money to the most qualified, asset-rich borrowers. Not necessarily entrepreneurs.

If small businesses can't grow, they can't hire.

"We could do something like our farmer loan program," suggested Vivek.

For years, Starbucks had been helping coffee farmers access credit so they could grow their businesses. In 2011, we'd made about $14.7 million in loan commitments, reaching more than 45,000 farmers in seven countries. We planned to increase farmer loans to $20 million by 2015. The loans were distributed to farmers via nonprofits.

Someone brought up microfinancing, which is the practice of making very small loans, even just a few hundred dollars, to people with no assets. As someone who started a company with no money, I'd been fascinated by how microfinancing was helping entrepreneurs and small business owners in developing countries become self-sufficient. The idea of using that model for America's entrepreneurs was intriguing.

However, it was one thing to loan money to our own suppliers. Loaning money to businesses that had nothing to do with Starbucks, well, that would turn us into a bank. And Starbucks was not in the banking business.

Adam lit up like a kid with a new toy. "That's why crowdfunding is so exciting!"

Thanks to the Internet, anyone could go onto a website like Kickstarter and ask friends and strangers for as little as one dollar to help raise money for a cause.

Maybe, he suggested, we could start a fund and ask people to contribute.

The next day, Adam sent us a long email proposing that Starbucks create a separate entity that solicited money, which Starbucks could collect and distribute to a nonprofit that specialized in employment.

"We could identify organizations that are 100 percent focused on job creation and job training," he wrote. He sketched an ambitious but rough plan.

I invited Adam, Vivek, and few others to my house for pizza on Sunday to think it through.

Six of us gathered around the large island in my kitchen. I'd picked up some pizzas, which sat in open boxes on the table, and my golden retrievers, Harper and Finn, were lying at our feet. Those of us assembled grabbed slices and began riffing off of Adam's memo.

We agreed that focusing on funding small businesses made sense to us. Starbucks had spent more than a decade as a small, private company before going public, and each of our stores operated, in many ways, like its own small business. Within our stores, countless customers ran their own businesses on laptops and phones while sitting at our tables. More than one had shown me a business idea sketched while sitting in a Starbucks.

We also agreed we needed a reputable partner, ideally a trusted nonprofit.

My mind moved on to how we would execute the program. Crowd sourcing funds made sense, but we needed a way to inspire people to donate—something tangible, a symbol. Not a product we profited from, but something physical that connected people to the cause.

An image came to my mind: the bright yellow gel bracelets with the word LIVESTRONG that had been such fashionable statements of support for cancer patients years ago.

"A wristband. We need a wristband!" Now I was the kid with the new toy.

An hour passed. The pizza boxes emptied and the dogs retired to the den.

Vivek paced the kitchen, head down and hands in his jeans pockets, and summed up where we were at: One, small businesses were the most likely source of new jobs in America, and we thought we could find a way to help entrepreneurs get access to funds so they could build their businesses. Two, we needed the right partner. And three, Howard wanted to have a signature piece of merchandise— maybe a bracelet—that was associated with a collective effort to create jobs in the country.

"It's a time for experimentation," encouraged Vivek, and I knew he would give direction to everyone's creativity. "We will do this," he added, "but we've got some big questions." How would we collect money? How would we communicate to customers so they saw our efforts as legitimate and not a marketing stunt? How would we measure results to ensure we made a real difference?

The scope of our ambition was revealing itself. We could turn back, call it a night, pat the dogs on the head, and agree that writing letters and checks was much easier than whatever it was we aimed to achieve. But we, not just I, wanted to do something real. Something together, and something bigger than just us.

The next day, I wrote an email to Starbucks' directors. "What we want to do is bold, it's complicated, and it's risky," I wrote. "But it's also Starbucks. Entrepreneurial, curious, and courageous. It's in our DNA."

Hours after the brainstorming session at my house, Adam Brotman was on the phone, researching our plan with Nia Zhang. A creative thinker, Nia had worked in investment banking at Merrill Lynch before joining Starbucks in our marketing department. She, too, was intrigued by the potential of microfinancing.

One of the people they talked to was Rodney Hines, a thoughtful, dedicated partner who had a history of working with underserved communities and in public policy. Three years prior, he had joined Starbucks from Microsoft, where he oversaw their community affairs efforts. Now Rodney helped choose which charitable causes Starbucks supported, and he knew a lot of people who worked in philanthropic endeavors around the country.

"I have someone you should talk to," Rodney told Adam. "Have you heard of CDFIs?" he asked.

The clunky acronym was unfamiliar. CDFI stood for Community Development Financial Institution. Clunkier still. Rodney explained that CDFIs were financial organizations that lent money to start-ups, small businesses, housing projects, and nonprofit organizations in low-income areas throughout the country.

"Basically, CDFIs invest in parts of the country that banks ignore," Rodney said. He also knew a guy from Pennsylvania who headed a CDFI umbrella group.

At 11 P.M. that Sunday in Philadelphia, Rodney sent a BlackBerry message to a man named Mark Pinsky. "We have an idea you might be able to help with, we would love to talk." The next day they were on the phone.

Mark's organization was called the Opportunity Finance Network, or OFN for short. OFN loaned money and made grants to specific CDFIs, using money it received from banks, wealthy individuals, and donors. CDFIs leveraged the funds they received to attract additional loans from other financial sources, which the CDFIs then lent out as low-interest loans to entrepreneurs in the community.

When I learned about it, I was skeptical. The names—OFN, CDFIs—were unfamiliar. Would our customers trust them? Could we trust Mark? It felt safer to engage a high-profile nonprofit whose leaders I knew. But we were moving too fast to reject any option out of hand. We invited Mark to Seattle.

Meanwhile, we reached out to two well-known nonprofits, but by the end of the week both organizations said no to our request to join our evolving effort. I was disappointed but quickly shifted my attention to the unfamiliar cluster of letters. *What are these CDFIs?* I was now very curious about what Mark Pinsky would say when he came to visit.

Three years earlier, in September 2008, high winds in the eye wall of Hurricane Ike passed through downtown Houston with enough force to rip apart the roof of the city's sports stadium. In Houston's Third Ward, Ike left some areas uninhabitable, including the building where Sunshine's Health Food Store and Vegetarian Deli had been located for years. When owner Arga Bourgeois learned that her landlord would not repair Ike's damage, she feared she'd have to shut down the restaurant her father founded. No bank would lend her money to rebuild.

"Arga Bourgeois is the kind of business owner that CDFIs help," explained Mark. He was a speedy talker and his enthusiasm streamed through my car's speakers as I drove. He was in a conference room at Starbucks offices explaining how CDFIs worked to about thirty people. I was on the road and had to call in to the meeting.

After Hurricane Ike, a Texas-based CDFI loaned Arga thirty thousand dollars. By the spring of 2009, Sunshine Deli was back in business. Arga and her staff were back at work.

Thousands of small businesses like hers could not build, grow, or hire because they couldn't get even ten thousand dollars from a bank, said Mark. "Basically, CDFIs customize business loans, sort of like how Starbucks customizes its drinks. But how we do it is complicated, and our industry does a lousy job communicating our model. That's why no one knows about us." I appreciated Mark's transparency. He seemed like a straight shooter.

Mark went on, "CDFIs lend to people that conventional financial wisdom says won't pay you back, but they do." Since the mid-1980s, CDFIs had invested $30 billion–plus to help more than fifty thousand organizations. Ninety-eight percent of their loans got repaid.

"How?" someone asked. CDFIs charge borrowers less than traditional lenders. CDFIs also don't have the same profit pressures. More important, they bend over backward to help their borrowers succeed by providing nitty-gritty, hands-on help like bookkeeping, marketing advice, technical assistance, and mentoring. They know their customers.

Mark was proposing money we raised in Starbucks stores could be given to his group, OFN, which would pass 100 percent of the funds to CDFIs around the country. That money would be equity the CDFIs would use to borrow more money against and lend to any organization that provided jobs in the community. On average, he said, CDFIs raised and then lent seven times the original amount of a grant they received.

All of this was a mouthful to explain to a customer as he paid for his latte.

I've always tried to surround myself with people who have an expertise beyond my own, and who also share my values. For these reasons, I was coming to trust Mark and believe that he and OFN, with its reputable network of low-cost lenders, would be ideal partners to help us create jobs.

OFN and the CDFIs could vet borrowers, distribute loans, and track jobs created, he said.

Starbucks, in turn, would reimburse OFN for its operating costs to ensure 100 percent of every dollar raised from our customers went into communities. In addition, the Starbucks Foundation would make an immediate donation of $5 million to the fund. That way, OFN could start distributing money as soon as we launched the program, rather than wait for customer donations to add up.

The meeting ended with many answers, and also more questions. I expected as much. When you do something for the first time, questions and problems are the two things you can count on.

Every entrepreneur faces challenges he or she can't predict. A hurricane destroys your store. A competitor copies your product. An investor tries to steal your business. In more than thirty years, I've confronted these challenges and many others. A handful still haunt me.

My first big entrepreneurial hurdle presented itself one year after I had raised the initial $1.65 million to start Il Giornale and build three stores in Seattle. Jerry Baldwin—Starbucks' cofounder, my former employer, and my first investor—came to me and said that he and Gordon Bowker had decided to sell the company, which included Starbucks' six stores, its roasting plant, and the Starbucks name.

"The good news," he said, "is that we think you're the right guy to acquire Starbucks, Howard."

The bad news, I thought to myself, *is that I don't have any money.*

Jerry said he and Gordon would sell the company to me for $3.8 million, the amount they needed to exit the business without debt. They gave me sixty days to raise the money and said they would not try to sell it to anyone else during that period. The opportunity felt like destiny. Il Giornale already served Starbucks coffee, and Starbucks whole-bean business would complement Il Giornale's beverage business. If the deal went through, I'd more than triple my store count overnight, with prime locations throughout the city. Elated, I crafted an acquisition plan that I shared with Il Giornale's investors.

About a month into the process, Jerry called and shocked me with the news that he and Gordon had another offer. "You said that you were offering it to me exclusively!" I said.

"Well, the offer is from one of your shareholders," he said. Someone I trusted had secretly offered Jerry and Gordon $4 million—all cash with no due diligence. Jerry asked how confident I was that I could raise $3.8 million.

I had to be honest. "It looks good, but I can't guarantee it."

Jerry was straight with me. "Howard, I can't afford to lose the $4 million. We'll give you thirty more days to raise the money. If you can't, I'm sorry."

Not only was I about to lose Starbucks, but my rival investor's grand ambition, I would soon learn, was to convince the existing Il Giornale shareholders to merge with Starbucks, and distribute shares of the new entity in a way that would dilute my ownership. As the founder of Il Giornale, I knew this was unfair. It was also infuriating. Even if I didn't get ousted from the company outright, my influence would be so diminished that I feared Starbucks would not grow into the kind of company I envisioned. As an entrepreneur and a new father, I was coming to believe that imprinting a business with values, and creating its culture, is like raising a child: a foundation of expected behaviors and beliefs must be set when the business is young. Il Giornale was a toddler, and growing fast. We'd already established a real sense of camaraderie and mutual respect in our stores and offices. We felt like a family united by a purpose: to create community and to uphold human dignity among ourselves and for our customers. We did not think of Il Giornale as just a coffee business that existed to make money, but as a people business that sold coffee—which meant that decisions about budgets, expansion, and policies took into account how our people would be affected. I feared this delicately cultivated mind-set would be lost if my shareholder won Starbucks and took over Il Giornale. Too much was at stake for me to lose this fight.

At first I freaked out, even telling Sheri we might lose it all. Then I pulled it together and got ready to fight, and to win. I just had to figure out how. One night, after playing a game of basketball in a recreational league, I shared my predicament with a teammate and friend, Scott Greenburg. He was a young lawyer.

"We have to go see the senior partner in my law firm," Scott declared after hearing my dilemma.

"Who?" I asked.

"Bill Gates." It was 1987 and Scott was referring to William H. Gates, Sr., the father of the cofounder of Microsoft, William H. Gates III. At the time, I did not know either Bill.

The next morning Scott and I walked into the office of one of Seattle's most prominent legal minds. At six feet seven inches tall, the senior Bill Gates was a towering figure, in person and in town.

"Sit down," he said, taking out a notepad. "Tell me the whole story." I shared everything. My trip to Italy, working at Starbucks, raising money to start Il Giornale, my opportunity to buy Starbucks, and, finally, the name of the shareholder who had bid against me. He was among Seattle's business titans.

"Howard, we don't know each other, and I have to ask, have you left anything out?" I shook my head no. "And is everything you told me true?"

"Yes, Mr. Gates, everything I have told you is the truth." We talked a bit more. Finally, he said, "Howard, I want you to come back in two hours. Alone."

I walked across the street and got something to eat. When I returned, Bill said, "Howard, I'm coming with you to see your investor." My heart started palpitating.

When we arrived at the office, I felt like the Cowardly Lion on his way to an audience with the Great Oz. The titan was furious. "We invested in you when you were nothing!" he shouted at me, in front of Bill Gates, Sr. "Now you have a chance to buy Starbucks, but it's our money. If you don't take the deal we want, you'll never work again in this town. You'll never raise another dollar. You'll be dog meat." I was appalled and nervous, but also angry. If I let him buy Starbucks, all my work and dreams would be destroyed.

"This was *my* idea," I said, my voice shaking. "I brought it to you!"

The towering man next to me spoke. "It's despicable," Bill said to my rival, and his peer, "that someone of your stature would be so un-principled as to try to steal this kid's dream." The two older men stared at each other until Bill spoke again: "You are going to stand down. Howard is going to raise the money. Do you understand me? Stand down." Then we walked out.

No one with the stature of Bill Gates, Sr., had ever stood up for me like that. In fact, no male figure in my life had spoken on my behalf with such gusto and integrity.

In the elevator ride down to the lobby, I started crying out of grati-tude but also fear. I was pretty sure we had just won, but I still needed to raise the cash. That's when Bill did something that changed my life, but also the lives of countless others.

"Howard, I'm going to invest in your business and help you raise more money." I couldn't believe my ears. Not only had this man who I had just met defended me, but he was promising to personally invest in my dream *and* come up with a plan to raise the rest.

Bill Gates, Sr., did more than invest in my business. He showed me that a stranger could change the life of another stranger. This was a revelation. Until I met and married Sheri, I'd always felt as if I was on my own as I tried to not just make a living but also make my mark. Then I worked for Jerry and Gordon, who helped seed my dream. Now a man I barely knew had swooped in to help save it. Bill had my back at a time that I believed no one else, aside from my wife, did. This profound gesture was not lost on me. I think I understood that it was not only my responsibility to protect Bill's investment and get him a good return, but to pay his gesture forward.

Almost losing Starbucks in 1987 was a harrowing experience. If I had failed, others would have suffered with me, including Sheri and my employees. In 2011, versions of my story were playing out in the lives of entrepreneurs across the country who were up against their own chal-lenges.

In Canterbury, New Hampshire, the owners of a small organic pro-duce company, Luke and Catarina Mahoney, were about to lose their business because their farmland's lease wasn't being renewed and they couldn't afford to buy a new plot.

In Seaside, Oregon, Jimmy Griffin envisioned opening a small brewery that would draw tourism to a town that had lost its fishing and logging industries. Jimmy had the perfect location, a ninety-nine-year-old building. But without a loan, he couldn't afford to renovate it.

In Troy, New York, Robyn Scotland had been turned down by multiple banks for a loan to help her start a daycare business.

In recession-ravaged Barre, Vermont, Cynthia Duprey had lost her home-based business when a rainstorm destroyed her property; for a new source of income, she wanted to buy the town's only bookstore before it shuttered, but she couldn't get a bank to lend her money.

And in Southern California, Miguel Gonzales was looking to secure a few million dollars in financing so that Gonzales Northgate Market could build a new store and create more than a hundred jobs.

I didn't need statistics to tell me that Miguel, Cynthia, Robyn, Jimmy, Luke, Catarina, and thousands more like them were on the brink of success or failure. I had been there myself. Their aspirations were as real as my own. So was their fear of failure; mine still haunted me.

CHAPTER 8

Better Angels

Less than a mile from Starbucks' headquarters, the Port of Seattle occupies a large swath of Puget Sound's eastern shore. Standing in my office, I could look out over the surrounding industrial area and see the port's enormous gantry cranes as they loaded intercontinental cargo containers from massive ships onto waiting truck beds and railcars headed for destinations all around the country. Packed inside the anonymous big boxes, fresh from their Pacific crossings, were billions of dollars' worth of cars, computers, clothing, toys, housewares, machinery, and massive slabs of iron and steel. This heaving flow of goods is but one view of American commerce. But it is not the full story.

Another aspect can be seen thousands of miles from Seattle's bustling shores, in East Liverpool, Ohio, a small town just over the Pennsylvania border, tucked in a bend in the Ohio River. Once known as the Pottery Capital of the Nation, East Liverpool used to have more than one hundred factories that produced a stunning array of ceramic goods, from fine china to perfume flasks. By 2011, "Crockery City" had just two working pottery factories. One, American Mug & Stein, was down to just three employees. It once had dozens. At that time, unemployment in East Liverpool was hovering near 10 percent.

None of us at Starbucks knew about American Mug & Stein when we began our project to fund the growth of small businesses, though we hoped that our endeavor would spur hiring in places like East Liverpool. But in the fall of 2011, outcomes like that were a big if.

My earliest memory of thinking like a merchant goes back to childhood, and the first time I remember going into Manhattan. My aunt took me to Radio City Music Hall. More than the show, I remember where we went to eat when it was over.

Inside the Horn & Hardart Automat in Times Square was a wall of dozens of small windows. Behind each window was a different food. A turkey sandwich. A bowl of Jell-O. A slice of apple pie. Even a cup of coffee. I watched as my aunt put a coin into a slot, opened one of the little windows, which was hinged at the top, and removed a piece of pie. After the window closed, a new piece of pie appeared in the chamber! My aunt convinced me that a magician was working behind the scenes. I had no clue there was actually a hardworking staff behind the vast wall, constantly refilling the empty chambers. The pie tasted delicious; just getting it was an enchanting event. The thrill of the automat was not the pie. It was the experience.

My merchant mind-set, which was the part of me that was fascinated by what captured the imagination of consumers, by what compelled them to make a purchase, understood the importance of symbols and stories in engaging people's emotions. Sounds, colors, and symbols can all conspire to give ideas fuller life and create that sense of magic. And magic is not reserved for selling pie and coffee. It can extend to any endeavor—like trying to create jobs.

On a late September afternoon, a dozen fabric and plastic bracelets lay scattered across the coffee table in my office. Five of us were picking them up and trying them on. Most of the bracelets were pricey. I picked up a nylon rope bracelet from Saks Fifth Avenue. It was lovely, but sold for seventy-five dollars, way too costly for us to produce and sell in our stores. We were going to make half a million bracelets.

"We need a unisex design as elegant as this," I said, pointing to a sleek band. "And, Nia, much less expensive to produce and buy." Nia Zhang had taken charge of designing and sourcing the bracelets. She, too, understood that the wristband wasn't some gimmick.

I picked up a flimsier bracelet. "We also need a thicker band than this." An extra millimeter mattered. If you weren't proud to wear it, you wouldn't want to wear it, which meant you wouldn't donate.

Because our jobs program was complex, we kept the name simple: Create Jobs for USA. Clear, but not particularly inspiring, so we wanted a tag line that captured the program's spirit. After tossing around bracelets, we tossed around words. *Unity. In It Together. United. One Nation.* Someone recited a line from the Pledge of Allegiance.

"What about 'indivisible'?" said Gina Woods. Gina was a six-year partner who handled special projects. She had a knack for logistical details and big-picture thinking. People, myself included, loved working with her. She had grown up in Iowa and shared my love of dogs. As I often do with people who can offer unfiltered perspectives, I'd pulled Gina onto the project's team. The word "indivisible" had yet to become a political catchphrase, and in the fall of 2011 it felt familiar yet fresh.

Beyond the bracelets, there was a more complicated detail we also had to figure out.

No economic model existed to quantify how many jobs a CDFI loan created, so Mark's OFN team consulted with many labor economists to construct a methodology, which helped us determine that a $21,000 loan allowed a small organization to create or keep one job. To ensure the model's validity, we had it endorsed by experts at Moody's Analytics. To make it meaningful to Create Jobs donors, we used the CDFI's multiplier of 7 and expressed the benefits in the lowest common denominator:

Every bracelet purchased for $5 would generate $35 for a CDFI, and every $3,000 a CDFI received would generate $21,000 in money loaned, which equated to one job created or sustained. A few bucks for a bracelet added up.

Decision by decision, the ideas bandied about over pizza in my kitchen were taking shape. Now we just had to tell people what we were up to, and try to get their support.

On October 27, 2011, I sat in Busch Stadium in St. Louis watching the sixth game of the World Series. The Fox cable network was broadcasting the games, and a top executive from Fox Sports was seated near me. At one point in the game, I told him about Create Jobs.

"Howard, if the World Series goes to Game Seven, we may be able to clear TV ad space for you tomorrow night. Great exposure," he said.

We had a commercial in development but it wasn't airing for another week, when Create Jobs was scheduled to launch. As Game 6 wore on, the thought of running an ad stayed with me. The exposure we'd get during the final game of the most enthralling World Series in years—the first one to go all seven games in a decade—was too good to pass up. But it was unclear if the Series would go to seven games—if the Texas Rangers beat the hometown Cardinals, the Series would be over. The game was still tied after nine innings.

In the tenth inning, both teams scored and the game remained tied. Finally, in the eleventh inning, David Freese hit a walk-off home run to give the Cardinals a win, and a shot at the title. The stadium erupted.

I called our offices in Seattle and ignited a scramble. Our creative team and ad agency had less than a day to finish the sixty-second commercial so it could air during Game 7 of the Series.

The next night, my son, Jordan, who was twenty-five at the time, stood with me in Busch Stadium along the first-base line and a ball-toss away from home plate. Everyone in the stadium was on their feet chanting, whooping, waving. Bundled up in a red hoodie, I could feel the cold, electric air. The Cardinals were just one out away from a glorious win.

By far, the highlight of the night was being with my son.

Jordy and I had been going to sporting events before he could even walk. I remember carrying him to baseball games at Seattle's old King-dome, where Mariners outfielder Ken Griffey, Jr., would become his Mickey Mantle. With Jordan and me, baseball was a signature aspect of a deeper relationship that included lots of talks, joking around, laughter, a love of dogs, and years of sharing family vacations and ordinary moments. Unlike me as a kid, Jordy enjoyed being home with family when he was growing up, and he and his friends, whom I liked, spent a lot of time at our house.

He also was a rabid sports fan. Once Jordan could pick up a bat and throw a ball, he began playing team sports. Sheri and I rarely missed his games. Sitting on risers in fluorescent-lit school gymnasiums, or wrapped in raincoats on wet bleachers, we reveled in Jordan's natural athleticism and the sheer joy he took in competition. He was especially good at baseball, but basketball was his passion. He was a well-liked and respected member of his teams, and, like my dad, Jordan was a student of sports, a collector of stats, and an astute observer and analyzer of strategy. Jordan played four years of college basketball, then turned his passion into his profession by pursuing a career in sports journalism. In 2018, he became an insider analyst for ESPN, where he currently serves as the correspondent for an ESPN+ show, *The Boardroom.* My son absolutely loves his work; reading his writing and listening to his broadcasts bring me tremendous pride and joy.

Being at that World Series together was something neither of us would forget—especially the moment when Cardinals left fielder Allen Craig caught a fly ball that brought his team their eleventh World Series win.

What I did not witness that night was the moment the Create Jobs commercial aired for 25 million viewers watching the World Series. But I'd seen it earlier. We'd decided against something loud and splashy or celebrity endorsed. Instead we wanted something that got to the heart of what we were trying to do. The spot opened with plucky violin music playing as a white animated cutout of the United States appeared on a red background while blue words danced across the screen:

9.1 percent of us remain out of work. Together, we can change that.

For the next fifty-eight seconds there was only music. The ad featured no people and no voice-over. Just animation. The commercial cut through the spectacle of the Series as it told a story:

Small business, it's the backbone of America's workforce. When it grows, jobs grow. We have an idea that can help. Donate five dollars to the Create Jobs for USA Fund at a Starbucks or at CreateJobsforUSA.org and 100 percent of the donations will go to create and sustain small business jobs in communities across America. You'll get a wristband to show support. The Starbucks Foundation will also donate $5 million to show ours. All of us, working together. Indivisible.

When something seems so simple, that's when you know it started out very complicated.

On the morning of Monday, November 1, eight weeks after gathering for pizza in my kitchen, the crew that had been heads down every day huddled around the computer screens in my office as CreateJobsforUSA .org officially launched. Throughout the country, our baristas had been briefed. In each of nearly seven thousand stores, colorful foldouts explained to customers how the money raised would go to fund the growth of small businesses so that they could hire. And in front of each store's registers, wristbands waited. The final design was a stretchy, sturdy, elegant braided rope of handwoven red, white, and blue threads that wrapped twice around the wrist. The centerpiece of the wristband was a block of brushed aluminum, imprinted with the word INDIVISI-BLE. Every day for almost a year, I would wear one on my wrist.

Mark Pinsky and I headed to New York City to promote Create Jobs. The media coverage gave CDFIs a level of national recognition the lenders had never received, but deserved. They were local heroes boosting small businesses.

I also hoped that every Starbucks partner who saw the coverage and the initial ad felt a sense of pride in the company.

After the thrill of the launch, I was excited to see results. Nothing mattered unless real donations flowed in and spurred businesses to hire. Daily, sometimes twice, I went to see Gina, who had assumed oversight of Create Jobs.

"Gina! How we doing?" She'd look at her computer and reel off the latest tallies. At company-wide meetings I asked her to stand up to share the amount of funds donated so everyone at Starbucks could feel a sense of pride in our progress.

During its first two weeks, Create Jobs surpassed $1 million in donations, and the numbers kept adding up: Ultimately, Create Jobs would sell more than 800,000 wristbands as hundreds of thousands of individuals—and companies including Google, Banana Republic, and Citi—donated more than $15.2 million, which CDFIs across the country turned into $106 million in financing for community businesses. Our idea helped create or sustain more than five thousand jobs.

Did we fix the jobs crisis? No. But we made dents, and the dents had names and faces:

In Oregon, Jimmy Griffin used a CDFI loan to renovate a ninety-nine-year-old building, buy brewing equipment, and hire nineteen people to work at his company, Seaside Brewing. In New Hampshire, the Mahoneys bought a parcel of land, financed new farming equipment, and kept their ten employees on the payroll. In New York, Robyn Scotland got $20,000 from a CDFI and opened Eco-Baby Day Care, which created four full-time and five part-time jobs. In California, Miguel Gonzalez received an $8.5 million CDFI loan and built another fresh-food market, hiring 118 full-time and 4 part-time employees, and creating 40 construction jobs. And on Main Street in Barre, Vermont, Cynthia Duprey got $40,000 just before Christmas and opened Next Chapter Books.

Create Jobs also reached East Liverpool, Ohio.

I'd first heard about East Liverpool when one of our Starbucks suppliers, an entrepreneur from California, Ulrich Honighausen, who had founded a design company called Hausenware, came to my office. Ulrich said that he'd seen me interviewed on CNN in September 2011.

"You were talking about politicians not doing their jobs, and you called on business leaders to start hiring in the U.S.," he recalled. The interview motivated him to find a U.S. manufacturer for Hausenware's products, which were made overseas. Ulrich's research led him to a small pottery maker in Ohio, near the Ohio River.

In East Liverpool, he met the owner of American Mug & Stein, a white-haired, easygoing entrepreneur named Clyde McClellan. Ulrich introduced Clyde to Starbucks just as we were looking for a U.S. pottery company to produce thousands of white ceramic mugs imprinted with the word INDIVISIBLE. The mugs' proceeds would be donated to Create Jobs. While in my office, Ulrich described East Liverpool as a once robust town that had never recovered from the loss of its only industry. I tried to picture the place but I felt that I had to see it for myself. If I wanted to understand, I had to be on the ground.

Driving into East Liverpool, we passed gutted factories, boarded-up storefronts, and dilapidated homes—reluctant monuments to industries that had moved away and settled overseas. The streets were barren. Empty lots were overgrown. Windows on houses and stores were gone or broken. It was a ghostly tract of America.

I walked into American Mug & Stein's 111-year-old building, a former furniture factory. Ceramic particles floated in the streams of faded sunlight that came in through the windows. White dust settled on the shoulders of my suit jacket as I walked through the space greeting smock-clad workers. I approached a young, ponytailed woman working next to rows of unfinished mugs and asked her if she would mind sharing her story. Her voice was quiet, so I leaned in to hear. She was a mother who had been unemployed for a long time until Clyde hired her to help fulfill Starbucks orders. She picked up a mug and showed me how she trimmed and polished it by hand. She smiled. Life in the Ohio Valley wasn't easy.

Clyde McClellan invited two of my colleagues and me to his second-floor office. The heat in the factory was astounding, and everything—Clyde's desk, his odd assortment of chairs—looked as if it had been here for decades. I took a seat. Clyde apologized, unnecessarily, for the messy factory.

"Most people who come here don't wear a dark suit," he said, eyeing mine. "It's a magnet for dust."

"That's the last thing on my mind," I said, and asked Clyde for his story.

He had been in the pottery industry for forty years. "The business model is simple," he said. "You get the order, you make the product, you get it out."

But it was a hot, dirty, physically demanding way to make a living. He explained that beneath the building, some 150,000 pounds of rock-hard clay and other materials from around the country sat in fifty-pound bags waiting to be dumped into two 800-gallon tanks on the fourth floor, which ground the rock into liquid. Every morning, the casters funneled clay from the fourth-floor tanks into plaster molds on the second floor. "It's a gravity-based system," Clyde explained.

Candidly, Clyde also shared that he had been in crisis mode for the past few years, and taken on a great deal of debt to stay in business. He was thrilled to have the Starbucks order, he said, but to meet our strict deadlines he had needed to staff up quickly and was frustrated that the bank he'd done business with for decades refused to lend him a penny to hire staff and update some equipment.

The bank had gone under during the recession and been bought by a bigger institution.

"I walked into the bank with $300,000 in purchase orders from Starbucks," he said, "and they turned me down." Without the loan, Clyde's small company was only achieving a slim profit margin. Still, Clyde was determined to deliver on his promise to us. Plus, he needed the work, and so did East Liverpool. When he had put word out that American Mug & Stein was hiring, almost one hundred people had shown up for twenty job openings. He'd had to turn many away.

After I assured Clyde that American Mug & Stein's relationship with Starbucks would not be short-term, I asked a question. "Have you heard of CDFIs?" He shook his head no. I turned to my colleague Virginia Tenpenny, whose role was to evaluate Starbucks suppliers to ensure they had fair and safe working conditions. Virginia did her job with a delicate mix of analytics and compassion, always getting to know the people be-hind a business. Months earlier, it was Virginia who had stopped me in the hall to introduce herself and tell me about Ulrich's efforts to find U.S. manufacturers. I had invited Virginia to tell me more, which is how I came to meet Ulrich. I'd also asked Virginia to come to East Liverpool. She already knew Clyde's circumstances quite well.

"Virginia, what do you think?" I asked, regarding Clyde's situation. "Might this be something for Mark and OFN?" She nodded and we told Clyde we could help. He smiled. He'd heard a lot of promises over the years.

As we flew home I gazed out the window at the Ohio Valley. There are so many East Liverpools in America, towns being left behind through no fault of residents like the ones I had met, people who desperately needed employment. Where I came from, there had never been thriving industry that disappeared; people in Bayview did not have a lot of money, but we also did not swing from one economic extreme to another.

Later that week, Clyde's mobile phone rang. It was Mark Pinsky. "I just got off the phone with Howard Schultz," Mark told him. "I'm going to put you in touch with a group called the Progress Fund in Greensburg, Pennsylvania."

Within days, suit-clad financiers from the Greensburg CDFI were walking American Mug & Stein's dusty floors.

"So, you had a few bad years," they said to Clyde, taking notes, "and now you're growing?" Clyde gave them the same stack of financials that he'd given his bank. Within a few weeks, the Progress Fund consolidated Clyde's debt, set up a payment schedule, and loaned him $150,000 to pay off his debt and outstanding bills. A couple of months later, thousands of smooth white mugs imprinted with INDIVISIBLE were on sale in Starbucks stores around the country. As I write, American Mug & Stein is still making mugs for Starbucks.

After Create Jobs launched, a few of Starbucks' investors called me to say they saw it as a diversion.

"You're in business to make money. Why spend time creating jobs for companies other than your own?" While many shareholders knew Starbucks' mission and values well, some still did not understand the heart of the company.

I tried to explain why Create Jobs was a good thing not just for the country, but for our company, and why, like providing comprehensive healthcare benefits to all of our partners, it was not an expense, but an investment. Another deposit in the reservoir of trust.

The partners who work in our stores are a microcosm of society. Whatever is happening in the country is usually touching the lives of our people, even if only indirectly. No doubt in 2011, many of our partners' friends and family members were experiencing the ache of joblessness and the uncertainty that comes with it. In Starbucks' efforts to help the United States create jobs, I hoped that our people felt a sense of pride knowing that their employer cared about more than selling coffee.

Create Jobs also helped to deepen our relevance and connection with customers. During times of crisis—and I believed our country was in a crisis of leadership as well as a crisis of unemployment in 2011—people want to feel better about circumstances beyond their control. Sometimes anxiety can be alleviated by fixing a problem. But when problems are complex, comfort can also come from a unifying experience or a single event that imparts a shared belief that "we're all in this together."

Think about how communities come together after a natural disaster, or citizens adopt a sense of patriotism after an attack on their country. By sparking a sense of unity and giving Americans a chance to help other Americans, Create Jobs made many people, including many Starbucks customers, feel part of something bigger than themselves while reinforcing the company's long-held values of community and compassion.

It's tempting to call Create Jobs an act of "corporate social responsibility." But that's a term I don't like applying to Starbucks, because it suggests that addressing social problems is an adjacent effort that is separate from decisions to enhance financial performance. At Starbucks, they are one and the same.

———

Raising money for America's small businesses was not something we would have done a decade earlier. But by 2011, we had become large enough that we considered the country itself to be among the communities we served. What I learned through Create Jobs was that Starbucks' role in serving the country was not to curtail political infighting in Washington, D.C., but to fight for basic human dignities by using the resources at our disposal.

For those who worried that Create Jobs was a sap on our resources, I pointed to the data. In the fiscal year that Create Jobs launched, October 2011 through September 2012, Starbucks had a record operating income of almost $2 billion on record global revenues of $13 billion. For investors, our earnings per share were up 10 percent from the previous period. Create Jobs, I reassured skeptics, had not hurt Starbucks.

We were doing a lot to grow the company: introducing new coffees, building mobile phone apps for customers, upgrading our in-store technology, improving our food products, hiring and promoting new leaders. Create Jobs was another tactic, and it sparked an expectation among our partners, and perhaps some of our customers, that Starbucks would continue to use its resources in creative ways to improve lives.

For me, Create Jobs was evidence of a simple point that was both humbling and empowering. I realized that "we" is a greater force than "me," a truth I knew as a business leader and a team builder, but I now realized was also true in the work we did outside the doors of our company. The diverse talent and collective will of a team has the potential to produce more than I could possibly pull off alone by writing letters. This was especially true of problems that were of indisputable national importance and tied to a universal need for basic human dignity—in other words, not my own personal passions, but the struggles that united all of us.

As I left East Liverpool, I reflected on America's dysfunctional politics, which showed no signs of letting up in 2012. Another fight about whether to raise the debt ceiling was inevitable, and a presidential election loomed.

Yet Create Jobs made me feel optimistic because the country had other sources of salvation, aside from government programs or politicians. We had what President Abraham Lincoln once referred to as our country's "better angels."

I thought back to Starbucks' founders, to Bill Gates, Sr., to my earliest investors, to Sheri, to her dad, to the countless people who had stepped in over the years to help Starbucks succeed. More recently, the actions of people like Ulrich Honighausen, Mark Pinsky, our Starbucks partners, and the men and women working at CDFIs proved that better angels were among us today, people willing to step up to help others.

The American Dream that my mother had introduced me to was not dead. It just needed a lifeline.

CHAPTER 9

Duty

M y mother did not want me to go to war. She wanted me to go to college.

But neither of us had much choice on February 2, 1972. That day, the U.S. government held its fourth draft lottery during the Vietnam War. The drawing, broadcast live, would determine the order in which American men born in 1953 would be called to serve in Vietnam.

The event took place inside the Commerce Department Auditorium in Washington, D.C. A slim man in a dark suit stood onstage at a microphone, his arms hanging awkwardly at his sides. Curtis Tarr was in charge of the draft. To his right was a clear drum containing 365 red capsules, each the size of a fortune cookie and housing a slip of paper inscribed with a date between January 1 and December 31. The clear drum to Tarr's left held blue capsules, each concealing a number between 1 and 365. Pairing two numbers, one from each capsule, picked simultaneously from each drum, determined the sequence of birthdates that would be called to serve in America's military, and sent to the jungles and rice paddies of Vietnam.

Speaking into the microphone, his voice rehearsed and oddly pleasant, Tarr explained the day's events to the journalists and other people seated in the auditorium, and to millions more tuning in around the country, including my mother and me.

I was eighteen, and this was the first year I was eligible for the draft. My family was in a different apartment in Bayview, and there was a palpable anxiety not only in our apartment but throughout the projects. I was not the only young man awaiting fate to reveal itself through a random drawing. Despite her patriotism and love of country, my mother prayed that my birthday, July 19, would be paired with a high draft number, at the very least a number over 125, which for some reason was believed by many civilians to be a safe bar that year. She was not alone in her prayers. By 1972, so many young men were still dying for a war whose purpose and mission were unclear and unsupported. Those who did return, even if wounded, were often met with indifference or saddled with a nation's rage.

I was as confused as the rest of the country. Whatever the initial justifications were for the war, they'd been obscured by years of grisly warfare and untrustworthy reports coming out of our nation's capital. I understood the fear of communism's spreading in Southeast Asia, but I had no sense that we were succeeding at combatting it. No voices out of Washington, D.C., moved me to want to go and continue the fight. Not from President Richard Nixon or, before him, from President Lyndon Johnson. I had joined my mother in her support of Robert F. Kennedy when he was running for president on a platform that included a pledge to pull the country out of Vietnam if elected. Bobby Kennedy was the voice of reason for me and a lot of other people in my generation, but after his assassination in 1968, his rousing compassion and steely purpose found no successor, at least not to my ears. I shared the country's antiwar sentiment and distrust of government and was vocal in my stance against Vietnam among friends and family, but I did not protest in the streets. Thinking back to that time, I suspect I was more focused on trying to get out of Canarsie than trying to get the country out of a conflict half a world away. I'm also sure that I wasn't yet comfortable raising my voice in dissent outside of the circle of my closest friends.

But I never viewed the men who fought during Vietnam with anything but respect. I knew guys ahead of me in high school who traded their letterman jackets for fatigues, and all I could think was how brave they had to be. By the time I was old enough for the draft, I was anxious about the idea that I would have to join them. Like many eighteen-year-olds, I did not see myself as someone who was equipped for combat. But if called, I knew I would be trained, and I would go and serve my country. My father expected it.

The lottery began with the slow, manual churning of each clear drum. For ten agonizing minutes, capsules containing the fates of thousands of lives collided and clumped and fell on top of one another inside each drum as it rotated round and round in a surreal game of chance. From California to Maine, Louisiana to North Dakota, the owners of 365 birth dates waited. There were more than two million of us.

The drums stopped moving and the capsules settled into place. One by one, a red and a blue capsule were plucked from their respective drums, their slips of paper removed by men in suits, and their numbers read aloud.

From a red capsule, "January 10." From a blue, "Thirty-seven."

Every American male born on January 10, 1953, now owned draft number 37. Capsule by capsule, fates were revealed and ceremoniously posted on two large boards at the back of the stage to document each date's order of assignment. Nothing was digitized or mechanical. The whole thing was conducted by hand.

When I share this process with young people today, they regard the entire production as primitive. Few know how the draft was done.

Sitting at home as the lottery proceeded at its dreadful pace, my mother smoked incessantly in panicked anticipation. With a cigarette in one hand, she held the telephone receiver to her ear with the other. Her sister, my aunt Rhoda, was on the other end of the line because my cousin Alan and I were the same age. With no clue when either of their sons' birth dates would be read, the two sisters were a mess of nerves. My own heart was palpitating, out of fear for myself and my cousin, but also for my mother. I was almost nineteen and understood just how fragile my mother had become.

When "October 26" was read aloud, my aunt Rhoda hung up the phone and called Alan, who was away at school. She told him through hysterical tears that he had draft number 78. When "July 19" was announced and paired with blue capsule number 332, my mother jumped from her seat and hugged me. The chance that I would be called was suddenly slim. In a matter of seconds, my future opened up for both of us. I felt two waves of relief. One for me, one for my mom.

As it turned out, none of the men conscripted for service in 1973 would be drafted. In June of '73, the government's authority to induct expired, and ever since then, the United States has relied on an all-volunteer military.

By the time the United States left Vietnam in 1975, more than fifty-eight thousand American lives had been lost.

The Vietnam draft lottery would be the closest I came to being exposed to military life for the next forty years. During my time growing Starbucks, my knowledge of the modern-day armed forces would be shaped by movies, documentaries, and books—and, of course, constant news reports as America engaged in a new series of wars, first in the Persian Gulf in the 1990s, and then in Iraq and Afghanistan after the terrorist attacks of September 11, 2001. But just as I felt during the Vietnam War, whether or not I agreed with a military action, I never wavered in my respect for our troops.

In the spring of 2011, I was asked to speak at the United States Military Academy at West Point. I was honored but also surprised to get the invitation, and unsure whether to accept. At fifty-seven, what did I know of military service? I had a father whose Army years were still a mystery to me. He had never talked about his World War II experience. None of my friends or their children served in the armed forces. I had never even spoken to anyone in uniform. In 2011, Starbucks certainly had partners who were military veterans, but I do not recall personally knowing anyone, inside or outside the company, who fought in Iraq or Afghanistan. What, I thought, could I possibly say to a group of young men and women on a path to serve in the Army during wartime, not because their birthdays were randomly chosen, but because they chose to do so?

The closest I had come, during my adult years, to connecting with military life was through a colleague and friend, John Culver, who joined Starbucks in 2002 and was overseeing our $2.6 billion international business. Both of John's grandfathers had served in World War II, and his father, a colonel, did two combat tours in Vietnam. Over the years, John had shared with me his memories of watching his dad in action as he directed troops during basic training exercises, and gathering at home with his siblings and his mother to listen to tape recordings that his father mailed from Vietnam. John was the only person I knew who grew up experiencing the pride, uncertainty, and fear that come with military family life.

Perhaps that's why my speaking at West Point seemed almost inappropriate—it was a stinging reminder of just how little I knew about our country's military institutions. I would be out of my element. But that was also a reason to go.

The cadet group I was invited to speak to was the Black and Gold Leadership Forum, a cadre of top West Point students that hosted leaders from many walks of life, including business. Once I accepted, I asked John Culver to join me. Sheri and my son, Jordan, who was twenty-five at the time, would also come. The visit was a chance for the three of us to learn.

On the almost sixty-mile drive from New York City to West Point in the Hudson Valley, my anticipation heightened, but I was not prepared for the feeling that came over me when we arrived. The meticulously manicured campus, with its massive granite buildings, was tucked amid New York State's rugged, leafy terrain, a stunning contrast of man-made and natural beauty.

When I sat down with the head of the academy, Superintendent Lieutenant General David H. Huntoon, Jr., he spoke to me about the character that each cadet must exemplify to be admitted—only 10 percent of applicants are accepted—and to eventually earn a place in the Long Gray Line, the prestigious corps of graduates, which, as President Theodore Roosevelt observed at the turn of the nineteenth century, "contributed to the honor roll of the nation's greatest citizens." Among its ranks were leaders that shaped America. From the class of 1843, President Ulysses S. Grant. From the class of 1903, General Douglas MacArthur. From the class of 1915, President Dwight D. Eisenhower. Other graduates included Olympians, artists, explorers. I had never visited a place with such connective tissue to the history of the country. At West Point, I felt as if I was on sacred ground.

On our guided tour, the academy's stated ideals—duty, honor, country—came to life in the campus's physical features: The overlook of the bend in the Hudson River, a strategic outpost during the Revolutionary War. The sprawling parade field, known as the Plain. The Gothic structures that housed classrooms and dormitories. The formidable monuments to past military and political leaders, which included an imposing bronze statue of George Washington on horseback. And the breathtaking stained-glass windows inside the century-old Cadet Chapel. I'd never encountered a place with such historic and stately proportions on American soil.

The intentional grandeur overwhelmed me with a reverence for America's past that I had not before experienced visiting museums or reading history books. My feelings stirred being on the grounds, however, were surpassed by the emotions I felt watching West Point's young cadets.

All around us, we'd see them as they walked to class in their crisp gray uniforms, rendering salutes or marching in precise formations. From a distance, I admired the disciplined elegance of their collective gait. More so, I was curious about what I could not see. What were these young men and women thinking and feeling? What motivates a teenager to attend such a rigorous institution as West Point? To forgo the typical college experiences and dedicate not just four years but almost a decade to serving in the military? Each West Point student commits to at least five years on active duty after graduation. How does a high school kid know military service is his or her calling? Particularly during a time of war.

Squinting, I tried to catch a glimpse of the cadets' faces, hoping for answers to my questions in their expressions, clues in their eyes.

When I was their age, the United States was also at war. I didn't want my number to be called to go to Vietnam, but if my number had been called I would have gone. Unlike the West Point cadets in our midst, however, I was not a young man who felt compelled to volunteer to serve my country in that capacity. Nor was I interested in committing to a military lifestyle of extreme rigor and sacrifice.

While I was proud of what Starbucks had accomplished, I also believed that the cadets' commitment to serve was more significant than anything I had done during my lifetime. I told Sheri I didn't feel I should be speaking to them about leadership.

An hour before my scheduled talk, I took General Huntoon aside and told him, with great respect, that I did not believe I was worthy to talk about leadership to the cadets. I asked to change the format to a more informal question-and-answer session. Today, we would all be students and learn from one another.

When I walked into the modest classroom, some thirty cadets in their two-tone gray uniforms were already seated. The group size felt about right for the more intimate discussion I hoped to have. When I pulled up a chair and joined them, I choked up a bit. I didn't know their individual stories yet, but I was in awe of the personal choices that had brought them to West Point, and the traits they surely possessed to be admitted. I also had never been among a group of young people so willing to sacrifice for their country. In the face of their valor, I felt embarrassed by my lack of it.

"It would be ill-advised for me to share any lessons of leadership with you," I said. "It is I who should be learning from you."

For the next hour, we just talked. My questions to them were not complicated. *Where are you from? Why did you come to West Point? What is it like to be a cadet, and where do you hope to go from here?* Some hailed from families with military legacies. Others were the first in their families to serve. They told me about school; their days were demanding and routinized, they said, their courses challenging, their homework copious. Their future plans were wide ranging: some anticipated military careers, others aimed for different types of public service or expected to join the private sector one day. They spoke eloquently and assuredly, yet many easily broke a smile if someone made a joke—

which they did. Beneath the polish, they were still kids, which made their maturity even more impressive.

When the cadets asked about Starbucks, I shared aspects of the company's history and lessons I had learned that seemed relevant to them, such as needing to have the courage of your convictions, and my recognition that leadership is easy when the wind is at your back, but much harder when facing into the headwinds. In business, leaders must often make decisions without perfect information. I told them I imagined the same was true in warfare.

No one cadet's story stood out. Mostly I was moved by their collective self-confidence and their sense of purpose: they were capable of committing themselves to something bigger than themselves at such a young age. These were students who could have chosen to attend other top schools that didn't require such a heavy dose of daily regulation and years of military service. Patriotism at West Point seemed a prerequisite.

Throughout the day, I had also seen or spoken with other cadets, of different genders, races, origins, economic backgrounds, even physical stature. Cadets were tall and short. Thin and muscular. Black, brown, and white. Many were female. They were majoring in a variety of subjects. The diversity of West Point's cadets also reminded me of what is so special about America: it's a country where very different people can come together in shared beliefs, practices, and purpose.

The day ended with a pensive drive back to the city. Regardless of how any of us felt about the politics of our post-9/11 wars, it was impossible not to respect these young people for choosing a path that put country first. Yes, they were gaining a first-rate education and access to many opportunities, but the hard work that earned them a spot at West Point, and the work and sacrifices ahead, demonstrated a level of responsibility and love of country that was hard to not admire, or want to emulate.

What struck me was not some display of American military might, but the ethos of service these young Americans embodied.

I realize in retrospect that my visit there in 2011 immediately preceded the period when I began speaking out about my frustration with some of our country's chronic social problems and what seemed to be a crisis in America's political leadership. I have to believe that observing the ideals and sense of responsibility on display at West Point gave me cause and courage to speak out. Military life, as I would come to better understand it, is not appropriate, desirable, or accessible to everyone. But there are multiple ways to serve one's country.

I was honored to call these cadets my fellow Americans, but I wondered if they would say the same about me. The day's visit revealed to me just how disconnected I was from our country's armed forces, her warriors old and new, and the wars in which we were currently engaged. That disconnect did not make me especially proud.

Nancy Kent had been my executive assistant since 1995. A perpetually steady presence in my working life, she herded the daily onslaught of requests, emails, calls, and meetings with deft warmth. She has a keen intuition and an infectious smile. Before people spoke to me, they usually had a lovely, at times in-depth, conversation with Nancy. My respect and admiration for her has always been immense.

One day in early 2012, Nancy popped her head into my office. "Howard, I have Arthur Levitt on the phone." I had no idea why the former and longest-serving chairman of the Securities and Exchange Commission was calling me. I had known Arthur for many years and thought highly of him. "Secretary Bob Gates is retiring and moving home to Seattle," he told me when I picked up the phone. "And he is interested in meeting with you."

Robert Gates had been the secretary of defense since 2006. I had not realized he was from the Pacific Northwest. Arthur had suggested to the secretary that the Starbucks board of directors might be one he consider joining once he left government. Apparently the secretary was interested. I figured he would have his choice of boards to serve on. Seattle and its environs were home to the headquarters of Amazon, Microsoft, Boeing, Costco, Nordstrom, and a lot of promising start-ups.

I knew the secretary was widely regarded as one of the country's most devoted public servants. He had held a variety of government roles under eight presidents, including Director of Central Intelligence. Gates seemed to be a rare leader in Washington, D.C., one who priori- tized the well-being of the country over his allegiance to any one party. In my mind, that cast him as a true patriot. I wanted to show him my respect.

Seattle is a city of casual dress. I wore a dark suit and tie to the office only for board meetings and visits from distinguished guests. The day Secretary Gates came to visit was such a day.

I immediately found Gates less imposing than his job title, espe- cially when he invited me to call him Bob, though this proved a hard request for me to follow.

Most of our conversation during his ninety-minute visit was not about Starbucks. I was far more interested in learning about the chal- lenges Secretary Gates faced leading the Department of Defense, es- pecially under two very different presidents and through two wars. He was personable and pragmatic. And a straight shooter. He, too, was disgusted with the hypocrisy and lack of transparency in Congress. We also shared a distaste for bureaucracies and political brinkmanship.

When I asked why he was interested in joining Starbucks' board, the secretary assured me it was not just because he enjoyed our coffee, although he did divulge that several times a week he drank a brewed dark roast with cream from a Starbucks store located inside the Penta- gon. He was impressed with how we treated our people, he told me, and he cited our history of providing healthcare coverage, as well as our values, mission, and culture of teamwork.

I was not alone in believing that the company would be lucky to have Secretary Gates on its board, and in May 2012 our existing eleven directors asked him to join them. Thankfully, Secretary Gates agreed.

As Bob and I came to know each other better, our conversations turned to America's active-duty troops and veterans. Not only was he a man who possessed great understanding of wartime strategy and the inner workings of the federal government, but the feelings he had for America's troops went beyond a professional respect. Bob regularly met with deployed soldiers overseas, and visited them in military hospitals as they recovered from life-changing injuries. Unlike at least one of his predecessors who sent impersonal form letters to families of fallen warriors, Bob wrote his own condolence letters. He also attended soldiers' funerals. He was very clear in describing how he felt about his fellow warriors. He described it as love.

Bob was especially concerned that the men and women of our armed forces were not returning home to more universal respect, sensitivity, and understanding about what they had experienced, risked, and could contribute to society.

Our talks added to my knowledge about the people who serve our country in battle as well as in thousands of noncombat positions. And yet, I didn't comprehend, at an intuitive level, the physical and emotional risks our troops take, and the strengths so many possess, until a wounded warrior arrived at my office door.

Sergeant First Class Leroy Petry was wearing a pristine Army uniform decorated with multicolored ribbon bars and gold chevrons. I did not know what the honors on his jacket represented, nor did I know the full story behind the five-pointed gold star that hung from a light blue ribbon around his neck. I did know that Starbucks Armed Forces Network, a group of partners and their spouses who had served in the military, which we called the AFN for short, had invited this recipient of the Medal of Honor, the nation's highest award for combat valor, to speak to the company.

Prior to Sergeant Petry's arrival, members of the AFN had told me that he was an Army Ranger, a member of the Army's most elite fighting force that trains for close combat in exceptionally dangerous operations. When he received the Medal of Honor, Sergeant Petry became the second living servicemember to be a recipient of the Medal of Honor since the Vietnam War.

We met in my office before he went out to speak to the rest of the company. Sergeant Petry was easy to talk to. When he told me he was stationed at Joint Base Lewis-McChord, a major military installation just over an hour from Starbucks' offices, I realized I knew very little about the base given its proximity. When we shook hands, his prosthetic right hand extended from his jacket's sleeve. I had already been told that he lost his hand in battle. I wondered if it was disrespectful to ask about his injury, or disrespectful not to. I chose not to broach it, although I would soon learn what happened. The sergeant was so humble that I was not prepared for the incredible story he was about to tell.

When we arrived at the ninth-floor atrium for his scheduled presentation, the large space was packed with hundreds of partners. Sun poured in from the skylights. People spilled down the open staircase to the eighth floor and stood shoulder to shoulder in the hallways. Sergeant Petry was introduced, and then a video produced by the Department of Defense began to play. One by one, his Army Ranger comrades appeared on camera, recounting what happened in the remote hills of Afghanistan the day that then–Staff Sergeant Petry and the rest of his Second Battalion of the Seventy-Fifth Ranger Regiment were called on a mission to pursue a key Al-Qaeda operative hiding in a remote cluster of homes.

On the morning of the assault, Sergeant Petry and his platoon boarded two Chinook helicopters, and from the moment they landed, they found themselves under fire from an unknown number of insurgents armed with AK-47s.

About two minutes into the video, a technical problem cut the film short and the screens in the atrium went black. Without missing a beat, Sergeant Petry picked up the story where the video left off. He turned to us and described, in his own words, the events that earned him the Medal of Honor. He had our full attention.

A few soldiers had accidentally entered the wrong compound, and Sergeant Petry followed them into an open courtyard to alert them of the mistake. Once inside the courtyard, he was joined by a younger member of his platoon, Private First Class Lucas Robinson. Petry and Robinson came under fire immediately. As bullets flew, Petry told us he felt a sudden impact, like a sledgehammer, as a bullet pierced his left thigh. It was the first time he'd ever been shot, but he didn't think the bullet had hit his bone, so he kept moving. I was standing not too far from him and glanced around the room. All eyes were pinned to our guest.

Petry said he and Robinson, who also had been shot, took cover behind a small building in a corner of the compound. Petry radioed his platoon mates to report that they had both been wounded, then he pulled a grenade from his vest and hurled it in the direction of the gunmen. It detonated, and the insurgents' gunfire stopped. Another Ranger, Sergeant Daniel Higgins, hustled over to help them. As Higgins checked Robinson's wounds, a grenade landed ten feet away from all three men. It exploded and knocked Higgins and Robinson to the ground. Petry, who was situated at the other end of the wall protecting them, peered around the corner to look for more insurgents, then looked over his shoulder to check on Higgins and Robinson. As he did, another grenade landed in the dirt, this one just a few feet away. In less than four seconds, Petry knew, the pineapple-shaped grenade would detonate with enough force to kill all three men.

The atrium was silent as Sergeant Petry described how he grabbed the explosive with his right hand to throw it away, but just as his fingers released the baseball-sized object, it exploded. Petry was propelled backward and onto the ground by the force of the blast. He opened his eyes, he told us, grateful to be alive. Then he sat up and looked at his right arm. It had been severed at the wrist, like someone had taken a saw and cut it off, he said. His right hand was gone and he could see his forearm's bones poking through debris-speckled flesh as the stump oozed blood.

"It sounds crazy," he said with a hint of a smile, "but this is what went through my mind when I saw my arm: 'How come it isn't spraying blood like in the movies?'" People laughed, almost relieved at a break in the tension.

Sitting in the dirt, Sergeant Petry cinched a tourniquet around his wrist to stop the bleeding, checked on the other people around him, then radioed the situation to his fellow Rangers. The gunfight continued. Only after he got back to a place of safety, but not before another one of his comrades would be fatally shot, did he realize that the bullet that had entered his left thigh had gone through that leg, exited, and then entered his right thigh.

I thought about what to say to Sergeant Petry that would do his bravery and sacrifice justice. Just thanking him for his service to our country seemed insufficient. I turned to Rob Porcarelli, one of Starbucks' in-house lawyers and a former lieutenant in the U.S. Navy.

"Rob, can I offer him a job?"

Rob, who was a cofounder of the AFN and had invited Petry to speak, looked at me somewhat incredulously, then grinned. "You're the boss," he said, "but I do think he may be set." Petry had reenlisted after he returned from Afghanistan, which Rob said was rare for a combat soldier who had survived such a harrowing incident and been so duly decorated.

Still, when I approached Petry, I extended an offer to come to work for Starbucks. Anytime he was ready, we would find a role for him. Then I asked what else we could do for him.

"What do you need?" I implored. We owed him everything. But instead of asking for so much as a cup of coffee, he replied with humor. "I could use some gas money to get home."

This was not a literal request, but a witty reference to his situation, which Rob later explained to me. As a Medal of Honor recipient, Petry was not required by the Army to conduct public outreach or accept speaking requests. He accepted invitations like ours out of his own sense of duty, usually sporting a newly dry-cleaned and pressed uniform and maybe a fresh haircut. The military did not pay for any of these expenses, including the gas to drive almost fifty miles to our headquarters, and he was not allowed to accept reimbursement or fees from us. Speaking here today was another way Sergeant Petry was serving his country.

As I walked back to my office, I thought about something Bob Gates had shared. He believed that Americans had a moral duty to take care of those who served and protected the country. I asked myself whether all of us listening to Sergeant Petry that day were living up to that duty as citizens. Some people surely were, but I knew in my heart that I was not.

CHAPTER 10

This Is Not Charity

In 2003, a U.S. Marine sergeant sent an email to his friends complaining that Starbucks refused to donate coffee to Marines serving in Iraq. He erroneously claimed the company did not support the war and "anyone in it." He asked his friends to forward the information and boycott Starbucks, and within weeks his email was circulating around the world, planting the false belief, especially among members of the armed forces, that Starbucks did not support America's troops.

His claim was a misinterpretation of an event he had heard about secondhand. A group of deployed Marines did indeed write to Starbucks asking for free coffee, and at the time Starbucks had a policy of only providing free products to charities. Our public affairs office sent the Marines a statement explaining the policy, and expressing regret that we had to decline their request because the U.S. military did not, by law, qualify as a charity.

In retrospect, our letter was poorly worded, and frankly insensitive, as was our decision not to send coffee to troops. But by no means did the mistake reflect any negative opinions about the military. Neither the company nor I ever took a public position on the wars after September 11, 2001.

When someone from Starbucks contacted the sergeant to explain what really happened, he apologized and, five months after sending his original email, wrote a correction to his friends. That correction, of course, did not go viral, and the original rumor continued to circulate for years, despite several websites and articles debunking the myth.

In 2004, Starbucks did what it should have done originally and donated fifty thousand pounds of free whole-bean coffee to troops in Kuwait, Iraq, and Afghanistan. In the years that followed, we continued to send care packages to deployed troops, and I have received many photos of soldiers brewing Starbucks coffee in the desert or in mountainous terrain.

This rumor has always upset me, but not until the summer of 2013 did I realize that, when it came to supporting the country's post-9/11 war veterans, something more egregious than a false rumor plagued the company.

That August, I gathered with Starbucks' senior leadership team at our monthly meeting. Starbucks had recently concluded the best across-the-board fiscal quarter in the company's forty-two-year history. We were growing our existing stores' sales, opening new stores, launching new products, announcing partnerships with other companies, and producing record earnings for our shareholders. With fall soon to be upon us, we were heading into Starbucks' busiest season.

Occasionally, partners from various parts of the company asked to speak to the leadership team, and on this day three members of our Armed Forces Network, or AFN, had come to the meeting. Vivek had alerted me that what they had to say needed my attention.

The data they posted on the boardroom screen was disappointing: fewer than one percent of Starbucks' 135,000 partners in the United States, about 950, had ever served in the military. While it was likely that we employed more veterans who had not self-identified as such, the number of veterans and reservists we did employ seemed to be a very low percentage of our workforce. Nationally, there were 10.4 million veterans under age sixty-five, who accounted for about 4 percent of the country's working-age population. We could do better.

Sharing this news were Rob Porcarelli, the former Navy lieutenant who had invited Leroy Petry to speak; Mick James, a former Marine who had joined Starbucks as a barista in 1993, had held many management positions, and cofounded the AFN with Rob; and Virginia Tenpenny, our partner now in public affairs who had been with me in East Liverpool. Virginia was not a member of the armed forces, but her father had served in Vietnam. She was here because she had been so moved by Leroy Petry's story that she became involved in the AFN.

The trio was quite determined to advance Starbucks' support of veterans, and had come to the boardroom to convince us to step up our efforts.

Virginia stated the situation bluntly: "We are not yet a veteran-friendly company."

Other companies, including many retailers, were doing more than we were. Many had hiring commitments.

The information was upsetting. Our passivity seemed especially hypocritical given our mission to be a positive force in communities. As grateful as I was that Rob, Virginia, and Mick had brought this to our attention, I was more pleased that they came with suggestions about how to fix it.

Their first idea was relatively easy to execute, although not substantial enough: on Veterans Day in November, Starbucks could offer free brewed coffee to customers who identified themselves as veterans or active-duty military personnel. Second, they proposed that Starbucks open new stores on or near military bases; these stores would share a portion of profits with the military community and be staffed solely by veterans and spouses of active-duty service members. Starbucks already had two stores sharing profits with groups in underdeveloped communities where they were situated, so extending that model to military bases seemed doable.

Their third recommendation was more controversial and complex. Starbucks, they said, should commit to hiring ten thousand veterans and military spouses over the next five years. This was a big ask. Never had the company set a public hiring goal or identified a specific population of people to employ, especially a cohort that many of us knew so little about. I sensed a quiet pulse of concern in the boardroom, but I also knew, intuitively, that we had to do something more than give away free coffee.

Looking back, I realize my ongoing conversations with Secretary Gates had primed me for this decision. While Bob never pushed or prodded, he had been educating me about the value that veterans bring to the workplace. War changes a person in many ways, he had said. Among the changes: People leave military service with qualities and transferable skills they might not have had previously and that employers need. Veterans, he explained, have gained extensive experience leading small groups in dynamic environments, and they are trained to be excellent team players. They are also creative problem-solvers, especially under stress, and have acquired an ingrained sense of accountability and reliability, as well as a goal-driven mentality. What company wouldn't want employees with these qualities?

Bob also pointed out that even though military jobs didn't directly align with most jobs in the private sector, military life bred fast learners. As he put it, a Navy flight officer who helped navigate an F-18 fighter onto the deck of an aircraft carrier in the middle of a violent storm could, at the very least, make espresso drinks during a morning rush.

Even more relevant, Bob had drawn cultural parallels between Starbucks and the military that I never could have recognized on my own. In combat, he said, troops are part of tight-knit groups. But that camaraderie and sense of family get lost when they leave the armed forces, and many veterans crave it in their civilian lives. Veterans also desire a sense of purpose. After they've spent years preserving the country's welfare, working for a business that only cares about making money can be rather uninspiring. Bob believed that Starbucks' emphasis on community service, combined with the sense of teamwork and family that we fostered, especially in our stores, made for a very comfortable environment for men and women once they were out of uniform. These were dots I hadn't connected on my own.

As Rob, Virginia, and Mick continued to make their case in the boardroom, I also reflected on what was going on in the country. By 2013, more than one million military personnel were in the process of returning to civilian life. This unusually high influx of veterans into society was the result of the drawdown of troops in Afghanistan and the overall reduction of the size of the Army. So many of these men and women needed jobs, and the country needed them to be employed.

Hiring more veterans seemed like the right thing to do, but it came with complications. Others around the boardroom table knew, perhaps better than I did, that Starbucks was not set up to achieve that goal. For one, we lacked expertise. Military résumés can read like a foreign language to people in the private sector, and our hiring managers were not prepared, or encouraged, to recognize how experiences in the armed forces could translate to a corporate or retail job.

Stereotypes about veterans could also affect hiring decisions. A recruiter might make assumptions about a soldier's emotional well-being, given all the attention to post-traumatic stress disorder, or PTSD. The myth that all or most veterans were somehow damaged—which the name itself perpetuates—needed to be dispelled in our own company, and in the country. Not all veterans experienced PTSD.

These concerns some of our leaders had about our ability to hire veterans were all legitimate.

"What if we fail?" I asked the AFN team, because the stakes were high. A hiring effort could not be an impulsive initiative, like writing "Come Together" on cups. It had to succeed, and endure.

Virginia didn't flinch. "This is going to be hard, but it's not failure when you are doing the right thing."

Sometimes people in leadership positions must make decisions with imperfect information. Despite not knowing how the company would solve the problems we knew about, and those we didn't, we agreed to offer free coffee on Veterans Day, to build military-focused stores, and to commit to hiring veterans and their spouses. The outstanding question was whether to commit to a number.

I called Bob Gates for his opinion. He felt strongly that having a milestone was more imperative than the actual number. Others I consulted agreed that a defined target would be a motivating force for our people, as well as hold us accountable. Still, ten thousand was daunting, especially to partners responsible for the stores' day-to-day operations. Many of them knew less about the military than I did.

The goal of ten thousand became more attainable when the AFN team explained why many of the country's 1.2 million military spouses were a cultural fit for Starbucks. As a group, military spouses were known to have a strong sense of community service, volunteering at a rate three times the national average. Because they moved from town to town, or base to base, so often, they had an unemployment rate twice the national average. But at Starbucks, a military spouse could transfer to another store if an active-duty husband or wife was assigned to a new U.S. base. We already employed many military spouses, and the possibility of actively trying to hire more was quite exciting.

Finally, Rob and Mick assured us, on behalf of the AFN, that veterans currently working for Starbucks would stand behind a concerted hiring effort whether or not we hit ten thousand. It was decided and in early November 2013, we announced that Starbucks would try to hire ten thousand veterans and active-duty spouses by 2018 as well as open five military-focused stores. Meanwhile, across the country, free brewed coffee was being offered to veterans and members of the armed services and their spouses.

"What we are doing today . . . this is not charity," I said at the time of the announcement. "This is not philanthropy. In fact, this is good business. This will be accretive to the culture of Starbucks, to work side by side with the people who have defended the country." I truly believed it would unleash a swell of pride, making another deposit in the reservoir of trust that is so vital to any organization. "We are doing something that is right for the country, right for our company, right for every stakeholder. But make no mistake. This is not a handout. We are going to benefit from hiring talented, experienced people who stand for something well beyond themselves."

Our current partners' willingness to open their minds, to learn, to overcome preconceived notions, and to adapt would ultimately determine the hiring initiative's success or failure.

———

The person with the most accountability for bringing ten thousand American veterans into Starbucks was Cliff Burrows, a Brit who was born in Wales and grew up in Zambia. Cliff had been working for Starbucks in Amsterdam when I asked him to move to Seattle in 2008 and run our then-struggling U.S. business. He is a talented retail operator and well respected, and without his support the hiring initiative would have died. Yet Cliff had his own learning curve; the U.S. military was an entirely foreign entity to him.

In addition to the stores, Cliff worked with departments that would also hire veterans, including supply-chain and legal. They brought in hiring experts. Starbucks retained a consultant and hired an in-house recruiter, both with military backgrounds, to help train our corporate hiring and store managers. We also created a field guide dubbed "Military 101" to demystify military life. Its pages explained, for example, the differences between commissioned and noncommissioned officers and the many military ranks. It was basic training for our civilian partners who would be hiring and working alongside veterans.

Then, in early 2014, Cliff arranged for and joined six busloads of district managers from around the country to tour Joint Base Lewis-McChord. I had visited the base a month prior and gleaned more insight and appreciation for how soldiers operate during combat. While touring the base, our managers watched as a gun line of soldiers worked together in crews of four and, with sequential precision, prepped, loaded, and fired explosive rounds from high-powered artillery pieces aimed at far-off targets. Our managers also met officers in charge of purchasing many millions of dollars' worth of defense equipment. In the dining hall, they lunched with soldiers, many having their first conversations with fellow countrymen in uniform.

Among the things our people observed were disciplined teams handling complex equipment as they worked in unison to achieve a mission. Among those they met were trained specialists who supported combat soldiers off the fields of battle. And among all the things our district managers heard were stories as diverse as the backgrounds of our own store partners. Some soldiers had enlisted out of a passion to serve their country, while others signed up because they needed the income or hoped for a fresh start after a history of bad choices. Some were compelled by the adrenaline rush of constant activity. Yet here they all were, developing an array of skills as part of a tight-knit group and feeling a sense of purpose.

Through education and conversation, our district managers began to make the same connection as Secretary Gates had made, as well as arrive at the same conclusions I'd come to: veterans are a good fit for Starbucks, and vice versa.

All of us were on a learning journey, and the hiring activities would not be without disappointments. Of course, not all veterans we hired would like the work or fit the culture. Not all would stay with us for long. Some would use a job at Starbucks as a stepping-stone and move on, and that was okay. But thousands would stay, and their stories have become part of the tapestry of the company.

Ted Warshaw was a veteran of the U.S. Air Force who had no job offers after a ten-year career as a military firefighter. He and his family were living in long-term-stay hotels as he searched for work. His money and his spirits were low when he attended a military job fair and a Starbucks recruiter approached him and asked if he had considered a career in coffee. Surprised but open-minded, Ted interviewed with a store manager. He showed up for his first day as a barista in November 2014. Within two years, Ted was managing his own store, had won his district's barista championship, and had bought a house for his family.

In April 2014, two weeks after getting married, Rachael Bialcak's husband, who would become an aircraft maintenance officer, was re-located to Vance Air Force Base in Enid, Oklahoma, a thousand miles from their families in Utah. Distraught and lonely, Rachael spent her first day in Enid sitting in a Starbucks store to escape the silence of her new apartment. She befriended the staff, who asked her about Utah, made her a drink on the house, and even gave her a hug after seeing her tears. Comforted by the spontaneous affection, Rachael applied for a job at the store that very day so she could, in her words, "be part of that feeling, and share it with others." The following words are also Rachael's, and I share them because they express, better than I ever could, the connections that exist among our partners and our customers:

> When I accepted this job, I didn't realize that I would be making lasting relationships with my partners. I didn't expect for a partner to invite me over for Thanksgiving dinner, or for my whole store to celebrate my birthday, or for my whole team to hug me in the back room the day I found out my dad had cancer, and I didn't expect a customer to bring me a box of golf balls because we talked about our golf game week after week, or to have a customer bring me Tums because my stomach hurt, or to create relationships with so many customers. I didn't realize that I could have family away from family.

When Rachael's husband was transferred to a base in New Jersey, she transferred to a nearby Starbucks. "My new store yet again felt like home," she said.

It's quite beautiful to consider that through Starbucks' aspiration to reach its goals, so many men and women have been able to reach their goals, too. This has been true of the company for over forty years, but is more pronounced, I think, among veterans and their spouses, a population in need of job opportunities to help them move forward with their lives.

Starbucks hit its ten-thousand-hires milestone in 2017, one year early. In response, we are committed to hiring twenty-five thousand veterans and military spouses by 2025. By 2018, the company was operating more than forty-five military-family stores in twenty-one states. Many veterans and spouses we employ also choose to wear a special green apron embroidered with the American flag. If you see someone in our stores wearing theirs, please thank him or her for their service and, if they seem open to it, ask them about their experience.

Some benefits are impossible to measure. Hiring from the military community begat more military hiring as happily employed veterans referred other talent, making our recruiters' jobs easier and more fruit-ful. And more partners are developing a deeper understanding of what it means to serve, as well as a deeper patriotism.

Starbucks' lessons in this area have been ongoing. While veterans share many traits, they are no less diverse in their style, strengths, and weaknesses than any other group that has a common thread. Bias works both ways—it can artificially inflate as well as denigrate. We may honor these men and women as heroes, but we must remember that they are also human.

Bob Gates told me that war changes a person, and while I had seen many of the military's positive influences, I had yet to come face-to-face with the brutal, life-altering wounds that war inflicts on the body, mind, and soul. In the months after we launched the hiring effort, my own education would continue. The people I would meet and the sto-ries I would hear would break my heart, but also propel me to chal-lenge perceived limits of how a company, and a citizen, can best support those who serve the country. Starbucks had proven we could do more than offer free coffee, but could we, and should I, do more than offer veterans good jobs?

CHAPTER 11

Unintended Consequences

On the streets of Canarsie, if a kid said to another kid a certain four-letter curse word followed by "off," a fistfight usually followed. When I was fifteen, I hurled the same profanity at my mother one day after school. I've scoured my mind to remember why. I'd heard the slang in the street hundreds of times. Did my mom say something to upset me? Was I in a foul mood? I still can't recall what triggered the disrespectful outburst.

Several hours later, just before our usual dinnertime at 5:30 P.M., I was in the shower. I did not hear my father come home, and I did not hear him enter the bathroom. I just saw the shower curtain whip open and my father's fists come at me. As he punched, water ran down my body and I wrapped my arms around my head and torso in self-defense before crumpling to the bathtub floor. Streams of blood raced for the drain. My father left the bathroom as swiftly and wordlessly as he'd entered. The whole thing happened so fast but seemed to go on forever. I can still feel it now.

I could barely stand up to turn off the shower. I was in shock and physical pain. He had never been this violent with me.

When I got out of the shower, I cleaned myself up, trying not to get blood on the towels we all shared. That night, I didn't join my family for dinner. Neither parent said good night to me, which was not unusual. I woke up the next morning and returned to the bathroom, where I saw my reflection in the mirror. The bruises were prominent enough that I chose to stay home from school for a couple of days.

I don't think I apologized to my mother for saying those horrible words to her. I should have. No child should speak to a parent that way. It was wrong and we both knew it. It also was uncharacteristic of our relationship during those years. We no longer did things like walk to the bookmobile together, but we loved and felt protective of each other. That day, I think, we both believed the other had broken an unspoken vow.

Mom never spoke about the incident to me, and my father never apologized to me for the beating. For many years, I could not bring myself to tell a soul about the episode, but the memory of being beaten up by my dad, the raw anger and at times the hatred I felt toward him, lived in me like a virus. It tainted my memories of him for decades.

My own experience growing up in a fraught family situation made me sensitive to others dealing with similar issues. In Bayview, living in such tight quarters with so many people meant I often saw others' challenges up close. But as I got older and moved into different worlds, opportunities for such intimate views were few. I was no longer living among people whose family histories were troubled in ways similar to my own—or worse. But that changed because of Sheri, who reintroduced me to that world.

In the mid-1990s, while I concentrated on growing Starbucks, Sheri was actively volunteering with community groups that helped kids who were at risk of dropping out of school, becoming homeless, getting lost in the foster-care system, or who were already living on the streets. She became especially involved in a wonderful nonprofit called YouthCare, and one winter night she joined some volunteers to distribute food, socks, and gloves to young people spending the night outside. The crew parked a van in Seattle's Capitol Hill neighborhood, behind Dick's Drive-In, a popular Seattle burger joint, and opened the back hatch. When kids walked up to the vehicle, Sheri and others would ask them what they needed and hand out the requested supplies, including clean needles to help prevent the spread of HIV and other diseases among those injecting drugs. A larger intent of the outreach was to introduce the kids to adults with whom they could begin to build trust and get the support they needed.

Sheri came home that first night distressed by what she had witnessed. The young people she met were in dire circumstances, and so appreciative for what they received from the volunteers. They were not insolent or dangerous, but hungry, tired, vulnerable kids and young adults. One boy in particular left a mark on Sheri's conscience. She handed him a pair of socks and they made eye contact. "Thank you," he said, "it's so cold outside."

"Howard," Sheri told me, "he could have been our son." She did not see a runaway or an addict, but a boy who was losing a chance to grow up safely because of circumstances he had likely been born or thrust into.

Sheri continued to volunteer on the streets of Seattle, getting to know the young people and their particular circumstances. Sitting next to them at shelters or on curbsides, she asked them questions and listened to what they had to say. They talked to her because she came to them with no pretense, just a genuine interest and a desire to assist. The more she understood, the more she felt for them, and the more she wanted to help them find a different path.

In 1996, Sheri and I established a family foundation to amplify our own philanthropic giving, and for the next fifteen years her compassion for young men and women in troubled circumstances drove our donations and determined how she spent her time. It was not a big organization—just a small board of advisors, Sheri, and myself. We had no office; Sheri worked out of our house. She was the foundation's leader and its heart, and over time she became more engaged with leaders of other community-based organizations. She began educating herself about how nonprofits operated, spent their money, and measured the effects of their work. She gravitated to groups that gave young people life tools, such as study skills and self-confidence. YouthCare, Mockingbird, and Treehouse were among her local favorites. She also had come to admire YouthBuild USA, a national organization that was effectively combining schoolwork and real work by having young people learn construction and get job training while pursuing a high school education. Beyond writing checks from the foundation, Sheri continued to keep her feet on the ground, in the streets, with the kids.

On the occasions I joined her, Sheri made sure I heard directly from the young people she was meeting. We would sit down and ask them to share a bit about themselves. Stories poured out—about abusive homes, drug use, parents who kicked them out for causing trouble or for being gay, or predators on the streets who tried to lure them into joining gangs, selling drugs, or prostitution. While I had never had to deal with their specific challenges, I could relate to feelings of isolation, fear, loneliness, even desperation. I was impressed with the level of detail they shared; I was not yet at a point in my life where I was ready to reveal my own history. More than anything, I recognized how the challenges of my upbringing paled in comparison to what these young people were dealing with. My family did not have much money, but I always had food to eat, clothes to wear, and a bed to sleep in.

Over time, Sheri's compassion was bolstered by a better understanding of the city's fractured social services system, its underfunded schools, and the well-meaning but often inefficient web of nonprofit programs designed to help kids in peril. She also became well versed in reasons why many young people find themselves homeless or out of high school, and which resources and services can best help them get back on track.

She shared what she observed and learned with me, and I came to agree with her perspectives. Sheri continued to see resourceful, tenacious young men and women who wanted what most kids want—to live in a safe home, to be in a good school, to have friends, to be heard, to have a new pair of shoes, to be financially secure, to feel loved. She also saw teenagers with the capability and the will to excel if given a chance and the right support. But what, exactly, did a chance look like for them?

"These kids should be working at Starbucks," Sheri said to me early on.

By 2013, Sheri was eager to expand a jobs program that she, Star-bucks, YouthCare, and YouthBuild USA had all become involved with. A 160-hour course taught young people how to be baristas so they could get their first job. The Barista Training and Education Program provided hands-on practice in stores. Graduates were prepared to work at any coffee shop that hired them, not just a Starbucks. They also earned high school credit toward a GED.

Sheri wanted to take the program to other cities so more kids with few options could gain skills and get jobs. The process of expanding the program, however, was frustrating. It required an expertise and a time commitment that was beyond our capacities. Rather than give up, we decided to get help.

In October 2013, we hired the foundation's first full-time executive director. Sheri had liked Daniel Pitasky immediately. He'd spent his career helping youth in distress. During the 1980s, Daniel had coun-seled some of the first kids to be diagnosed with HIV on the streets of Los Angeles, and developed and managed two of the most effective high-risk-youth-focused organizations. He had also worked in national strategic roles, most recently at the Bill and Melinda Gates Founda-tion, creating student support programs for low-income and minority youth so they could complete high school and be productive after grad-uating. Daniel was a passionate and pragmatic advocate for young peo-ple and, like Sheri, quite personable.

In addition to a master's in social work, he had a business degree. I especially liked the fact that he approached social services with an emphasis on achieving measurable results.

When we hired Daniel, the original plan was for him to help Sheri expand the barista training program, increase the foundation's finan-cial commitments, and help us to become more strategic in our giving.

Veterans were not a population on the Schultz Family Foundation's radar. But during our nightly dinners together, I'd been telling Sheri what I had been learning and experiencing during the past year. She, too, had come to know and respect Bob Gates, and after one particu-larly moving conversation I'd had with Bob that fall, I had gone home and asked Sheri if she thought the foundation could also find a way to support veterans. By the end of the night, we agreed that we should do something through the foundation. But we had no idea what. We just knew that writing a check was not enough to ensure real change.

We shared our intention with Daniel, whose interest mirrored our own. So only weeks after he became the foundation's head, the three of us embarked on a learning tour. Before doing anything meaningful for veterans, we had to understand military culture and the challenges they faced. In the months that followed, much of what we saw and heard would not be at all what we anticipated.

"I would be more nervous about interviewing for a job than I would be about doing another tour in Afghanistan."

These words were spoken by a sergeant major—the highest rank an enlisted soldier can achieve—sitting at a large table with me, Sheri, and Daniel, as well as a dozen of his comrades, all dressed in muted green-and-tan combat attire. I had just asked the man how long he planned to stay in the Army. I was surprised to hear him suggest that war was less daunting to him than trying to get a job.

I looked at Sheri, who seemed just as taken aback.

It was a cool, overcast January day and we had come to Joint Base Lewis-McChord to learn about the process by which service members transition from active duty to nonmilitary life. We'd had a busy few hours, and the staff at the base, including Major General Kenneth Dahl, had been generous with their time.

When we asked the soldier why a job interview would make him more anxious than another tour of duty, he was not the only one around the table to provide an answer. The military had programs to help soldiers write résumés, but many of them still had no clue what career to pursue, or even what they could do in the world beyond the base. They didn't all know how the skills and training they had received during their service transferred to the civilian sector, or how to describe their experience and qualifications in nonmilitary language that a corporate recruiter would understand. Given all I had learned about my own company, their fears made sense.

Transitioning to civilian life posed other challenges, too. Military life was intensely regimented; members of the armed forces are told when to wake up, where to report for duty, and what to do during their waking hours. Civilian life has much less structure, fewer rules, and is more self-directed. For a veteran, as for many people, it takes time to readjust—and the return to the suddenly daunting freedoms of civilian life can lead to a sense of isolation.

Sheri, Daniel, and I were coming to understand that while the military was excellent at many things, it was not as effective as it could be at providing smooth passage for its members into civilian life. For soldiers like those we met at Lewis-McChord, adjusting was challenging not just because companies lacked the expertise and incentive to hire veterans, but because veterans and their families had a variety of their own particular issues to work through. Being nervous about a job interview was the tip of that iceberg.

The first time I met retired four-star general Peter Chiarelli, in 2012, he had asked for a favor.

Pete is a Seattle native who attended college and graduate school in Washington State. At twenty-two, he was commissioned as a second lieutenant, and during his long military career he was stationed on bases abroad and throughout the U.S., including at the Pentagon, where he was working when terrorists piloting American Airlines Flight 77 deliberately crashed into the massive building on September 11, 2001.

In the years following the terrorist attacks, Pete had led an Army division in Baghdad, and eight months later commanded the multinational corps in Iraq. In 2008, he was appointed the thirty-second vice chief of staff of the Army. His duties included overseeing the training and equipping of all soldiers, managing the Army's budget, and ensuring the well-being of half a million men and women.

He also oversaw the critical work of trying to reduce the Army's rising suicide rate. After years spent commanding forces, he was shocked to learn that the majority of soldiers the Army classified as disabled were not amputees or burn victims, but those diagnosed with post-traumatic stress disorder (PTSD), or traumatic brain injuries (TBI). Pete quickly became an expert on both, and was my teacher.

PTSD is a condition that people sometimes experience after being exposed to physical harm or threatened by it, and its symptoms include flashbacks, nightmares, and feelings of anger, anxiety, or disorientation. TBI can be suffered after a concussion, which often occurs when the brain is rocked by the explosion of a bomb. Both PTSD and TBI can easily go undiagnosed, and the effects include depression, destructive behavior, and attempts to take one's own life.

Unfortunately, the psychological wounds soldiers bore after returning from their post-9/11 deployments were not being treated with the same rigor as the Army was treating troops' physical wounds. For four years, Pete worked to reshape how PTSD and TBI were cared for in the military. He kept at it after retiring in 2012, when he moved back to Seattle and became the chief executive of One Mind for Research, a nonprofit that advanced treatment of brain injuries. The former Army general's new job was raising money to fund research, which was why he had come to see me. He'd asked for financial support. I promised to find a way to support One Mind.

In person, Pete is a broad-shouldered, steady presence, and when we met again in 2013, I told Pete about Starbucks' efforts to hire more veterans. He was pleased to hear it, but he was also saddened, and somewhat dismayed, that my own exposure to America's troops had been so thin. People in my position of influence, he thought, should not be so detached from the military. I will never forget when Pete looked me in the eyes and said, "Howard, if you're serious about helping veterans, if you really want to understand them, you must go to Walter Reed."

He cautioned me that visiting the U.S. military hospital that treated the most severely injured and ill members of the armed forces would not be easy, but I'd heard the general and knew I had to go.

———

Pete was right. But even with his caution, I was unprepared for what I would see and hear.

The Walter Reed National Military Medical Center at Bethesda exists as the result of a 2011 merger between two medical facilities, one for the Army, the other for the Navy. Patients ranged from Army privates to U.S. presidents. John F. Kennedy's autopsy had been conducted at the Bethesda Naval Medical Center. It's also where President Ronald Reagan underwent a surgery in 1985. More recently, Walter Reed was where the late Senator John McCain was treated for brain cancer.

I knew a bit about Walter Reed's history from Bob Gates, who played a significant role in rehabilitating the facility, its outpatient care, and its reputation when its operations were revealed to have major problems, including dirty conditions in the buildings where outpatient wounded warriors were housed, and a crippling bureaucracy.

Pete and I arrived together at Walter Reed's sprawling concrete campus, just ten miles outside Washington, D.C., on a chilly February morning. We were joined by Vivek, Daniel, and John Kelly. Sheri was unable to come and had planned a tour at a later date.

The first stop on our tour was a newer building, the National Intrepid Center of Excellence, a seventy-two-thousand-square-foot research, diagnosis, and treatment facility that had been envisioned by Arnold Fisher, a commercial real estate developer and philanthropist. Arnold's family founded Fisher Houses, which provide free housing for military families near veterans' hospitals around the country. The Intrepid was the second Fisher facility designed to treat soldiers with psychological health problems. Its calm, wavelike glass façade signaled it was a different type of healing place.

The interior was designed with the building's unique pool of patients in mind. Curved walls softened its open spaces, while recessed windows prevented exposure to direct sunlight for those with debilitating headaches. There was a yoga studio and an art room.

The patients we passed in the halls appeared to be no different from us. They wore civilian clothes. You would never know these veterans were suffering. In fact, I saw only one sign that the Intrepid's patients were in grave pain.

On several walls throughout the building there hung a collection of multicolored papier-mâché faces that had been decorated by patients as part of their rehabilitation therapy. The art helped them to "externalize their demons," a guide told us, and express distressing memories of war and its aftermath when speech did not come. And what stories the masks told.

Most were abstract versions of facial features. The eyes on some masks were closed, some were missing, and some wept blood. Some mouths were wide open, as if in mid-scream, while some had been sewn shut. Skin was black, brown, white, and ripped. Many faces had symbols on their cheeks and chins. A sun. A white tombstone. Various depictions of the American flag. Many masks were covered in words. *Frustration. Stress. Sad. Lonely. Bitter. Pray. Music. Hope. Friend. Wife. Jessica.* On one mask, in place of lips, all-capital letters read WHAT MATTERS MOST. Another face was painted to look like a brick wall. One mask had a pink heart on its scalp.

"Physical wounds take your breath away," Pete had said, "but you can't see brain injuries." The painted masks revealed invisible distress. They also reminded me of something Bob Gates had written about his own visits to Walter Reed, that wounded warriors are the real faces of war.

Quietly, our group left the Intrepid and headed to another building.

America's military hospitals were not prepared for the influx of patients they received as the wars in Iraq and then Afghanistan dragged on. Never before had so many soldiers survived such extensive physical injuries, from multiple amputations to debilitating gunshot wounds to severe burns. Survival was possible in part because of improvements in protective gear that shielded vital organs from otherwise deadly blasts, even when limbs were blown off, and because of medicine administered mid-battle to stanch blood loss, as well as the speed with which the injured were evacuated to hospitals. These and other advances made it possible for soldiers such as Master Sergeant Cedric King to live.

I didn't know a thing about Cedric King when I walked into the Warrior Café, which was the sunlit cafeteria located in one of Walter Reed's many buildings. Our small group was scheduled to eat lunch with patients who were in the midst of physical rehabilitation. At a long table draped with a white tablecloth, half a dozen service members and a few of their spouses were already seated, awaiting our arrival. I sat down next to a square-jawed, grinning man in a wheelchair. When he extended his right hand, I noticed that a slice of his arm was missing.

"Master Sergeant Cedric King," he said. "It's an honor to meet you, Mr. Schultz." His grip was strong and his voice boomed. After the subdued visit to the Intrepid, his energy caught me a bit off guard. Then came his rapid-fire questions.

Apparently, Cedric knew who I was and had even read my first book. He told me he was very interested in how I built the company. This conversation also surprised me. Starbucks was not a topic I thought I'd be discussing at Walter Reed. But Cedric was curious.

"You turned your nothing into something!" he said.

Cedric recalled my persistence with investors when so few believed in the idea of building Italian espresso bars, and said he felt the same way about his predicament, which at first I did not understand. My business history had inspired other entrepreneurs, but a soldier? Then he explained, "I know I'm going to run the Boston Marathon even if no one believes it but me." The conviction in his voice gave me no reason to doubt him, and our conversation was so lively, Cedric's unexpected jubilance so entrancing, that I almost forgot we were in a hospital.

When our guide announced it was time for all of us to get lunch, I stood up, Pete Chiarelli stood up, Daniel and Vivek stood up, the wives stood up, but Cedric and several of his comrades did not. Instead, they pushed themselves back from the table and for the first time since we had arrived at the café I realized that most of our lunch companions did not have legs. Cedric was missing two. As he heaved himself into a standing position, his breezy expression transformed into the knotted brow and tight lips of someone negotiating tremendous discomfort. He was struggling to stand on his prosthetics.

I knew, of course, that we would meet men and women whose limbs had been amputated, but the sudden view of so many young men missing pieces of themselves was a shock. For these men and their loved ones, for Cedric and his wife, lifelong battles were just beginning. The sight of such physical trauma did indeed take my breath away.

As Cedric slowly made his way to the chow line, I realized I wanted to know all about this man whose body had been torn apart but whose heart seemed so intact, and whose spirit certainly did not seem broken. Quite the opposite, in fact. When we returned to the table with full plates, I peppered Cedric with questions about his past, the incident that took his legs, and how his life had changed since coming home. He answered all with candor.

Cedric had been raised by a single mom in a mobile home in North Carolina. As a kid, he had been teased and school had not come easy. He enlisted in the Army after barely graduating high school, and was a dedicated soldier who fought hard to become an Army Ranger. He eventually graduated from all but one of the Army's leadership academies—and he would have completed the final academy if he had not been injured. Cedric loved the military as much as his family, and no less now than prior to July 25, 2012, when he was leading a reconnaissance mission into an abandoned Afghan village and stepped on a land mine. The bomb's blast ripped through his legs at the knees and stole part of his right arm. Cedric was so critically injured that doctors put him in a medically induced coma. When he awoke seven days later at Landstuhl Regional Medical Center in Germany, his wife and mother were by his bedside.

"They had to take your legs," his wife told him.

In the year and a half since, Cedric had undergone multiple surgeries. He said he had seen the abyss, but his faith in God, the support of his family, and a deep-seated belief that something good might come of his tragedy urged him on.

He had a whimsical way of expressing himself. Not only, he said, was he reprogramming his brain to learn how to walk on prosthetics, he was reprogramming his life. Cedric's wife had quit her job and moved with their two young daughters to Bethesda. They now lived in one of the small apartments at Walter Reed's Tranquility Hall, a residential building for rehabilitating soldiers and their families. He began most mornings at 6 A.M., here at the Warrior Café, getting breakfast for his family—his daughters were now six and ten—while his wife brushed their hair and helped them dress for school. After breakfast, Cedric took the girls to their bus stop before spending his day in physical therapy and medical appointments.

If recuperating was Cedric's new job, pain was his coworker. The severed bones in his legs continued growing through his muscle tissue, which made walking on prosthetics feel like walking on glass. And yet he was training for a marathon.

I was in awe not only of Cedric's trials but also of his buoyancy. This man truly believed he was a better person because he had lost so much. As he put it, he had no choice but to learn to operate with less, "like a chef who has to cook with whatever he's got in the kitchen and comes up with delicacies," he said.

Cedric told me that he wouldn't change a thing about his life. His story and attitude so moved me that I asked Cedric if we could stay in touch and, in the months ahead, we would show up for each other in ways neither of us could have predicted that day in the Warrior Café.

Later that day, our group passed a chunk of rusty steel on display behind a red rope and under a painting depicting the scene of the fallen World Trade Center—ground zero of America's longest war. The heat-mangled beam had been taken from one of the Twin Towers.

I left Walter Reed weighed down with questions. How does a country assess the costs of combat, or measure success in a "war on terror"? By the absence of another major attack on American soil? In the killing of a terrorist leader? One thing I was now certain about was that our dignity as a country should not only be measured by the validity of the choice to go to war, but also by how well those who volunteer to serve are treated while they serve and when they come home.

From the young cadets at West Point to meeting Sergeant Leroy

Petry to visiting Walter Reed, I had been exposed to a continuum of American commitment and sacrifice. The cost of war had been laid raw before me in lost limbs and howling masks, in wounds seen and unseen.

Was the cost worth it? I grappled with the question as I had not previously. I believe militaries should be deployed when genuine national security threats put America and her allies at real risk. Warfare should be an act of true necessity, not a rash choice stemming from partisanship, hunches, ego, or impatience.

The wars in Iraq and Afghanistan had been launched for different reasons. In 2001, President George W. Bush and other government leaders initiated military action in Afghanistan to fight the Taliban, which was harboring Al-Qaeda terrorists responsible for 9/11. Launching that conflict, I believe, was a just and necessary decision to preserve the safety of the country. However, the invasion of Iraq in 2003 was based on faulty intelligence and wrongheaded assumptions. At Walter Reed, I had seen the life-altering consequences of both decisions and conflicts, and the weight of war coated me like tar.

Those deployed were not the ones who launched and sustained the invasions. Members of our military follow the orders handed down by civilian leaders, foremost the president of the United States. Whether or not the service members who fought agreed with the reasons to go to war, they had nonetheless served. For that, I believe, they unquestionably deserve to come home to a country that welcomes them, cares for them, and extends hands of compassion and opportunity.

While in D.C., Vivek had arranged for us to have dinner with his old friend Rajiv Chandrasekaran. Rajiv was a senior correspondent and associate editor of *The Washington Post*, where he had worked for two decades, reporting from more than three dozen countries. He had been a bureau chief in Baghdad, as well as Cairo and Southeast Asia.

When Rajiv had called Vivek in early January to check in with his friend, he casually mentioned that he was writing a series of articles about veterans. The series was based on a groundbreaking study the

Post had conducted with the Kaiser Family Foundation, a nonprofit focused on health issues. Rajiv did not think the topic of veterans would interest someone who worked for a coffee company, until Vivek told him about Starbucks' hiring commitment and my evolving interest in veterans. Rajiv accepted Vivek's invitation to meet with us in D.C. to talk about the study.

When Pete, Vivek, Daniel, Rajiv, and I sat down at Rasika, a popular Indian restaurant in D.C., Rajiv and Pete immediately began comparing notes about their respective stints in Iraq, when Pete was a war commander and Rajiv a war correspondent. As the food arrived, the conversation turned to the results of the *Post*-Kaiser poll.

Of the 2.6 million Americans dispatched to fight in the post-9/11 wars, Rajiv told us, 43 percent said that their physical health was worse than before they deployed. Thirty-one percent said their mental or emotional health was worse

One in two knew a fellow service member who had attempted or committed suicide, and more than one million suffered from relationship problems and outbursts of anger. Hearing these numbers, Pete shook his head. He was not surprised by the stats, but they still troubled him.

Rajiv had interpreted the results through the lens of his own experience. As the author of an acclaimed book documenting the transfer of power back to Iraqis at the end of the U.S. invasion, he had a working knowledge of the post-9/11 conflicts and their politics. And as a boots-on-the-ground war reporter, he had been embedded with troops and knew firsthand the dangers they faced in combat. All in all, he had great respect for the risks soldiers voluntarily assumed, which was one reason why he was surprised and upset by another of the poll's findings: that 55 percent of veterans—about 1.4 million among this generation's service members—said they felt disconnected from civilian life in America.

The soldier from Joint Base Lewis-McChord came to my mind— *I would be more nervous about interviewing for a job than I would be about doing another tour in Afghanistan*—as did Starbucks' own hiring challenges, and the high suicide rates among returning soldiers. Dots were connecting, and the picture showed an unfortunate but gaping divide between the country's military and civilian populations.

For the next two hours, we talked about the reasons for the so-called civilian-military divide. Since 2001, the burdens and horrors of warfare had fallen disproportionately on a fraction of U.S. families. Less than 7 percent of the nation's citizens were either in the military or had an immediate family member who was. Less than one percent of the population—*one percent*—had directly participated in the war, and all on a volunteer basis and for a war that had already lasted longer than any other war in American history. Previous conflicts—World War I, World War II, the Korean War, Vietnam—touched so many more people in part because of the draft. Conscription forced more of us to pay attention because we, too, might find ourselves or friends and family engaged in battle. There is no doubt that more Americans played a role in past war efforts, on the front lines and the home front. But for the last decade, few of us had had any personal involvement, and thus we did not fully understand war's human consequences.

By the time the meal ended, the five of us had concluded that more needed to be done to break through to the vast majority of Americans who had no real understanding of what our nation's veterans had done in battle and could do back home. It was an important conversation that did not end once we left the restaurant.

My father never spoke to me about his military service during World War II. To this day, I do not know exactly what he did, what he saw, or what he felt when he was stationed in the South Pacific, except that he contracted two mosquito-borne illnesses common in the region, malaria and yellow fever. Aside from that, I knew of no physical injuries. How his service affected his state of mind, however, I can only speculate.

My father was not among those who came home after World War II and seized on the opportunities made available by the G.I. Bill. As far as I could see, my father chose to remain uneducated and unskilled, and I observed in him traits that I intuitively knew I did not want to emulate. A willingness to cut corners. A lack of a work ethic. A habit of spending money he did not have. A violent temper. Something had defeated my father, but I never knew what.

For much of my life, it was hard for me to really respect him, even if I did sympathize when he was injured and humiliated by circumstances beyond his control. Still, anger at my dad eclipsed other emotions.

In 2014, my late-in-life exposure to the experiences of those who serve in the military was suggesting a new lens through which I could choose to view my father. Today, I can imagine a young, scared Fred Schultz who was drafted and stationed thousands of miles from his family in a remote, dangerous part of the world. I can see a kid who experienced fears and perhaps witnessed horrors of war that may have followed him home. Did he suffer PTSD? Did his wartime experience exacerbate his demons and color his choices? Perhaps.

I had to wonder: How might my dad have painted his mask?

CHAPTER 12

Role and Responsibility

Liliane Kamikazi wasn't afraid of death. At ten, it was the machetes she feared.

In the spring of 1994, Liliane was just a girl when the mass slaughter of men, women, and children broke out in her home country of Rwanda. It was a vicious, brutal, fast-paced genocide perpetrated by the government and the country's ruling Hutu class against all Rwandans of Tutsi ethnicity.

At the time, Liliane's father was working far from home, in the capital city of Kigali. There was a day when Liliane's mother told Liliane and her older sister to pack small bags so they could stay at their uncle's house and hide.

"Now go," her mother said. "You have to run!" Liliane's family was Tutsi. She never saw her mother or her father again.

"I was the best runner," Liliane would eventually tell me. "But the first day they came I couldn't run."

It was sunny when more than fifty men with machetes arrived at her uncle's home. The men were singing. "They called it 'going to work,'" Liliane later recalled. The men surrounded the house and ordered everyone outside. Her sister ran into the forest. But fear paralyzed Liliane. The men lined up her aunts, uncles, and cousins, but for some reason pulled Liliane, her grandmother, and her little cousin aside and told them to watch while their loved ones were beaten with machetes, and murdered. They were the only ones left alive that horrific day in May.

When I first met Liliane in 2012, I knew nothing about her unimaginably painful past. All I knew was that she was a barista at the Starbucks store in our headquarters. She was quite tall, but I noticed Liliane because she made very little eye contact and moved with a quiet grace behind the coffee bar. When she took my order or handed me my drink, I sensed a sadness about her.

One day I saw her sitting at a table, reading a book. She was on a break. I walked up and said hello. For the first time I saw her smile. "I heard you speak during your book tour," she told me, referring to *Onward*, which came out in 2011. I sat down and asked how she had come to work at Starbucks.

It would be a while before Liliane revealed her family tragedy. That day, she simply told me that she was from Rwanda and had come to the United States to attend college in Seattle. After she graduated, she wanted to work for Starbucks, in marketing. She applied online but never heard back, so she interviewed for a job as a barista thinking it would get her foot in the door.

I asked Liliane if she had met with people in our marketing department.

"Howard, it's not that easy to just meet with people in marketing!" She said this with a polite spunk. I liked Liliane. She was clearly smart and driven. It takes a lot to move so far from home and begin a new life. I'd moved across the country with Sheri. Liliane had traveled around the world, with no one.

"I'll make sure you meet someone in marketing," I told her, and sent Gina Woods her way.

In the summer of 2013, Liliane hung up her green apron and accepted a job in our public affairs department.

Almost daily I would walk past Liliane's desk on the way to my office. I usually stopped to say hello and ask how things were going. Sometimes we'd have lunch. I also introduced her to Sheri, and several times Liliane joined us for dinner. When I hosted holiday dinners at our house for some of my Starbucks colleagues, I often included Liliane.

I came to see that while she carried the tragedy of her past in her bones, she had the heart of an angel and the inner strength of a lion. But not until we sat in my office one day, and she told me the horror of her childhood, did I more fully see and understand her.

The day after Liliane's family members were murdered in front of her eyes, two men returned to the house, with machetes. "Run!" her grandmother yelled. That day Liliane ran. She tripped on a stone and fell and the skin on her knee broke open. But she got up and kept running. Liliane never saw her grandmother or little cousin again.

The Rwandan genocide ended after approximately one hundred days. An estimated eight hundred thousand to one million people had been killed, including most of Liliane's family. She spent her teenage years living with another uncle and his family, as well as her sister, who had also miraculously survived. Liliane went to school and tried to be a good student and a grateful survivor. But the past haunted her. Grief clung to her soul and she longed for her mother. She missed the way her mother called her Cheri, which meant honey. She also missed her mother's vanilla pudding. Some days Liliane made the pudding for herself, and its sweet taste filled her for a while.

But the gruesome images of her family's death couldn't be erased. She tried to escape them by watching television. In her darkest moments, there was one show she turned to: *Oprah*. Liliane couldn't understand English, but the vivacious warmth of Oprah Winfrey hosting her talk show transcended language. The sound of Oprah's voice—booming and soothing at the same time—leapt from the screen into Liliane's cavernous heart. There was something about the way Oprah hugged people, the way she cried with people, and smiled so easily, that drew Liliane in. Sometimes she woke up in the middle of the night and turned the TV on at low volume. She'd sit inches from the screen, watching *Oprah* reruns.

Liliane later said that Oprah gave her a reason to want to see tomorrow. She also gave Liliane a desire to see America. At fifteen, Liliane set her sights on moving to the United States.

She'd graduated and been working for Starbucks for two years when, in the fall of 2013, the company was preparing to launch a new product: Oprah Chai Tea.

About that time, Oprah was in Seattle, at Starbucks headquarters. Our offices were electric. Everyone wanted to meet Oprah. Between meetings, during a quiet moment, I asked Oprah if she might do me a personal favor. There was someone I wanted her to meet.

I walked with Liliane into the boardroom. Oprah stood up. Liliane stared, wide-eyed, and walked toward her, falling into her arms. Oprah enveloped her. Clinging to the woman from the TV, Liliane thanked her for saving her life.

That Thanksgiving, Oprah invited Liliane to her home. It was the first of many holidays that Liliane would spend with Oprah, and among her family and friends.

Liliane still works for Starbucks, as a program manager for our digital news efforts.

Knowing Liliane has taught me about the resilience of the human spirit, about our ability to move on after tremendous loss, and the responsibility we all have to bring others along with us. In 2017, Liliane founded a nonprofit organization, A Bridge for Girls, to train Rwandan women how to sew and sell their own goods so they can support themselves. By the fall of 2018, Bridge for Girls had thirty-two participants.

At age thirty-four, Liliane would tell you that many of her dreams have come true. But she also knows that dreaming is not enough. "People need a path," she says. "And you have to give them one."

In 2014, paving paths for others was a responsibility I was beginning to take more seriously. And not just for people who had suffered, or who possessed the courage and strength of someone like Liliane. Everyone deserves a first, and often even a second, chance.

In March, I began the 2014 annual meeting of Starbucks shareholders with an anecdote that was not about coffee. Standing onstage, I told the full auditorium how, several years earlier, I'd been in London visiting Starbucks stores, and after spending a day meeting with hundreds of partners I decided to walk the streets alone, which is still among my favorite things to do in cities I visit.

I went from one store to another in downtown London, hoping to be inspired by what other merchants were doing. Eventually I found myself on a very fashionable street in a high-rent district, and out of the corner of my eye I saw a storefront that did not look like it belonged. The façade could not have been more than fifteen feet wide. There was no fancy sign, just one word above the door: CHEESE. My curiosity got the better of me, plus I was hungry, so I walked in.

It was like stepping back in time. The peeling walls and the worn floor. The musty air that smelled like history and blue cheese. The man behind the counter must have been at least seventy years old. He was unshaven and wore a flannel shirt that was ripped at the elbow. We started talking and he began giving me samples of different cheeses, telling me about each slice with expertise and passion as he described its acidity, body, how it would taste with wine. He was so friendly that I got up the nerve to ask him a personal question.

"How do you afford the rent on this street?"

He smiled. "I don't afford the rent," he said. "I own the building."

A laugh wafted through the auditorium, but that punch line was not the point. The proprietor went on to tell me about his father and his grandfather, who had both worked in that shop and made the cheese; the business had been going for over a century. Today, his son made the cheese, about a hundred miles outside London. The proprietor could easily have made more money by renting the space. He said he worked to honor his family, and the legacy of responsibility and the pride he had in the generations that came before him. That was the punch line, but it was no joke.

We never know when we're going to have a learning moment, when something unexpected occurs to enhance our perspective. And this serendipitous conversation, I told the audience, still reminded me to ask myself, in the context of Starbucks, *What is our core purpose? What is our reason for being?*

I asked our shareholders to keep that story in mind throughout the three-hour meeting. We would review another year in which Starbucks had achieved record revenue and profit, and announce plans to launch new products and open more stores. We would also discuss the theme of the day, which appeared on a sixty-six-foot-wide screen behind me: WHAT IS THE ROLE AND RESPONSIBILITY OF A FOR-PROFIT PUBLIC COMPANY?

That question implied a company's role in society went beyond making money, a concept Starbucks had been expressing in many ways, going all the way back to the first mission statement as Il Giornale. As we opened more stores, we always strove to achieve the fragile balance between profitability and a social conscience. As we went global, we tried to use our scale for good. More recently, I described Starbucks as a company that is performance-driven through the lens of humanity. I also liked the way Vivek put it, that Starbucks is built for something bigger. These aren't mere platitudes; this language has inspired our people and guided the decisions that we make.

At the 2014 shareholder meeting, framing our purpose as an open-ended question felt authentic to me because I did not have a definitive answer. I just knew that, at this point in our history, we had to do more.

Why, after three decades, was the company wading into territories that other public companies deemed too risky or off course? For a few reasons, I explained to shareholders. But the biggest was a void of leadership in America.

"Whether you are Republican or Democrat or independent or Libertarian, it doesn't matter," I said. "I think we all have a sense that there's something not quite right [in the country], that we're drifting toward mediocrity."

I was in my early twenties when I opened the door of our home one night and heard my parents arguing. When my mom saw me, she grabbed my arms and began talking at me through hysterical sobs.

"The shylocks," she kept saying, "the shylocks are going to come for your father and hurt him." "Shylock" is a derogatory term for a loan shark, and perceived as anti-Semitic when used by people who are not Jewish. Apparently, my father had borrowed five thousand dollars from some unsavory people. The money had been used to pay for my younger brother's bar mitzvah party, and although I was upset to learn about it, I was not surprised.

In Jewish tradition, at age thirteen, a boy becomes a *bar mitzvah,* a young man capable of assuming responsibility for adhering to the morals and values that make up Jewish law. In short, he becomes, in theory, an adult. My family was not religious. We did not keep kosher or attend temple regularly. But the bar mitzvah ceremony—or, for girls, the bat mitzvah ceremony—was a common practice among most Jewish families we knew, and one my parents wanted for their children. I had gone to Hebrew school for years at a temple in Canarsie, and did a lot of preparation to learn Hebrew so I could read a portion from the Torah aloud to the congregation during my bar mitzvah service.

The ceremony is traditionally followed by a celebration, which can be as simple as a casual lunch for friends and family, though some families put on much more extravagant affairs. To my astonishment, my parents had insisted on throwing a nighttime party after my bar mitzvah at a banquet hall in Long Island. They could barely pay our bills, but I don't recall asking where they got the money for the hall, my dad's tuxedo, or the matching gold-toned suit jackets that my younger brother and I wore. I had never been so dressed up, and I felt proud as we posed for pictures for a professional photographer my parents had hired. I remember being surrounded by relatives and friends of my parents, and my own friends, including Billy. All night long, people hugged me and congratulated me.

"Mazel tov, mazel tov, Howard!" they said as they handed me envelopes with money inside, because that's what you gave as a gift. The assumption was that the money would help pay for a future college education.

At one point, my father told me to give him all the envelopes, which of course I did because I thought he was holding them for me. Later, at home, I asked to have the envelopes back.

"The money's gone," he said. Then he told me that all of it was used to pay for the party.

My joy deflated. I had worked hard to prepare for the day. And while I loved the fancy celebration, I had not asked for it. The money to help me afford college, and maybe to buy a treat or two at thirteen, had been hijacked to pay for a night that did not have to happen. I came to believe that my parents threw the affair to impress friends and family, some of whom had more money than we did. Even with my gift money, they didn't have enough to cover the costs. The photographer was never paid and refused to hand over any of the pictures. The only shots of the event I ever saw were a handful of photos taken by guests.

The loss of the money, but more so the loss of trust, sparked an internal fury. That was about the time I began doing less forgiving and more judging of my father's behaviors.

Eight years after my bar mitzvah, my mother was pleading with me. "Please, Howard," she said, "go to the Levys' house. Ask to borrow the money for your father." I knew the Levys. Their son was my friend and the family owned a furrier business in Manhattan where I had worked during high school to earn my own money. They were perhaps the only wealthy family my parents knew. The thought of going to the Levys' home in their nicer Canarsie neighborhood and asking for money made my skin crawl. I couldn't do it. I looked at my parents and considered rebelling. I was over six feet tall—taller than my father. But he still had his temper.

My mother pleaded, "Please, Howard, the shylocks are going to come." I did not know these people she was talking about, but I also did not want my father to be hurt. I loved him still. But the thought of going to the Levys' . . .

My father began scribbling on a piece of paper, writing an I.O.U. note for five thousand dollars, which included a promise to pay interest. He handed me the paper. I can still hear my mother saying, "Please, Howard . . ."

Mrs. Levy answered the door and invited me inside. We sat down in the kitchen and I told her why I was there and handed her the I.O.U. Frozen, I could barely bring myself to say the words. Shame was like ice in my veins. Waiting alone while she disappeared to talk to Mr. Levy was almost unbearable. I seethed. I felt like my parents were using me to shoulder their mistakes. My stomach churned. When Mrs.

Levy returned and handed me five thousand in cash, it was hard for me to look at her. I never returned to the Levys' house. I couldn't.

No one ever came to hurt my father, to my knowledge. At his funeral, in 1987, Mrs. Levy walked up to me and handed me my father's I.O.U. note. As I looked at the fifteen-year-old piece of paper with his recognizable handwriting, she said to me, "I wonder, at some point, if we can talk about this." Embarrassed once again, I repaid her the money, with the interest she was due.

I cannot pinpoint the moment I realized that my own life would change because of having money. Starbucks became a public company in 1992, and the day of our initial public offering the corporation was valued at $250 million. I owned 10 percent. On paper, I was an overnight millionaire. Of course, Starbucks would have to continue to be financially successful for me to ever realize the value of my shares. But I felt a sense of security like nothing I'd ever known.

I must say that writing about my own experience with money as a wealthy adult is less comfortable for me than writing about life as a child with my struggling father. But like my father, it's part of who I am.

Coming into a lot of money very quickly is an odd phenomenon. I remember feeling like we had won the lottery. So many forces had conspired to bring me to the point in my life where in one day the shares I owned in a company that I led were valued by the market at millions of dollars. All entrepreneurs are subject to elements beyond their control. Consumer trends. Macroeconomics. Personally, I'd endured the treachery of an investor who tried to steal Starbucks out from under me, but also benefited from the support of people like Bill Gates, Sr. I felt grateful that hard work and original ideas had merged with good fortune.

In a short period of time, Sheri and I went from renting a small house to being able to build our dream home. We began to exercise our new financial freedoms while trying to be good parents. Money did make it easier to be the kind of parents we wanted to be—the kind of parents I never had when I was growing up. Financial worries were the backbeat to so many of my parents' fights when I was a child. It was, in part, a lack of money that demoralized my father and stressed out my mother.

So while having money made things easier and gave our family choices, Sheri and I did not want our children's values or self-worth shaped by money. As Sheri put it, it was important that our children grow up seeing the world through a wide-angle lens.

We talked about and tried to demonstrate to our kids the responsibilities that went along with financial privilege, even as we continued to figure it out for ourselves. We tried to attune them to the challenges faced by those who were less fortunate, and we tried to emphasize, through conversation and our own actions, the importance of being involved in the community. Sheri was regularly volunteering with homeless youth. And through Starbucks, I hoped the kids absorbed the lesson that treating people well could be part of the fabric of human and corporate behavior. That it was just what you did.

As they eyed college, we also encouraged them to follow their passions. Our hope and expectation was that, as adults, both Jordy and Addy would find fulfillment through hard work and careers, as well as family. Today, Addy is a social worker and Jordan is a sports journalist. Both are married to exceptional individuals. Jordan's wife, Breanna, and Addison's husband, Tal, are extremely kind, generous, bright people who have become integral members of our growing family. They share our kids' values, and the six of us, along with my two grandchildren, spend a lot of time together. We all treasure family.

Money can fundamentally change things in our most intimate spaces, and in our own minds and hearts. Not having money isn't just about a number in your bank account. It's a blow to your body and soul. It can translate to a lack of security, a lack of opportunity, a lack of mobility, a lack of health, a lack of information, a lack of time, a lack of dignity. It can be as inescapable and suffocating as the air in our Canarsie apartment on days when the money was tight and my parents were undone by their own anxiety and humiliation.

I have lived at both ends of this country's unbalanced economic spectrum. The suffering that some people in America endure, and which others are shielded from because of seemingly endless resources, is the untold story of wealth inequality.

I am not ashamed of the wealth I have accumulated through Starbucks' success. But I have never been interested in broadcasting my personal net worth. I'm very private in that regard. Money is not a measure by which I judge myself or want others to judge me. At the end of the day, we must each close our eyes and find peace with the decisions we have made.

Among the things I have come to understand is how money can too easily amplify the best and worst of human nature. People with vast wealth are not immune to the heartbreaks of life, some of which are brought about by that wealth. There are also emotional aches that no amount of money can possibly ease. And while money can afford us our dreams, it can also imbue our failures with the destructive breadth of a tsunami.

As a kid, I never imagined I would ever own a professional sports team, but later on it became a dream of mine. Sports had played such an essential role in my life, from the Canarsie courts and forging my path out of the projects, to watching games with my dad and going to games with my son. In 2001, Seattle had four major sports franchises. The Mariners for baseball. The Seahawks for football. And for basketball, the women's NBA team, the Seattle Storm, and the NBA's SuperSonics. The Sonics had brought Seattle its first professional title, the world championship in 1979. The city's pride for that team never faded.

I'd turned down a chance to own a minority stake in the Seattle Mariners. I'd regretted the decision, so when the Sonics became available for purchase, it seemed like another chance. Even though baseball is my first love, basketball is a close second. Once during high school, I waited outside all night to buy tickets to see the New York Knicks in a playoff game. I'd held season tickets to Sonics games since I'd moved to the city, and still played basketball every week. In 2001, the timing to get involved in the business of sports was also right; I was no longer the CEO of Starbucks. I was still busy as chairman and chief global strategist, but I had more bandwidth than usual to pay attention to things outside the company.

I couldn't afford to buy the team on my own, so another lead buyer and I pulled together two investor groups, and more than fifty of us came together to buy the Sonics. As the largest shareholder—although not the majority owner—I became the public face of the franchise. At the press conference announcing the sale, I said that I viewed my ownership of the team as a public trust. At the time, though, I did not fully appreciate what that meant.

I wanted to learn how to run the franchise from one of the other new owners, who had been the Sonics' general manager for many years. He oversaw the day-to-day operations, while I assumed responsibility for one of the franchise's biggest challenges. The Sonics had what many considered to be one of the league's worst business arrangements with city government. The team's lease to play at the outdated KeyArena for many more years had terms that made it very hard for the franchise to be profitable; even if every home game sold out, which rarely happened, we still would have lost money. In addition to needing a new arrangement with the city, we needed to give the arena a multimillion-dollar renovation, or find a new arena, to attract more spectators and bring in the kind of revenue that would help make the Sonics as profitable a business as other NBA franchises.

Seattle taxpayers had recently funded new football and baseball stadiums, and the city was not keen about paying tens of millions of dollars to help build another sports facility. I bought the team believing that we could win government and public support for a new arena, or at a minimum, renegotiate the adverse lease agreement with the city in a way that balanced the needs and desires of all parties—owners, the local government, and fans.

My assumptions were a mistake. The back-and-forth conversations I had with the mayor, the city council, and the state legislature could fill another book. At times, I felt as if I was up against a brick wall. One influential member of the city council was so adamantly against public funding for a new stadium that he told *Sports Illustrated* that the city of Seattle would suffer no lasting damage if the Sonics ever left. "On an economic basis, near zero," he said. "On a cultural basis, close to zero." I thought he was just being blind to the value that sports brings to a city, from economic revenue to bringing members of the community together. In retrospect, I can see he had other priorities for taxpayers' dollars.

We never did reach an agreement with the city on sharing in the costs of a new arena. Meanwhile, the team continued to lose money. To keep the franchise operating and paying the players, we owners kept putting more of our own funds in. I became hyper-focused on stopping the bleeding and saving the business. The need to keep writing checks, however, unsettled many of my fellow owners and me.

What I did not appreciate at the time was that owning a public sports team is not the same as operating a private or even public company. The obligations are different. The Sonics only existed because so many people in the city had supported the team for years, and they supported it not because it was always winning, but because the team represented the city itself. That is the beauty of sports in America. The team belongs to the city it represents, not just to the owners. The fans, while not shareholders, are the most precious stakeholders.

As all this went on, I was also doing my job as Starbucks chairman. The two roles consumed my time and my brain. And once Orin left the company, retiring as long planned in 2005, the departure of my mentor, fellow leader, and friend left a void in me. I missed him dearly.

As the Sonics' economic problems mounted, other team owners, myself included, did not want to keep putting in more money. For me, operating the team had become financially and emotionally debilitating. After five years with the Sonics, I felt as if I'd done the best I could at that period in my life, but my best was not good enough. I decided to sell my stake. I assumed at least some of the other owners who did not want to sell the team would buy me out, but they didn't want to. The only way for me to exit was if a majority of owners agreed to sell the team to another buyer. Few local people could afford to buy it, or were willing to buy a franchise that was saddled with such a horrible lease arrangement.

At one point, a local chief executive verbally agreed to purchase the team. For a moment, I thought the problem was solved. When he rescinded his offer a few days later, I was crushed. With few options in Seattle, then-head of the NBA, David Stern, put me in touch with potential buyers in other cities. One well-known tech CEO would have paid a premium to buy the franchise but I turned him down because he insisted on moving the Sonics to another state. I saw a path forward when I met the head of an investment firm in Oklahoma who agreed to spend a year working in good faith with the city and state officials to try to get a new arena deal. If he could, he said, he would keep the Sonics in their hometown. Someone from outside Seattle, I thought, might have a better chance of negotiating a new arena deal because the threat of losing the team could push city officials to come to the table with more favorable terms. In retrospect, this was not a fair position to impose upon the city.

In 2006, the SuperSonics were sold to the Oklahoma ownership group, which never did reach a new deal with the city. In 2008, the new owners relocated the Sonics to Oklahoma City and renamed the team the Thunder.

The loss of Seattle's professional basketball team devastated Sonics fans. They were brokenhearted. And furious. Almost everyone blamed me, and after some initial denial, I realized they were right to do so. I had squandered the very public trust that I had bought into.

The ire on sports radio, on the pages of the local newspaper, and on the streets of the city was relentless. People who recognized me would shout expletives, sometimes cursing me out in front of my kids.

Selling the Sonics as I did is one of the biggest regrets of my professional life. In retrospect, I believe that I was so focused on getting myself and other investors out of a bad financial situation that I did not abide by one of my own guiding principles, which is to try to balance profit and people's needs, and make decisions that are not purely economic. A sports team's true purpose—to bring people together as it had for me and my dad when I was young—had receded from my thoughts, even though as an owner I was a guardian of that purpose.

I also made a tremendous mistake selling to an outsider; I should have been willing to lose money until a local buyer emerged. Instead, I made a financial decision hoping for the best. The choice cost a city its beloved sports team.

I have spent countless hours trying to learn from the experience. In America, there is an outsized power that people, especially those with wealth, are often afforded. Prior to my experience with the Sonics, so many of my decisions had resulted in positive outcomes for others. The eventual outcome of selling the team, however, made me more aware than ever of the negative ramifications attached to power. The experience also imprinted upon me the searing knowledge of how a single decision can adversely affect thousands of lives. In the years since, I have thought about and questioned the very nature of power, and the enormous responsibility of those who have it.

More than a decade later, in 2018, the Seattle city council approved a privately funded $700 million renovation of KeyArena to help the city land a new National Hockey League franchise. If the renovation happens, a new basketball team could follow.

The loss of the Sonics continues to reverberate throughout Seattle. Lingering anger is still directed at me, and I don't deny anyone his or her rage.

The sharpest pains hit me not when I'm publicly insulted, but when I'm walking or driving and see someone wearing a SuperSonics T-shirt or cap. If it's a boy with his dad, it's like a stake through my heart. Losing the Sonics has been tragic for generations of fans, especially kids who are growing up without the benefit of an NBA team in their city. It's a public wound I cannot heal. For that I will forever be deeply sorry.

CHAPTER 13

For Love of Country

Pouring rain arrived with more than one hundred fifty guests.

It was an eclectic gathering that filled our home on that damp spring evening. They included Starbucks board members and senior leaders, Major General Dahl from Joint Base Lewis-McChord, Secretary Gates, Arizona congresswoman Gabrielle Giffords, and her husband, astronaut Mark Kelly. Also there was Oprah Winfrey, who had attended the Starbucks shareholder meeting that morning to announce a new, eponymous tea Starbucks was selling, Oprah Chai.

Sheri and I were hosting the event to heighten awareness of the veteran community.

Together with Daniel Pitasky, we had acquired a deeper understanding of veterans' issues through our travels—in addition to visiting Joint Base Lewis-McChord and Walter Reed, we toured military facilities in Georgia, San Antonio, San Diego, and Kuwait. We had also consulted with experts and funded a national analysis to identify areas where veterans' and their families' needs were not being met. This due diligence helped Sheri and Daniel develop the foundation's first long-term strategic plan, which they announced in March 2014, to focus on youth *and* veterans.

That evening at our home, Sheri announced that the Schultz Family Foundation would make an initial pledge of $30 million to help address the three greatest barriers veterans and their families face in transitioning to civilian life: their employment, their health, and the reintegration of their families.

First, the foundation would invest its time and resources to develop specialized job training and placement programs that put veterans on paths to successful, sustainable careers. Second, we would invest in organizations—including One Mind for Research, fulfilling General Pete Chiarelli's request of me—to better understand and evaluate post-traumatic stress disorder and traumatic brain injury research and alternative treatments. Third, we would develop comprehensive transition programs for veterans, as well as their families. Military spouses also make tremendous sacrifices, often giving up educations and careers as they constantly relocate to support an active-duty spouse. The foundation would invest in helping families navigate the real world once they left the base. We would do all of these things in partnership with a variety of veterans' service programs.

As guests said their goodbyes that night, I looked for someone I had invited but had not yet seen.

After our dinner in Washington, D.C., Rajiv, Vivek, and Daniel had continued to explore what else could be done to reach people who were unaware of our troops' valor in wartime, as well as their value once they left the service. At their urging, I began speaking with Rajiv about writing a book that would feature stories of upstanding veterans, and we discussed collaborating. That evening, we agreed we could make a complementary team. Plus, we both believed that sharing veterans' stories was the best way to help people grasp their issues.

We had three months to write a book if we wanted to publish by Veterans Day. To make the deadline, Rajiv took a leave of absence from *The Washington Post*.

Our intent was to highlight the good that veterans bring into society by telling true stories of their valor and contributions, in combat and stateside. Doing so would help serve one of the foundation's goals, which was creating successful transitions to civilian life. We believed that the better understanding Americans had of today's veterans, the more inclined they might be to reach out to them not just with a polite "Thank you for your service," but with real opportunities, like jobs.

The two of us met with veterans and active-duty service members around the country. The interview that struck me most, however, was with Dr. Bill Krissoff, an orthopedic surgeon in his late sixties who sat in my office and told us about one of his two sons, Nathan, a Marine who, at twenty-five, became the 2,924th American killed in Operation Iraqi Freedom when his Humvee was blasted by a bomb. Dr. Krissoff described how he answered the front door of his home at 8 A.M. on a Saturday morning and saw three Marines and an Army chaplain who had come to deliver the wrenching news.

Bill, who had no prior military service, received a rare age waiver at sixty-one to join the Navy medical corps. After training to be a combat surgeon, Lieutenant Commander Krissoff deployed to Iraq and Afghanistan, where he performed or assisted on more than two hundred combat surgeries and saved countless lives of other parents' children. When Bill told us that his seven months in Afghanistan were the most rewarding in his three-decade-long orthopedic career, I was in awe of his and his wife Christine's commitment to their son and to the country. They did not want Nate to have died in vain.

The stories of Dr. Krissoff, Leroy Petry, Cedric King, and many others are featured in *For Love of Country: What Our Veterans Can Teach Us about Citizenship, Heroism, and Sacrifice.* The book was a slim volume that wove a tapestry of human spirits. Bravery. Fortitude. Will. Honor. Selflessness. Love for fellow human beings. Duty to country.

Starbucks stores in all fifty states carried the book, as did traditional outlets. Proceeds from sales of the book were donated to organizations that support veterans.

After the book project, Rajiv left *The Washington Post* and moved his family to Seattle so we could continue to explore new ways to leverage the powerful combination of storytelling and Starbucks.

We were brainstorming when it occurred to me that we did not have to limit the stories in *For Love of Country* to the pages of a book. There was another way to reach people. We could bring them together, and I knew just the place.

On Veterans Day 2014, Jennifer Hudson sang the national anthem in front of an estimated 800,000 people gathered on the National Mall in Washington, D.C., for a concert to honor service members and veterans and raise awareness of their sacrifices.

Nowhere in America seemed a more fitting place to bring American citizens and service members together than the iconic park of green grass between the Capitol Building and the Washington Monument. For years, I'd dreamed of holding an event on the Mall. Here, people of all backgrounds and political persuasions have gathered over the decades to inaugurate presidents, to protest, to champion beliefs.

Until now, nothing I had been involved with was important enough to justify using the massive, historic space. Getting the permits was a complex undertaking, as was orchestrating the entire event. More than a concert *for* veterans, we wanted to raise awareness *about* veterans by getting people from around the country to watch the concert and hear their stories.

We could not pull it off alone, and two people in particular stepped up. Richard Plepler, the CEO of HBO, offered to produce and broadcast the two-hour event live, and Jamie Dimon, the CEO of JPMorgan Chase, agreed to have his financial institution sponsor the event with Starbucks and the Schultz Family Foundation. A diverse roster of talent also volunteered to perform for free. Everyone I asked said yes.

The night was clear and comfortable, and the nation's Capitol glowed in the distance as musicians, actors, and public figures followed each other onto the stage. Rihanna, Carrie Underwood, the Black Keys, Jessie J, Metallica, Dave Grohl, Eminem, Bruce Springsteen, Jamie Foxx, John Oliver, Jack Black, and George Lopez were among those who performed or spoke.

But the true stars of the evening were not celebrities. Between acts, short videos, which HBO produced, profiled several of the veterans who appeared in the book *For Love of Country*. The videos aired on massive screens posted up and down the Mall, as well as on HBO. Each video was narrated by a famous voice. Among them, Steven Spielberg shared the story of Bill Krissoff's late-in-life tour of duty. Oprah Winfrey recalled Leroy Petry's gunfight. Michelle Obama spoke about Cedric King's physical and spiritual rehabilitation.

I could see Cedric stand up from his seat near the stage and acknowledge the applause when his name was announced. When Leroy waved his right hand, he had his Medal of Honor around his neck.

At one point, Meryl Streep stood onstage. Her father, her father-in-law, and two of her nephews had all served, she told us. She continued:

> "Valor" is a powerful word. It resides in those good, simple things we do for one another, and it is found in those courageous acts that leave us in awe, wondering where such bravery comes from. Valor is at work tonight in our effort here, to find a way to celebrate, honor, and support the 2.6 million new veterans since 9/11.

The concert was watched by more than 1.1 million viewers.

Funds raised were distributed to sixteen organizations whose names and missions were broadcast during the concert. The exposure increased their public awareness, web traffic, donations, and memberships.

I hoped that those who watched would be moved as well as learn some of what I had learned. Valor deserves respect, but it is not the purpose of the military. Valor is a by-product of decisions made to engage the military. Yet whether or not we agree with the decision-makers of our post-9/11 wars, those who served valiantly in them deserve the same support the nation showed its World War II veterans.

I wondered if those who tuned in to the concert would also consider a larger truth. In addition to moral and economic imperatives, there exists a national security reason for caring for our veterans. A volunteer military force is a privilege for any society, but if we want our country to continue to attract men and women of the highest caliber to voluntarily defend the nation, then we must honor those who already have. Not just with a "thank you," but with top-notch medical care and employment support. Future generations must believe, because it is true, that time spent in uniform contributes to a thriving, dignified civilian life. Ensuring this is a solemn responsibility we all share.

There was a moment during the Concert for Valor when Bruce Springsteen sang an acoustic version of his 1978 ballad "The Promised Land":

> *Mister I ain't a boy, no, I'm a man*
> *And I believe in a promised land*
> *I've done my best to live the right way*
> *I get up every morning and go to work each day . . .*
> *And I believe in a promised land*
> *I believe in a promised land*

The lyrics made me think about my mom and my dad.

They also made me think about the country, and how we could each, in our way, work toward that promised land.

CHAPTER 14

A Promise Made

Back in 2012, Markelle Cullom-Herbison walked into the one-bedroom apartment she shared with her mother, collapsed onto her knees, and cried. She was working three jobs, while attending her second year of community college, and had just found out that financial aid for her third year had been denied. Her family's income was not enough to pay tuition out of pocket, but it was too high to qualify her for aid. She felt utterly depleted.

The 2008 financial crisis had hit the Cullom-Herbison family hard. Markelle's mother, a social worker, lost her job. Her father had to close his flooring business. The family had dealt with lean times in the past. There were years the kids shopped for new clothes at the mall and years they bought shoes at Goodwill. Some nights, an array of healthy food had crowded Markelle's dinner plate. Then, for weeks, it was macaroni and cheese. But the Great Recession was different, and Phoenix was among the areas of the country hardest hit. The Cullom-Herbisons lost their house and two cars were repossessed. Amid these pressures, Markelle's parents got divorced and moved into separate apartments. Markelle was working as a sales clerk in a clothing store, a nanny, and a caretaker for children with disabilities to help pay for her mom's groceries and rent. But she never did stop earning A's in high school, or clinging to her dream of one day going to college.

"Where did Barbie go to school?" her mom would ask when Markelle played with dolls as a youngster. "What's Barbie's job?" Markelle grew up believing that she would earn a degree and have a career. But when she graduated from high school—one semester early, in December 2012—college was unaffordable for her family, after being upended by the Great Recession.

Markelle got a job as a barista at Starbucks. Six months later, a community college awarded her a two-year academic scholarship. She stayed at Starbucks, balancing work with homework. She planned to major in speech and hearing pathology. During lunch breaks, she studied. While she drove, she listened to class lectures that she'd recorded. When her scholarships ran out, Markelle applied for financial aid to help pay for her junior year, but the request was denied. The frustration, the disappointment, the hard work, and the stress of the years overcame Markelle that day she sank to her knees in tears.

"I just don't know how else to help myself," she told her mother. For this bright, ambitious young woman, the door to college had slammed shut, locking her out of the rest of her life.

I did not know Markelle at that time, but I did know what it feels like to be young and to want to help yourself.

My mother believed a college degree was my path to a more financially secure, even happier life. But at seventeen, I just viewed college as my chance to fulfill the desire I'd had since my youngest days: to escape. So while my mom assumed I'd attend one of the free, or almost free, city colleges for residents of New York City, I was determined to go far away. Of course, my family couldn't afford tuition for an out-of-state or private university, and an academic scholarship was not an option for me. I was not a stellar student.

Football, I decided, was my best chance to leave.

I played high school football for three years. During my senior year, I was the starting quarterback for the Canarsie Chiefs. Although not a strong team, the Chiefs had a dedicated coach. We also had an assistant coach who often filmed our games so we could watch our performance and strategize for the next opponent. Without telling my friends and family, I asked our assistant coach to edit together my best moves and plays of the year to create a highlight film. He graciously agreed and produced a black-and-white reel that showcased a tall, athletic kid in a number 18 jersey passing, running, scoring, and taking some hits and jumping right back up. I felt good about it. I had a few copies made using money from part-time jobs, and mailed them to some schools.

My clandestine pursuit of an athletic scholarship resulted in a few letters of acknowledgment from coaches offering to keep me in mind as they built their teams, but nothing that would deliver me from Canarsie. One day, a college football recruiter came to scout a player on an opposing team at one of our games. I didn't know the recruiter was there. A few days later, I received a letter from Frank Novak, the assistant football coach at Northern Michigan University, a Division 2 school located in a part of the country that seemed a world away. I remember calling Frank and talking to him directly, then sending him my reel. He invited me to come to the campus and train with the team during the summer months. If I made the NMU Wildcats, I would receive a scholarship.

I convinced myself that this was it, I had a football scholarship. What I actually had was the makings of one.

I told my parents. My mother was elated because her son was going to get an education. My father? He was visibly proud that I might be playing college ball.

In a move that surprised me back then, my parents cobbled together money to drive us hundreds of miles from Canarsie to NMU during my last year of high school. The university is located on Michigan's Upper Peninsula, a chunk of land north of Green Bay, Wisconsin, between Lake Superior and Lake Michigan. Aside from a trip to Los Angeles that I had taken with my grandmother when I was about thirteen, I had never traveled so far from New York City.

Later that year, in the summer of 1971, I boarded a flight to Detroit, connected to a smaller plane, then took a bus to Marquette. My canvas duffel bag was my only companion.

During the first days of football practice, I knew. I saw the truth in the size and agility of the NMU players and new recruits, in the speed and the throwing distance of the quarterbacks I'd be competing with. I was not good enough to be a quarterback for Northern Michigan. Coach Novak saw it, too. My performance didn't live up to the highlights on my reel, and he and his staff began talking to me about becoming a defensive back, which was not a position I wanted to play.

Not good enough. The words throbbed as I phoned my parents. I didn't get a cascade of sympathy from my father. If anything, he was disappointed. But as usual, he had few words to share. I quickly reassured my anxious mother that I was still going to pursue a degree. But I also told her I was not going back home to Canarsie. I'd given up on football, but not an out-of-state college. I promised my mom, and myself, that I would find a way to stay at NMU and finish.

For more than thirty years, the benefits of health insurance and Bean Stock have contributed to what Starbucks calls its comprehensive compensation package, and helped the company employ many talented people who consider it a pleasure to serve customers. But in 2013, we were overdue for a new benefit, a new way to let our people know we cared. Health insurance was still valuable to many of our people, especially those who worked part-time. While the Affordable Care Act had made healthcare more accessible, it only required companies to provide healthcare insurance to employees working thirty or more hours a week. Starbucks provided it for people who worked as few as twenty hours. We could have easily changed our policy. Covering fewer people would have saved us millions of dollars a year and kept us in compliance with the new law. Instead, we chose to do the right thing, which was to keep thousands of part-time partners insured.

That year, I explicitly told our leadership team that we had to figure out how to "innovate the partner experience, not just the customer experience." A recent company-wide survey we'd conducted provided insight into our current partner population: 72 percent of our partners did not have a bachelor's degree. We wondered, *How many of our baristas want to go to college?*

Then we learned another statistic, this one about the country: 50 percent of Americans who pursued higher education never actually got a degree. We asked ourselves, *How many of our people had started college but not finished?*

But it was a third data point that blew us away: student loan debt in America was nearing $1.1 trillion, almost double consumer credit card debt. *How many of our partners,* we asked, *are burdened by student loan debt?*

From my years shielding my parents from the calls of bill collectors, and from asking the Levys for five thousand dollars to cover my father's ill-gotten loan, I was painfully familiar with the feelings of fear, guilt, and embarrassment that come with owing money you cannot repay. So the stunning knowledge that young people in America owed such a massive amount of money, many to pay for degrees they did not even have, was heartbreaking.

Student loans were crippling a generation. And yet, for previous generations, including my own, student loans had jump-started lives.

Although the potential football scholarship that had lured me so far from home to the northernmost part of the country did not materialize, I was determined to stay at Northern Michigan, so I figured out how to apply for student loans from the federal government.

In 1971, the year I started at NMU, the tuition, fees, room, and board for a public four-year college cost about $1,410 a year. Adjusted for inflation, that's about $8,800. For a freshman who showed up to college with a single duffel bag, it was a fortune. The only way to stay at NMU was to borrow money. So at eighteen, I was among the early cohort of U.S. college students to benefit from the government's first civilian student loan program.

When President Lyndon B. Johnson signed the Higher Education Act in 1965, he called the legislation "the most important door that will ever open" for young Americans. By helping to fund education for the poor as well as the middle class, Johnson said "a promise has been made" to the nation's children and grandchildren. As a beneficiary of that promise, I was grateful, even though I did not like the idea of having debt.

Student loans did not cover all my living expenses, and I had no money arriving by mail from Canarsie to help me pay for food, books, or the warm jacket I needed once the biting winter descended. To afford all that, I worked as a bartender at two popular student hangouts, Andy's Bar and the Traffic Jam Lounge. I also gave blood in exchange for cash as often as I could. I wasn't the only NMU student visiting the blood bank to put a few bucks in my pocket.

It took me a bit of time to find my rhythm at college. The Midwest's landscape, and the campus's staid academic buildings and wide streets, lacked the hum and grit of Brooklyn. I could go days without hearing a car horn honk, but I could look up at the night sky and see endless stars, not just faint twinkles in the haze of city lights. Michigan's weather and terrain lent themselves to different activities than the ones I grew up with. On hot days, students trekked to Lake Superior and plunged from twenty-foot volcanic cliffs into the cold water. During frigid winters, we leapt from third-story dorm room windows into massive white snowdrifts. Brooklyn snow was never as deep or as clean.

I was the only Jewish resident in my freshman dorm, and one of the few students from out of state. There were others who came from families with little money, but also kids from wealthy households, who did not have loans or part-time jobs, and who definitely weren't selling their blood to stay in school.

Despite these differences, I came to feel at home at NMU, and I began to figure out who I was away from my family. I grew a mustache and let my hair grow longer and get shaggy. Surrounded by Midwesterners, I began to shed my Brooklyn accent. I also joined a fraternity, Tau Kappa Epsilon, whose members excelled at sports, and our flag football games against other teams could get as rough as those I played back home. I became Howie to my friends.

My grades were good enough to keep me enrolled, but I did not do as well as I could have, or should have. I disliked statistics and accounting but did well in communications courses. People, I thought, were much more fascinating to study than numbers. Even outside class, I was known as the inquisitor, always asking friends about their lives, where they were going, what they were up to. But I did not display the same curiosity in class. Perhaps, in college, I was just happy to be on my own. And at that age, being free for the first time was good enough.

On Saturday, May 10, 1975, some seven hundred students donned NMU-green caps and gowns and filed into the Wildcats football stadium. I was among them. But I was not among the graduates who were craning their necks to try to spot parents, siblings, grandparents, aunts, or uncles in the bleachers. My parents did not come to my college graduation. I recall feeling embarrassed and disappointed that I had no family present on the auspicious occasion. The reason was simple and obvious: they couldn't afford to come.

Our commencement speaker was George Romney, the former governor of Michigan and the father of Mitt Romney, a future governor of Massachusetts and Republican nominee for president.

America was a great nation, Romney said in his speech, but we were living in a cynical age. The country needed a revival of faith—in ourselves, in our fellow man, and in our country. Restoring the spirit of America, he told us, must start with the individual. My generation, he said, held "the fate of America in the balance," and what we did would set the course of the country for decades to come.

What a shame she was not there.

My mother was a big reason I pursued a college education. I did not graduate *for* her, but *because* of her. Her dreams had become my own, and she more than anyone else deserved to witness me become the first in our family to get a college diploma.

CHAPTER 15

A Promise Kept

It was 2013, and in a cold conference room on a hot summer day in Colorado, forty experts from business, technology, academia, and government were talking about how to solve a crisis: globalization and technology were continuing to change the job landscape in the United States, eliminating millions of manufacturing jobs and creating new jobs that not enough people in the country had the skills or education to fill. In the next five years, the U.S. would need a total of at least eight million more graduates than it was currently anticipated to have to stay competitive in the global economy.

I was at the gathering, doing a lot of listening as people more informed than I aired their perspectives.

During a break in the meeting, I met up with another participant, someone I'd known for years, Dr. Michael Crow, the president of one of the country's largest public universities, Arizona State. We'd initially met when Craig Weatherup, a Starbucks board member and an ASU alum, and the former president of Pepsi-Cola North America, asked me to speak to ASU's business students. Michael believed that America's university system had become unfairly selective by providing people with money more access to educational options. This was harming the country by failing to make education more accessible to students at the low end of the socioeconomic spectrum. Public universities especially, he contended, were defaulting on their duty to serve the public good.

After assuming his post at ASU, Michael had restructured the university and rewritten its mission. ASU would be judged "not by whom it *excludes,* but by whom it *includes,* and how they succeed." Under Michael, ASU had already more than doubled the proportion of its students from low-income families.

Not surprisingly, academics considered Michael Crow a bull in their china shop. He was trampling the traditional model of education, which is based on the notion that learning has to be delivered in person, in classrooms. ASU had a top-ranked online degree program with the same content taught by many of its award-winning on-campus faculty in more than sixty fields of study. To earn a degree, a student never had to step foot on campus, or in the state.

When Michael and I first met, we'd quickly discovered our common ground. He, too, was the first in his family to graduate college, and for a period as a boy, he lived in public housing. His father was a Navy man and his mother had died when Michael was nine. Like me, he grew up believing that education could improve his life. But even as a kid, he also understood that education wasn't just a means to a better life for individuals, but a way to elevate whole societies.

He once told me the roots of this epiphany. One day just before Christmas in 1968, when Michael was thirteen, he and his father had volunteered to deliver food to families living in a poor, rural area of their town. One home, he recalled, was a shack with a tarpaper roof, dirt floor, and a potbelly stove. That night, Michael was back at his own home, sitting spellbound in front of the television watching news coverage of Apollo 8, the first manned spacecraft to leave Earth's orbit and circle the moon. The juxtaposition of the day's events struck Michael with its patent unfairness. *How is it,* he thought, *that people can live in a shack in a world where we can send people to the moon?*

"Howard," he had said when we first met, "it's insane if we cannot figure out how to use every single tool we have to drive people forward." At fifty-eight, Michael Crow was still fighting for the family in the shack, for the boy he once was, for all underdogs.

Seeing each other in Colorado, we migrated to a corner of the conference room, and our conversation veered to the state of education in the country. I told him how many Starbucks partners did not yet have a college degree, and shared my shock at the enormity of student loans as well as the rising cost of college tuition. We were both appalled that a generation of Americans was drowning in debt. It was unconscionable, and unnecessary.

And yet money was not the sole challenge, he said. Young people entering school with loans also arrived without support. No one was helping these kids navigate the administrative maze and emotional ups and downs of collegiate life. No one was advising them how to choose majors and classes or spend their money and time wisely. Their families lacked the knowledge or the time. Most universities were set up to recruit and enroll but not to help students succeed once they arrived. It was a model with devastating consequences. An undergraduate degree is the single greatest factor in determining someone's ability to jump from one income bracket to another. Upward mobility, the heart of the promise of America, was stalling as students left school. Many who did so with debt to repay were saddled with shame and a deflated sense of confidence. It's hard to go back to school when you feel as if you've already failed.

The country didn't just have a college debt crisis, I was realizing. It had a college completion crisis.

After the conference in Colorado, Michael and I stayed in closer touch. Our joint frustration turned into a joint calling.

Back in Seattle, I shared Michael's insights with Starbucks' new head of strategy, Matt Ryan, who had recently joined the company from Disney, where he was head of brand management. Matt has a quick intellect and a brisk walk, and prefers a workplace that matches his pace. He'd come to Starbucks to do groundbreaking work, he told me, and wasted no time getting started.

When senior executives join Starbucks, they spend time working in stores. After tying on a green apron, they learn how to make espresso beverages behind the coffee bar, stock the pastry case, and serve customers. During Matt's store immersion, he had made it a point to get to know his fellow baristas. How old were they? Why did they choose to work at Starbucks? Where were they in their own life journeys? He'd also popped into other Starbucks stores and chatted up our people behind the counter. Listening, Matt picked up a few common threads. A lot of partners had begun college but not finished, or they were enrolled but struggling to balance classes with work.

Their questions to him, about how to get ahead in their own careers, revealed their ambition. If they hadn't completed their college education, Matt concluded, it wasn't for lack of trying. His anecdotal observations matched the data from our company-wide survey.

Matt had been in the boardroom the day I called for our leaders to innovate the partner experience. Now, upon hearing about my conversations with Michael Crow, his mind churned with the possibility of a new partner benefit that paved a path to college completion. Our current program only provided partners one thousand dollars toward tuition. Could we find a way to get our full- and part-time partners a degree without significant cost to them, or to the company? Such an employee benefit would be as rare and innovative as providing all employees with healthcare insurance and stock ownership in the 1980s and early 1990s. I gave Matt free rein to figure it out.

He pulled together a three-person team led by Dervala Hanley, another whip-smart partner with an imaginative bent, whose pace could match his own.

Online education immediately intrigued them as a possible solution. Economically, it could be less costly than if students spent four years on a college campus. Without expenses for housing, food, and general living, the prospect of helping partners pay for school was more affordable for Starbucks. Online courses are also accessible anywhere, ideal for a large, nationwide workforce like ours.

As Matt and Dervala investigated ASU, they discovered the school's established online program offered a wide variety of respected, accredited degrees. And given the relationship I had established with Michael Crow and our like-minded values, ASU seemed a slam-dunk choice as an educational partner.

But as more people got word of our thinking, questions arose. Was online education the best way to go? And if Starbucks affiliated itself with only one school, would partners sign up if they couldn't choose their academic institution?

The team's due diligence dispelled some of these concerns. In focus groups, we learned that our partners' strong desire to get a degree, their financial constraints, their lifestyles, and their need for flexibility trumped a desire for school choice or a traditional university experience. If a reputable online university delivered degrees that matched their interests and constraints, they were excited.

The team also researched other schools' online programs. In 2014, many colleges were not yet taking online education seriously. Some only slapped videos of lectures on the Internet. Many academics also interpreted online teaching as a threat, or were hesitant to embrace the digital medium's potential for interactive and custom learning, for collaboration with students, and for the integration of compelling visuals and graphics into their lessons. America's colleges were not yet meeting students' demands for more affordable, flexible high-education options, even though the digital tools to do so were readily available.

I was coming to fully appreciate Michael Crow's vision for a new type of American university, one that met more students where they were in life, and with faculty equal to that of brick-and-mortar universities.

Working with Starbucks appealed to a lot of schools. Universities spend an incredible amount of money trying to acquire students. Starbucks was offering a way to reduce those expenses with immediate access to a huge pool of would-be online learners: tens of thousands of our partners. In turn, our partners could gain access to college courses at reduced tuition because, ideally, the school's marketing expenses could be stripped out of the price tag. And that lower tuition also helped make the benefit one that Starbucks could afford to contribute to.

It took one more element, however, to really make the proposition doable.

The federal government's Higher Education Act had long provided financial assistance to students from low-income households, in the form of subsidies known as Pell Grants. Many of Starbucks' store partners were the very people that Pell Grants were created to serve: those for whom a college degree—and with it, a lifetime of higher earning potential and self-sufficiency—would be unattainable without financial assistance. If a partner qualified for a Pell Grant, it would further help cover his or her tuition.

Other companies provided their employees access to online education, but the programs we heard about had limits we did not want: too few employees were eligible, there were few course options, or the tuition discount was capped.

No such public-private funding model to provide debt-free college tuition—where students, a sponsoring company, and a university all had a stake in the outcome—existed. We had to create it.

ASU was willing to help us invent a new way to get people through school. Michael Crow and his staff understood the link between economies of scale and educating more people. Increasing ASU's population of online students reduced the cost for each student, making college more affordable for all participants. That's why ASU was willing to reduce its tuition for Starbucks partners up front: easy access to a pool of potential students through Starbucks' workforce could help ASU achieve scale faster.

Matt had crunched the numbers. The mix of tuition adjustments by ASU and the likelihood of our partners' qualifying for Pell Grants made providing a college benefit more affordable for Starbucks. Whatever costs we did incur we would likely make up in the reduced turnover we anticipated such a benefit would yield. Whenever a person leaves the company, it costs us money to rehire and train someone new. We believed that our costs to help send partners to ASU would be comparable to the costs we would save by not having to replace as many partners.

Educating a workforce is smart business. A company is only as strong as its people. Baristas pursuing degrees could bring more knowledge and energy to our operations. More entry-level partners could advance into management roles. Helping provide a college education for baristas could establish a pipeline of potential leaders who began their Starbucks careers immersed in the daily life of the stores.

A college benefit could also attract higher numbers of ambitious, talented job applicants. Even those who left the company after earning a degree could be ambassadors of our brand. Plus, we'd be funneling college graduates into the marketplace at a time when education was a competitive advantage and key to higher lifetime earnings—and for a company like Starbucks, what's good for the country as a whole is good for business, too.

Providing such unprecedented access to college would also make our partners proud to work for a company that made it possible. This, I believed, would be true for partners that attended ASU as well as those who observed their fellow partners completing their education.

These outcomes were enticing, but it would just be wishful thinking if partners did not stay enrolled in school. Paying for college was but one hurdle. Students also needed to finish.

One week after Markelle Cullom-Herbison had collapsed in grief about not having the money to finish her college degree, she logged on to Facebook. As she scrolled through friends' updates, a newly posted link about Starbucks caught her attention. She read in disbelief. Starbucks, her employer, had just announced a new benefit for its partners, and if what Markelle read was true, she could soon be back in school finishing her degree, debt-free. The door that had slammed shut clicked open.

Markelle began to cry. Staring at her computer screen, with her mother standing by her side, she digested the new benefit for which she was eligible: 100 percent tuition coverage for ASU's online university for juniors and seniors, beginning in the fall of 2014.

This is it, she thought, *this is my opportunity.*

Days later, she attended an information session to learn the details

of the Starbucks College Achievement Plan. Her tuition would ultimately be 100 percent paid for through a combination of sources: ASU,
financial aid, and Starbucks. An ASU scholarship automatically covered at least 42 percent of the costs for every Starbucks partner that
enrolled as a junior or senior. Freshmen and sophomores would get 22
percent covered.

Our original College Achievement Plan only provided full tuition
coverage for juniors and seniors; the ASU team had told us those were
their most successful online students, since they already knew how to
study and manage their time. And most of our partners already had
some college. Partners with fewer than sixty credits—freshmen and
sophomores—were offered a partial scholarship by ASU to get them on
the path to a degree.

Markelle had enough credit to enroll as a junior. Any financial aid
she was qualified to receive would be applied toward the remainder of
her tuition. If the scholarship and financial aid did not cover full tuition, Markelle would have to cover that cost herself—either with a
standard student loan or out of pocket—*but only temporarily.* After six
months, Starbucks would reimburse Markelle so she could pay back
the loan and any tuition she had paid for herself.

Asking students to make an up-front, temporary payment was originally intended to incentivize partners like Markelle to stay enrolled. If
Markelle quit Starbucks prior to getting paid back, she forfeited the
reimbursement. But she also had no obligation to stay with the company after she graduated.

When Markelle enrolled, she discovered the program's other dis-
tinguishing feature: each student was assigned three advisors.

First, she met with a financial coach, who walked her through
ASU's online application, helped transfer her credits, and guided her as
she reapplied for financial aid.

Next, she was paired with an academic advisor, who asked Markelle
about her passions and what she hoped to achieve in life. Together they
determined that psychology was a better fit than her previous major,
speech and hearing pathology, because it allowed for a wider variety of
job options. Plus, more credits from Markelle's general studies classes

at community college counted toward that major at ASU. Without the advisor, Markelle might have selected a less suitable major. Together, they also picked her first-semester classes.

Then Markelle met with her "success coach," who would check in with her periodically, email her reminders about university deadlines, offer encouragement after a tough test, celebrate good grades, and suggest ways to reduce stress and balance school and life.

Markelle told friends that her college journey had never felt easier.

Unfortunately, not every eager or eligible partner was as quick to enroll. The College Achievement Plan's website had more than two million views in the days following its launch, but our partners did not sign up in the droves we expected.

Beth Valdez was thirty-one and for ten years she had dreamed of finishing her college degree.

She had grown up in a rural Ohio town so small that it didn't have its own ZIP code. Her parents had not attended college, and in 2004 Beth had left college early to pursue a full-time career in restaurant management. She was just one semester and one class shy of graduating—and fifty thousand dollars in debt. A decade later, Beth was a store manager at a Starbucks in Akron and a mother with two young children. She enjoyed her work, but the shame of having quit college and still owing student loans weighed on her. And although she knew a degree would position her for jobs with higher income, the thought of taking out another loan to pay for ASU—even temporarily— was a burden she could not stomach. So Beth did not apply.

That six-month waiting period, we realized, was among the College Achievement Plan's early shortcomings. Another mistake: we underestimated the weight of the decision to return to school. Even when it's paid for, even if it's part-time, college is a life-altering move. Many partners required more time than the program originally allotted to adjust their schedules, hunt down old transcripts, or just make the mental shift. We changed the waiting period and other rules, first extending the sign-up deadline in 2014. Then, in 2015, we announced

1. As a toddler. 2. The bookmobile. 3. My mother, Elaine Schultz. 4. Michael Nadel (top left), me, and Billy Block, about age 13. 5. College graduation day, 1975, Northern Michigan University. 6. My father, Fred Schultz, a World War II veteran. 7. In our Bayview apartment, age 9. 8. With my sister, Ronnie.

Early Years

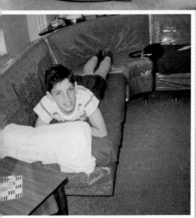

Onward to Seattle

1. Our wedding day with our parents. 2. In front of Mount Rushmore on our drive to Seattle, 1982. 3. Il Giornale's menu. 4. My father and brother outside the first Il Giornale. 5. Sheri and Jonas.

6. Me and Dave Olsen in Guatemala, 1992.
7. The first Starbucks in Seattle's Pike Place Market. **8.** Howard Behar, Orin Smith, and me (H2O). **9.** Leading the transformation, 2008. **10.** Eight thousand store managers rally in the New Orleans Arena, 2008. **11.** My first time in Milan, 1983.

Creative Civic Engagement

1. Delivering signatures to Capitol Hill. **2.** Counting signatures on petitions calling for an end to the government shutdown in 2013. **3.** Selling 8,000 wristbands to help fund small-business hiring. **4.** The Concert for Valor on the National Mall. **5.** Loan recipient Cynthia Duprey outside her Vermont bookstore. **6.** Inside American Mug & Stein in East Liverpool, Ohio. **7.** The INDIVISIBLE mug we sold in stores.

Honoring Heroes

8. With Robert Gates, board member and former secretary of defense. **9.** Retired General Pete Chiarelli. **10.** Visiting troops at Fort Benning, Georgia. **11.** Many veterans and military spouses wear green aprons embroidered with the American flag. **12.** Rajiv Chandrasekaran and I sign copies of *For Love of Country*. **13.** Master Sergeant Cedric King.

A Pathway to College

5

1. With Arizona State University president Michael Crow. **2.** Markelle Cullom-Herbison graduates in 2017. **3.** At graduation, partners celebrate. **4.** Giving the commencement address at Sun Devil Stadium. **5.** Starbucks ASU grads decorate mortarboards.

3

4

MELLODY HOBSON
President of Ariel Investments,
Starbucks Board of Directors

of a for-profit, public company?

Tough Conversations

6. Talking about race with partners at an open forum. **7.** Board member Mellody Hobson gives her TED Talk, "Color Brave," at our Annual Shareholders Meeting. **8.** Speaking at our 2013 Annual Shareholders Meeting. **9.** Rodney Hines and Cordell Lewis open a Starbucks in Ferguson, Missouri. **10.** Using cups to spark discussion in our stores.

Opportunities for All

1. The entrance of the 100,000 Opportunities Fair and Forum in Washington, D.C. **2.** On a bustling floor of a fair, attendees write résumés and meet recruiters. **3.** A recruiter and Sheri conduct mock interviews. **4.** Helping young men dress for interviews. **5.** Thousands wait to enter the Los Angeles fair.

6

In It Together

11

7

10

9

8

12

6. Our annual meeting with some current and former board members in the front row: from left, Javier Teruel, Clara Shih, Satya Nadella, Craig Weatherup, Secretary Robert Gates, Mellody Hobson, and Senator Bill Bradley. **7.** Vivek Varma, executive vice president of public affairs. **8.** The Pride Flag waves atop our Seattle headquarters. **9.** Daniel Pitasky, executive director of the Schultz Family Foundation (left), with Sheri. **10.** Nancy Kent and Tim Donlan have worked with me for a combined 39 years. **11.** Liliane Kamikazi, Starbucks partner and friend. **12.** Liz Muller, the creative genius and my partner in bringing the Roasteries to life.

Upstanders

1. Speaking to partners about immigration after President Trump issued his travel ban. **2.** Speaking with former coal miners in West Virginia. **3.** Meeting refugees who resettled in Seattle. **4.** In 2018, gathering with our Chinese partners to say goodbye. **5.** Brandon Dennison (right), founder of Coalfield Development Corporation. **6.** With Mary Poole (center), who founded Soft Landing Missoula.

7. Alibaba founder Jack Ma at a Partner Family Forum in China. **8.** With Belinda Wong, president of Starbucks China. **9. & 10.** Outside and inside the 30,000-square-foot Shanghai Reserve Roastery. **11.** Families of Starbucks partners in China.

Coffee in China

1

3

1. With Senator John McCain in 2017.
2. Speaking at the National Constitution Center to honor McCain in 2017.
3. Reading Dr. Martin Luther King, Jr.'s papers at Morehouse College. **4.** Partners gather for anti-bias training in our stores, 2018. **5.** Visiting Morehouse College.

A More Perfect Union

5

4

A New Chapter

6. With Starbucks CEO Kevin Johnson on my last day; thousands of partners suprised me to say goodbye. **7.** With dear friend Plácido Arango in Milan. **8.** Crowds in Milan snaked around the block, waiting to enter the Roastery. **9.** Sheri celebrates with me in Milan. **10.** The grand opening of the Roastery in Milan, in the Piazza Cordusio.

Family

1. With Jordan and Addison, early nineties. 2. A Thanksgiving together. 3. Me and Addy, during high school. 4. With the love of my life, Sheri, at a friend's wedding, 2018. 5. Jordan, his wife, Breanna, me, Sheri, Addison, and her husband, Tal. 6. Jordan and me, 2018.

Back to the Past

7. My apartment building in Brooklyn's Bayview Housing Projects. **8.** Back in the stairwell. **9.** The hallway outside apartment 7G. **10.** With Dakota Keyes, the principal of my old elementary school. **11.** Watching kids play ball in Canarsie.

1. Sheri and I visit Omaha Beach, 2017.
2. Normandy American Cemetery and Memorial.

that tuition reimbursements would arrive in partners' paychecks after each semester and before the next tuition bill came due.

That's when Beth gathered her courage. *It's time,* she told herself.

Standing in front of her staff, she admitted to them, for the first time, that she had never finished college. Then she asked for their support as she embarked on a rigorous new routine.

She regularly arrived at work at 4:30 A.M., worked until midafternoon, then studied before heading home to see her son and daughter. Now divorced, she ate dinner with the kids, then went to bed when they did, at about 8 P.M. When an alarm awakened her three hours later, she made herself an iced coffee and sat down with her laptop and books at the dining room table. For the next few hours, in the peace of night, as her children slept, Beth attended ASU classes, wrote papers, submitted assignments, and took tests online. At 4 A.M., her parents arrived to take care of the kids, and the routine restarted. It was a grueling pace Beth took on to hasten her graduation date, and it armed her with credentials that would pave a path to the higher-paying, more challenging career she wanted.

Within seventeen months, Beth had earned a B.A. in organizational studies.

In the winter of 2016, Starbucks held a contest for all graduating partners. The winner would be awarded an all-expenses-paid trip to Tempe, Arizona, to attend ASU's commencement ceremony in the Sun Devils' massive stadium. Excerpts from Beth's submission letter capture her second college experience:

I began classes in the fall 2015 . . . afraid and nervous. The last thing I wanted to do was to let myself down again.

At first I felt awkward and unsure, but once I opened my mind and books, everything started to feel right. Term by term, my energy rose.

My SCAP journey has been nothing short of sleepless nights, a coffee addiction worth working on, hours after work at my favorite Starbucks stores, and pages upon pages of reading and writing.

I joyfully share my story with any partner and customer, hoping that anyone and everyone who is ready to take the adventure do so. Knowing how special it is for partners to pursue their dreams all while knowing they won't be graduating with the debt that comes with traditional higher education is incredible.

I did it. I did it for me. I did it for my kids. I did it because someone believed I could . . . and I will pay it forward.

Beth won the competition, and attended a commencement ceremony with fifty-four other Starbucks graduates who also came to Tempe. Five months later, she was promoted to senior regional coordinator, a role that put her on a career path to having a larger impact at the company.

One year later, more than seven thousand Starbucks partners were participating in the College Achievement Plan. Our original goal was to have twenty-five thousand graduates by 2025. Despite a slower-than-expected start, momentum continued to build. In 2017, Starbucks celebrated its one thousandth graduate.

For all its symbolism, and for all that my degree afforded, my own college graduation ceremony never meant much to me. That was not true when I returned to Northern Michigan to give the commencement address in 1998, and when, in 2017, I delivered the commencement address at Arizona State at Michael Crow's request. The event began at 7:30 P.M., but first, I attended other events on ASU's sprawling campus.

At a luncheon for university administrators, alumni, and Starbucks partners, Michael Crow presented me with an honorary degree from ASU. After I accepted the framed diploma and spoke a few words, a colleague approached me. Mary Dixon had been overseeing the College Achievement Plan since February 2015; she and her team continued to collaborate with ASU to improve it.

Mary told me there was someone she wanted me to meet and led me to one of the round tables in the bustling room. A petite young woman with blond shoulder-length hair rose from her seat, smiling. I reached out to shake her hand and she introduced herself.

"Hi, I'm Markelle."

I did not know anything about Markelle Cullom-Herbison's long road to this day. She glowed with confidence and joy as she told me she was graduating with a B.A. in psychology, cum laude. I congratulated her. She thanked me, and asked if I would sign her mortarboard. On it she had painted the Starbucks logo and, in gold, the word ONWARD. I smiled when I saw it, because "onward" was a word I had invoked for decades. I signed company-wide letters to partners with the word above my signature. *Onward* was also the title of my second book, which documented the company's battle to return to sustainable growth.

"Onward" had always been a rallying cry for me, a word that connoted the necessity of hope and hard work on any worthwhile journey, and the dual motivations of purpose and passion. Seeing the word on Markelle's cap on that momentous day, I realized how apt "onward" was to describe the courage, confidence, and sacrifice required to return to college, to stay in school, to move forward after graduation. I had so much admiration for everyone who took that on, especially those who were going back as returning students. Pulling a black pen from my pocket, I wrote my name on Markelle's cap.

Later that week, Markelle's district manager offered her a new job, as the office manager of a technology center Starbucks was opening on ASU's campus. She would receive a salary increase. Was she interested? Markelle accepted.

I learned about Markelle's full story from a letter she sent to me. In it, she candidly described her family's financial challenges—the loss of their home, the repossessed cars, the pooling of family money to pay for meals—and her own uncertainty about how she would complete her education. She also wrote this:

> I am sure you can understand the joy that overcame us when the College Achievement Plan was announced. However, I didn't know how truly life-changing the experience would be.

I would not have made it through some of my toughest days without the support that you and your team provide. From success coaches in school, to investments made in store; I was able to find a balance through challenging times.

When a company invests in you the way Starbucks has, you cannot help but feel an extra sense of pressure to be successful. I want to show the world and other business leaders what can come from making investments in one another.

When the College Achievement Plan first launched, a shareholder asked me if Starbucks was in the charity business. I told him that Starbucks was in the business of investing in people. In 2017, the partners who enrolled at ASU were staying with the company one and a half times longer than the average partner. Half of all our ASU graduates were still employed at Starbucks, despite having no obligation to stay. And those who participated in the College Achievement Plan were being promoted at two and a half times the regular rate.

The individual who so blindly posed that question needed to meet Markelle.

Michael Crow has many favored sayings, but one he repeats to me more often than others. "I criticize by creation, not by finding fault." He is quoting Cicero, the Roman philosopher. The idea that solutions speak louder than words is a concept that, Michael and I agree, is not being exercised enough, especially at the seat of government in Washington, D.C., where criticism regularly eclipses creativity.

We continue to try to make the College Achievement Plan better. Today, freshman and sophomore partners entering ASU can also receive 100 percent tuition reimbursement, along with juniors and seniors. Also, veterans employed at Starbucks can extend the College Achievement benefit to a family member and send a child or spouse to college. For our partners who apply to ASU but do not yet qualify, we offer Pathway to Admission, a customized curriculum to raise their GPA to earn enrollment. ASU professors also designed a leadership course for Starbucks partners, taught with input and participation from Starbucks executives.

Michael and I do not consider the program proprietary to our institutions. We want the model to be copied, adopted, and customized by other schools and corporations.

It is our hope that business leaders will see that companies can play a role in extending learning opportunities to more Americans, be it a college education, vocational training, niche certifications, or instruction in other skills such as communication, financial literacy, and even how to interview for a job. Multiple forms of educational opportunities—not just four-year degrees—can help people get ahead.

It is also our hope that leaders in the academic world open their minds to alternate ways of teaching, learning, and discovery, and be courageous in using technology to expand access to knowledge and to educators.

And finally, it is our hope that the plan's success will encourage more partnerships between public and private entities to stimulate more collaborative and entrepreneurial thinking. Instead of just getting angry about broken systems, people can come together, further examine what's broken, try to understand why, consult experts, and embark on more constructive problem solving. The College Achievement Plan certainly is not the only way to extend educational opportunities, but to paraphrase another insight from my wise friend Michael Crow, it proves that new solutions can exist.

Perched high above the stands on the south end of ASU's football field is an enclosed viewing area where I waited before the university's 2017 commencement ceremony began. Large windows overlooking the field offered a sweeping view of Sun Devil Stadium, where eight huge sections of white folding chairs awaited the day's graduates. From the window, I watched as thousands milled about the stadium floor, greeting their friends, straining to locate loved ones in the stands, and finally taking their seats. As the crowd grew I called Sheri from my phone to share the awe-inspiring view, and the moment.

At the appointed time, I walked down to the field with Michael Crow and his colleagues and took a seat on the stage. I was reviewing my speech in my mind when a beautiful sight captured my attention. At the front of the sea of graduates that stretched to the far end of the field was a patch of 230 Starbucks partners who sat side by side several rows deep. It was easy to see them: draped around every partner's neck was a special gold-colored stole trimmed in green and featuring the logos of ASU and Starbucks. It was a smiling, proud crew. I fixed on their faces, and a surge of admiration and delight overtook me. Each of them had a backstory like Markelle's, or like mine, a history of setbacks and surprises, of grit and goals, that brought them to this moment.

I heard my name, walked to the podium, and told thirty thousand people a story.

The previous year, Starbucks opened its first two stores in Johannesburg, South Africa. The day before we opened, I had gathered the fifty young people who would be working in our new stores. They went around the room introducing themselves, telling tales of hardship and of family, and also expressing appreciation. Working for Starbucks was, for most, their very first job. They also kept repeating a word I did not know. *Ubuntu.* Again and again, *ubuntu.* Finally I asked. "Please tell me, what does it mean?"

One young man smiled, and in unison they all said, "I am because of you."

"I am because of you," I repeated to ASU's class of 2017. "I ask you to keep this story in mind, because everything I am going to share with you today is through the lens of *ubuntu.*"

I revealed a bit about my own life history because I assumed a lot of young people only knew me as the head of Starbucks, not the son of parents who never finished high school, and who was the first in his family to graduate college. I told them my life was proof that the American Dream is real and that those of us who had achieved it—as many of them were doing by receiving a degree—had a responsibility to pay the dream forward.

You each possess an entrepreneurial spirit, the passion and the commitment to create the future you deserve.

However, don't stop there. Try not to rely only on what you have learned in the classroom.

Summon your compassion, your curiosity, your empathy toward others and your commitment to service.

Give more than you receive. I promise it will come back to you in ways you cannot possibly imagine.

I urged them to remember that we were all here today because of someone else. A parent. A sibling. A teacher. A neighbor. A mentor. Someone who had faith and confidence in us, like my mother had in me. And I posed three questions to consider not just on that day, but throughout their lives:

How will you respect your parents and honor your family?
How will you share your success and serve others with dignity?
How will you lead with humility and moral courage?

What I did not say, what the graduates would discover for themselves, was that arriving at answers to these questions would at times be a thorny, complicated endeavor. The choices they made would elicit satisfaction and pride, but also regret. Some of their actions would be misunderstood by those they loved, and voicing their opinions would at times invite criticism or be met with contempt, even unleash venom from strangers, regardless of their intent. All this I knew to be true. But I did not say so that night.

Instead, as the glow of the stadium lit the graduates, I encouraged them to trust themselves.

The speech ended where it began, *"Ubuntu."* We are because of each other.

PART THREE

Bridging Divides

CHAPTER 16

Discuss

My father didn't like us having our friends over for dinner, but he never turned away Michael Nadel.

For as long as I could remember, Michael had lived on the floor below us, in apartment 6B. His adoptive parents didn't tell Michael, at least not when he was young, that he wasn't their biological son. But those of us who grew up with him eventually came to realize that our friend with light brown skin was half black and half white, even though his parents were white.

Michael's roots didn't matter to me—or to my parents. My mom and dad were not bigoted people. They raised me to accept others who were different colors and religions from us. And there was plenty of diversity around us.

Our apartment building housed about seventy families on eight floors, and all of us shared a single, steel-encased elevator. The door had a slit of thick, cloudy glass, and during my later years it carried the stench of urine. On any given day, those of us packed inside the claustrophobic box reflected the makeup of Brooklyn's public-housing residents in the 1950s. The majority were of Irish, Italian, and Jewish descent. About a third were African Americans, and a smaller percentage were Puerto Rican.

Growing up in this urban melting pot meant getting along with people whose complexions were different, whose language was different, who celebrated different holidays, and whose apartments smelled of different foods. Conducting ourselves with civility toward one another in our shared living spaces, even when standing skin to sweaty skin in a tiny elevator stuck between floors, was mandatory. Bonded by circumstance, there was a comforting sense of community.

People had disputes and some neighbors didn't like each other. But for the most part, I grew up feeling that adults would lend a hand if someone got in trouble, and that any kid could become my friend. But Michael Nadel was more than that. In schoolyards and playgrounds where the hierarchy of boyhood was still tested with fistfights, Michael held top rank. He was the one other kids feared because he was faster, stronger, and a better fighter.

Michael was known for his daredevil antics. Once, he climbed up to the roof of our eight-story building from the outside by scaling the fencing that enclosed each floor's terrace. Our shared athleticism was one reason the two of us bonded. Another was that we helped each other out. When skirmishes broke out in the common areas of the projects, Michael was a protector to me and Billy and the rest of his friends. In turn, we welcomed him into our apartments on nights his father kicked him out because of his violent outbursts. I think he felt as safe inside our homes as he made us feel on the playground. Michael had our backs. And we had his.

Michael Nadel was known throughout the entirety of the Bayview projects but also misunderstood by many. The Michael I fondly remember was a fun, loyal, tough buddy who stood by those of us who were kind to him and respected him out of friendship, not fear. It didn't occur to me at the time that maybe he was treated poorly not because he was a bully, but because he was of mixed race.

I grew up thinking that everybody in the elevator, regardless of where they came from or where they were going, should try to get along, and that a boy of any race should be welcome in any home. I never shed this ideal, even when reality contradicted it.

———

On July 17, 2014, an unarmed forty-three-year-old black man named Eric Garner was approached by white police officers on a sidewalk in Staten Island, New York, on suspicion of illegally selling cigarettes. When an officer tried to handcuff Eric, he struggled and the officer put him in a choke hold. An amateur video of the incident shows Eric facedown on the sidewalk, telling the police that he cannot breathe, while an officer is pushing his head against the ground. Eric died one hour after the incident.

The video of Eric's brutal arrest was more than hard to watch. It was horrific.

His death came two years after seventeen-year-old Trayvon Martin was fatally shot by a white neighborhood watch volunteer who was later acquitted. Trayvon's death, and the subsequent court ruling, sparked the Black Lives Matter movement, bringing issues of violence toward black people and systemic racism to the forefront of the nation's attention.

When a grand jury chose not to indict the police officer who killed Eric Garner, in December 2014, the decision further exacerbated the sense of distrust black communities had for police and provoked demonstrations by protestors. Most of the demonstrations were peaceful, if angry; some were unruly; a few violent. Many were purposefully disruptive, with people—white, brown, and black—blocking traffic on highways to ensure their calls for justice got the attention they deserved.

As the events unfolded, I began to ask myself and others what the tragic deaths, court rulings, and uprisings revealed about the plight of black people in America today. I remember asking several black friends and colleagues for their perspectives.

"We've been having a lot of conversations at the dinner table," said Chris Carr, an eight-year partner and an executive vice president who oversaw a significant portion of our retail operations. Chris and his wife had a daughter in high school and a son in middle school. A few nights prior, his daughter had said something that Chris found hurtful. "She said that my generation of African Americans had let her generation of African Americans down by not being the social activists that

we should have been, by not having a voice." Chris countered by pointing out to his daughter the progress people of color had made in America, and listed prominent black individuals.

"Dad," she told him, "if you look at the black community as a pie, what
you've just described is a sliver of that pie." Chris had disagreed with his
daughter, but admired her conviction. I appreciated both perspectives.

I admitted to Chris that, from my vantage point, there seemed to
be an absence of strong, individual voices. Why weren't we seeing a
singular person representing or speaking for the nation's black community, not even President Obama? Unable to recognize a Martin Luther King, Jr., figure in 2014, I was genuinely puzzled. Over the years,
through my travels, I had met many black civic and religious leaders,
but no one seemed to be rising up.

Chris responded, "The leadership is there, but it shows up differently today, especially for the younger generation. It comes through
social media, for instance. It's the voices of many."

With the bullhorn of Twitter, a 140-characters-or-less remark in
2015 by anyone could take flight in seconds and spark a movement.
Chris was right. The leadership was there, I just didn't see it, in part
because I was not yet active on social media.

Talking with Chris and others had been enlightening. It felt good
to broach the stymied, divisive topic of race. Almost like a release valve
amid what I was perceiving as increasing chaos in the country.

On December 9, I headed to bed wondering if I was in a position
to give people inside the company another outlet to share their own
perspectives and to hear what others were thinking and feeling, too.
We were all living in America, and what was happening in the country
was part of our shared experience. The more I thought about it, the
more I believed that doing or saying nothing was an abdication of my
responsibility as Starbucks CEO. Convening people to address what
was happening in the country reflected our mission to be involved in
our communities.

The next morning, I arrived at work and told a few people that I
wanted to hold an open forum in the ninth-floor atrium. I only shared
the topic with three or four people. When eyebrows rose, I said not to

worry. This was a conversation we could have. I knew this because of our tradition of holding open forums since the early 1990s.

The forums had evolved into quarterly and impromptu gatherings where company announcements were made and partners could share opinions, concerns, or ideas without fear of retribution. No one had to worry about losing a job or losing face or being reprimanded for airing problems or a personal truth. At past forums, partners had questioned decisions made by others and myself. They had expressed anger and disappointment with policies. Over time, the nature of the forums bred internal trust. Partners knew any topic was fair game, and that acting respectfully toward one another was part of the deal. Providing a space for our people to discuss controversial, emotionally fraught current events was new, but not out of character for the company.

Climbing the stairs to join the hundreds of people milling about the sky-lit atrium, I asked someone walking beside me if he knew what the forum was about.

"Holiday promotions?"

"No," I said, "not even close."

"The last few weeks," I began, "I've felt a burden of personal responsibility, not about the company but about what is going on in America. . . . It seems like something is not right, and whether you are black or white, it feels that, as Americans, this is not our best day. For that reason, I felt like we should come together and have an opportunity to discuss this among ourselves. If we just keep going about our business and ringing the Starbucks register every day and ignoring this moment in our country, then we are part of the problem."

I admitted that I did not know where the discussion would go. Then I opened it up to anyone who wanted to share. Maybe 20 percent of the five hundred gathered in the atrium were people of color or ethnic minorities.

There were about six seconds of silence. People were taken aback, I could tell, but those who had been with Starbucks for a while probably weren't surprised. They knew me. They knew the company.

Finally, someone said, "Hello, my name is Rachel."

A young, white female partner stood up, and I walked over to be closer as she spoke into a microphone. "I am going to be nervous because I have a lot of feelings about this," she began. Over the past few weeks, she said, she had felt a sense of powerlessness. "I think it comes from how segregated our society still is. Our schools and workplaces have become more diverse, but our society as a whole, our personal lives, are incredibly segregated." She apologized for shaking. "I don't know how can I help young people of color if I am not a part of their personal lives. . . . Despite the movement of the sixties, racism has not truly ended in our culture and society."

I thanked her. For the next hour, microphones passed as partners from all corners of the building—men and women, black as well as white—stood up and shared stories, opinions, and emotions. Some spoke for one or two minutes. Others talked longer. One partner had been at Starbucks for seventeen years, another for three weeks. Some faces I knew well; some I'd only seen once or twice; some were new. Together, their voices revealed the scope of the concerns, and questions, on people's minds.

A fifteen-year partner stood up. He had come to America from Africa at the age of twenty-two. He said he had two boys and had discussed with them what they were witnessing on TV—the images we had all seen. "The current state of racism in our country, it is almost like a humidity at times," he said to the room. "You can't see it but you feel it."

Midway through the hour, a white woman with short brown hair stood up. "I remember one time many years ago, way before I realized that there were middle-class black people, just from everything I knew, I thought everybody grew up in slums who was not white, and I very innocently asked someone what was it like to grow up in a slum, and she looked at me and she was furious. It was my ignorance."

She sat down and another woman motioned for the microphone. She was black. She inhaled, then spoke slowly. "I am very touched, moved, and inspired by this conversation." She closed her eyes, placed her hand to her chest, and again breathed deeply. "This is why I joined this company ten months ago," she said, her voice rising, "because we have the courage to talk about the things that matter for humanity. This is not just a conversation about race relations. This is a conversation about humanity, and the fact that humanity has not processed how to manage pain, how to deal with hurt, and how to deal with what it means to love folks that don't look like us or come from the same background."

She looked across the room at the white coworker who moments earlier had confessed ignorance. "Thank you for being so honest about your experience. I think the more honest we are, the more we can connect at the human level and break down those biases and break down those stereotypes." Her attention turned back to the room.

"There is something powerful about intentionally putting yourself in proximity to those who are different than you, and to say, 'I may not agree with you, I may not understand you. You may not agree with or understand me. But I have value, you have value, and your perspective matters, and we will hash this out in a safe space.'"

There was no shouting or whispering. No one hurled insults at others or walked out. I did not expect so much emotion. It was illuminating, as well as a relief at times, to hear what people thought and felt.

I ended the forum by encouraging partners to begin their smaller meetings throughout the day by continuing to share. I also said the company would not stay quiet about the issue of racism. "We are going to find a way to thread our values and sense of humanity into the national conversation, and perhaps we can have some effect on the national discourse."

As people dispersed, the black woman who had spoken so eloquently came up to introduce herself. Saunjah Powell-Pointer had recently moved to Seattle from New Jersey to join Starbucks after fourteen years in the pharmaceutical industry. I thanked her for speaking, and asked Saunjah to email me so we could stay in touch.

Walking back to my office, I felt more hopeful than I had an hour ago. What had transpired felt like a moment of unity amid discord. Other people also left the forum with a feeling of connectedness, that something positive had been achieved. I think the fact that such a meeting even occurred made as strong an impression as what was said.

Someone would later comment that I was lucky that the unplanned forum went as well as it did, but I didn't think it was luck. Starbucks had spent more than twenty years nurturing a culture of respectful discussion where this kind of group conversation could exist. Because of that history of speaking freely at open forums, I had no doubt in my mind that even if people disagreed with each other or felt angry about the subject matter, the tone would stay civil.

At eight the next morning, I sat in the boardroom with a new team that included Chris Carr; Tony Byers, our head of diversity and inclusion; Matt Ryan, who had brought the College Achievement Plan to life; Adam Brotman and Gina Woods, who had steered Create Jobs; Vivek Varma, who had been at my side since I wrote the letters calling out elected officials in D.C. in 2011; and Blair Taylor, our head of community outreach, who had come to Starbucks from the Urban League in Los Angeles. Also at the table was Saunjah Powell-Pointer, whom I asked to join us.

People agreed that the tone of the forum was positive. Blair said he'd witnessed countless gatherings in community centers and churches in black communities where race was discussed, but he had not heard the topic being talked about at a company, especially in such an unscripted way. More public, meaningful dialogues about race needed to happen, he added, not only among African Americans.

By day's end, we came to two decisions:

We'd explore if there was a way to translate the forum's respectful sharing. More than one partner who spoke had suggested that Starbucks stores could be catalysts for similar conversations and bonding.

For the Create Jobs campaign, we had designed a colorful foldout that explained the economics behind the endeavor, so that our customers would understand how their donations were helping to grow small businesses. With that model in mind, we decided to develop a compendium about race in America that we could distribute in stores. Vivek took the lead. He would work with outside experts as well as Rajiv Chandrasekaran, the newly hired journalist who had done such a beautiful job writing *For Love of Country*, to create insightful, compelling, legitimate content.

I had not initiated the forum just so I could get my own emotions off my chest, or to impose my own agenda on others. Granted, people did not know what the forum was about when they arrived, but if those who sat through it were ruffled or angry, I knew I would hear about it eventually. Complaints from all levels of the company often found their way to me, but after the forum nothing negative filtered up. If anything, the feedback was the opposite. Partner emails to me and comments I heard as I walked through the halls that day expressed gratitude for initiating the conversation.

We also agreed to do more forums. I had faith that many Starbucks partners in other cities would be as interested, and as respectful.

Oakland. New York. Chicago. Los Angeles. St. Louis. In these cities, from January 2015 to March 2015, almost two thousand Starbucks partners voluntarily attended open forums about race relations. As at the Seattle forum, attendance was not mandatory. Some partners came during their regularly scheduled work hours, others during their free time. Unlike in Seattle, however, we announced the topic ahead of time. Those who showed up had self-selected to be there.

We held each forum at a location other than a Starbucks store, like an empty airplane hangar or a university auditorium. Some partners drove for hours to attend. Some brought family members. Some cities' forums were more diverse than others, but at each, people of various colors and ethnicities stood up to speak. The hunger to do so among those in the room was undeniable, given the size and length of most of the forums, which usually went for two hours and included anywhere from one hundred to five hundred people.

The format was the same in each city as it had been in Seattle. Region to region, comments were consistent in their candor. Everyone was willing to listen. We had created a platform for people to share, and what resulted was a flow of bottled-up emotions and experiences.

A white female partner said it wasn't until she was twelve that she was told that racial slurs were wrong. One black mother said she felt compelled by current events to explain racism to her six-year-old son, years before she expected he'd encounter it. Another black woman explained that each morning she reminds her teenage son not to wear his hoodie over his head when he walks to and from school. Several partners in mixed-race relationships brought up the discrimination they'd experienced, including from their own families. Spouses, siblings, and children of police officers, black as well as white, said they worried about their loved ones amid that job's inherent dangers.

In one city, a soft-spoken black female partner stood up and quietly told us she had been beaten up by police not far from where we were meeting.

The comments were raw. A lot of them, I had a hunch, weren't things that people had articulated before to anyone other than friends and family. I think this was especially true for our white partners. I could hear many of them, as well as myself, grasping for language to capture what they were trying to say, being careful not to offend others. Talking about race in mixed company was not common, or easy.

In St. Louis, the open forum was one of our largest and longest. Twice in the past six months, protests, fiery riots, and looting had ravaged the nearby town of Ferguson, Missouri, first after a young black man named Michael Brown was shot dead by a white police officer, and again after the grand jury decision not to indict the officer who killed him. Damage to retail businesses in Ferguson had been extensive. Buildings were burned beyond repair, and stores were shuttered after looting left nothing to sell. The governor had declared a state of emergency and imposed a midnight curfew. The National Guard was deployed. Ferguson had become a symbol of racial inequality and the distrust between communities and police.

At the forum, a young black female partner stood up and took the mic. Her family, she said, had been in St. Louis for generations:

> I lived about a block away from the worst gang violence in the city. Whenever there would be an issue, you would call your neighbors first. You would never call the police. If someone hurt you, you'd call your friends, because you couldn't trust that the police would come quickly. That is what creates a lack of trust. . . . There is an

understanding that community comes first, and police officers aren't part of the community. That is such a great divide in the African American community and it needs to be bridged before any real dialogue can really seep in.

Her comments reminded me of a conversation I'd had with the chief executive of another company, who was African American.

"Howard, how did you teach your son to drive a car?" he had asked me when we got together to talk about race relations. I said that I probably taught Jordan how to ease up on the gas, parallel park, and mind the rules of the road. He told me that his driving rules for his son included instructing him to always keep both hands visible on the steering wheel when he was pulled over.

Bias, profiling, and the sometimes violent and illegitimate exercise of law enforcement had become central to the national dialogue around race. And at the open forums, partners continued to bring up the topic of police.

As we visited more cities, I began to read up. A colleague gave me a new memoir titled *Just Mercy* by Bryan Stevenson. Bryan is a renowned public defense lawyer whose nonprofit organization, the Equal Justice Initiative, provides free legal counsel to defendants who are otherwise denied fair legal treatment. In his book, Bryan writes about being a twenty-eight-year-old civil rights attorney in Atlanta in the late nineties when two police officers approached him as he got out of his car, which was parked in front of his apartment building. One of the officers pointed a gun at his head and threatened him.

"Move and I'll blow your head off!" the officer shouted. They ordered Bryan to put his hands up while they conducted an illegal search of his car. They had no probable cause. He was just coming home after a long day at the office.

When one of the officers questioned what he was doing in the neighborhood, Bryan calmly explained that he lived there. Eventually they let him go.

As Bryan filed a complaint with the Atlanta Police Department, he found Bureau of Justice statistics reporting that in 1998 black men were eight times more likely to be killed by police than whites. As he expressed it, the history of police brutality in America was the latest manifestation of a four-hundred-year-old problem in America.

I was so moved by the book that I found Bryan's number and called him cold to introduce myself. We spoke for a bit. Bryan was a gentle yet adamant voice crusading for equal justice. I told him about the forums and asked what he thought about where the country was at. Unfortunately, he pointed out, the prevailing belief in America that black people were presumptively guilty and dangerous continued to compromise law enforcement. The ramifications were not new, he said, just being more widely exposed.

I did not know much about policing in America. As part of my own self-education, I arranged to meet with local law enforcement officials in many of the cities where we held open forums.

In New York City, Police Commissioner William Bratton and Community Affairs Bureau Chief Joanne Jaffe talked to me about their police retraining program.

In Los Angeles, Chief of Police Charlie Beck described efforts to reduce violence in public housing by permanently placing LAPD officers—instead of public-housing security personnel—in those areas so cops could get to know the residents, and vice versa. Chief Beck opened a cabinet and took out a handgun. "It's not real," he said, placing the lightweight mock weapon in my hand. It was being sold in the streets, he explained, and his officers couldn't tell the difference between a real gun and a fake one, which made it hard to know whether or not to shoot their own weapons in self-defense.

In Seattle, which has a well-documented history of biased policing, I met with then–Chief of Police Kathleen O'Toole, who had been recruited to turn the police force around. She wanted to try to restore public trust in the police department by bringing more diversity to the force, improving training, and employing more officers who lived in the city they policed. Her ideas, she told me, did face dissent among some in the department. Kathleen also spoke up for her peers. During her decades in law enforcement, she had seen how even well-intentioned officers were cast in a dim light when corruption or abuses were uncovered.

"Nobody dislikes bad cops more than good cops," she said. And we agreed that despite a long history of prejudiced law enforcement in America, there were and are good police.

Before we left St. Louis, I asked to visit the town of Ferguson. Thirty-seven buildings had been looted and vandalized during the riots, including a Family Dollar store, a Walmart, a Foot Locker, and a locally owned beauty supply store. A gas station and an auto parts store were gutted by fire, their signs broken and hanging askew.

Rodney Hines was among those with me in the car as we drove through the quiet streets. He had steered us to CDFIs for Create Jobs and had led our community programs for years. Rodney was African American, and had grown up in West Philadelphia. His father, a meat-packer for Oscar Mayer, and his mother, a seamstress, had raised him to help bring out the strength, resilience, and potential of people living in poor communities. He had spent his career trying.

As we passed building façades that had been spray-painted with X's or O's to indicate whether they were inhabitable or not, Rodney was reminded of New Orleans in the aftermath of Hurricane Katrina, back in 2005. That devastation had resulted from a natural disaster. What we were seeing in Ferguson, he said, was a disaster of a different kind, the result of people trying to tell the world about injustices oppressing them and their families for generations, through overt racism and systemic segregation. Millions of African Americans had been born into impoverished neighborhoods that felt inescapable, especially for young people, who felt cut off from jobs and good schools and even fresh food. In Ferguson, the helplessness so many were feeling exploded in moments of rage that had been built up over lifetimes.

That's what it took to get the world's attention, I thought. *Including mine.*

Starbucks had eight stores near Ferguson, but the only one in the city itself was inside a Target. There was no stand-alone store in which people could gather. As we headed to the airport, I said, "We have to open a store here." People in the car nodded. They were thinking the same thing.

The fiery destruction of communities, the open forums, and the private conversations with friends and coworkers were exposing me, at the age of sixty-one, to the brutal reality of racism, ethnic discrimination, and economic inequality in America, which were far more prevalent and embedded in the consciousness of the country than I had recognized. I'd experienced anti-Semitism in the form of derogatory comments, and probably in subtle ways I'd not realized, but I knew nothing about what it's like to be a racial minority in the United States. Which meant I'd also taken for granted the privileges of being in the racial majority, and the hundred little ways that whiteness had benefited me and made my path easier. My attention was overdue. Now that I was waking up, I was eager to learn more and felt a responsibility to act. The forums were a start. But what else?

Around this time, someone reminded me of a 2006 television campaign that an advertising agency had developed for Starbucks but that we never ran. It was titled "Discuss." Six spots filmed actual customers and partners looking into a camera and answering, extemporaneously, a question. *What is the American Dream? Are we talking about things that really matter?*

In one spot, eleven green-apron-clad baristas give their take on the societal role of cafés.

"I think it's a place for all types of conversations," says one young woman.

"It's a good place to be able to sit down and compare and contrast ideas," offers another. "We don't all think the same, but you know if we listen to one another maybe we'll come up with good ideas. . . ."

The final response comes from a genial older barista: "The only way that we can solve problems is by getting the problems out there and discussing them. And who knows? You might learn something from somebody else, and maybe if we all just talked a little bit more about the things we don't want to talk about, maybe things could happen."

Seven years after that campaign was nixed by colleagues who said it was irrelevant, I was asking myself that same question: *Are we talking about the things that matter?*

The answer had crystallized for me as I attended the open forums.

An hour into the St. Louis gathering, a store manager in a gray sweatshirt and a baseball cap stood up. He had been skeptical about coming, he said, assuming this would be another hollow effort to dampen racial tensions in his city.

"Now I believe we are taking it seriously. Thank you for using your voice. I would like to see it used on a national scale, because I think that Starbucks should be the third place. We can have those conversations, not just in St. Louis."

"Why *not* in our stores?" asked the next speaker. This notion came up again and again.

I'd started the company not just to serve coffee, but to create places of connection and community, a place where all belonged and could get along, and stand side by side in a respectful fashion, like in the elevator of my youth.

If the rules of social engagement for corporations really needed to change in the country, as I'd been saying, then perhaps the time had come to discuss something as divisive as race in Starbucks stores, in a way that would bring people together.

On March 5, 2015, while traveling with a small team to icy cold Chicago to attend our sixth open forum about race, I received an email that would lead to one of the most contentious periods in Starbucks' history.

CHAPTER 17

The Third Rail in the Third Place

We were planning to launch a campaign in our stores about race relations in America. And we were calling it Race Together.

"Race Together" was also the title of the discussion guide we were co-creating with *USA Today*. The eight-page pamphlet, printed on twelve-by-twenty-three-inch newsprint, would be distributed for free in Starbucks stores. *USA Today* would also include the guide in the national newspaper's weekend edition.

Rather than outsource the guide's creation, we had decided to produce it ourselves. Its pages would be filled with facts, statistics, personal anecdotes, and questions designed to provoke thought and induce conversation. The content was researched and collected by *USA Today* journalists, people inside Starbucks, and several topical experts we reached out to.

A timeline tracked one hundred years of racial injustice and progress. A quiz highlighted trends in immigration and the uneven concentrations of wealth in America. First-person anecdotes from six Americans—a social worker in Reno, an auto repair shop owner in South Carolina, and a healthcare company worker in Louisville, among others—recounted when each individual first became aware of his or her own race. Three maps of the U.S. depicted the growth of the country's ethnic and racial populations between 1960 and what was projected for 2060. In fifty years, America would have no majority race.

On my way to Chicago for another open forum, I got an email from the team in Seattle that was working on the campaign. They asked what I thought about an idea: baristas could write "Race Together" on cups to draw attention to the discussion guides. It was intriguing, and played off the Come Together campaign in 2012, when we had last used our cups' real estate for a social purpose.

I forwarded the email to solicit feedback. Vivek, traveling in India, was among the first to respond: "I don't like it," he said unequivocally. He warned it was vague and easy to misinterpret without explanation. The first page of the compendium articulated the guide's intent for readers, but the phrase "Race Together" on cups would arrive in customers' hands without context. I also heard others' concerns about whether our baristas would be put in an awkward spot if customers responded with confusion, anger, or questions. There was internal debate about how various regions of the country might react differently. And would all that writing slow service, especially during morning rush?

I checked in with members of our board of directors, including Mellody Hobson. Mellody was the president of Ariel Investments, a money management firm with $13 billion in assets, and a director at Estée Lauder and several nonprofits. She had joined the Starbucks board in 2005 and was one of two African American directors. Mellody had a ruthless pragmatism, and her direct candor was often paired with a warm smile. In her widely viewed 2014 TED talk titled "Color Brave," she revealed her own experiences with racial bias in the corporate world, and urged more people to summon the courage to talk about race among people who were different from themselves. I had asked Mellody if she would give the talk at Starbucks' annual meeting the week we launched the Race Together campaign. She agreed. The two of us also had a frank exchange about bringing up race in our stores.

When I told Mellody I felt like a bystander and wanted to get more involved with the issue, she was a cautious advocate regarding how I chose to engage.

"Howard, it is one thing for a person of color to take up this cause, in many ways it is expected," she wrote me in an email. "It is another for a global corporation and its leadership to deal with this issue head on."

While she conceded that Starbucks was in a unique position to foster constructive dialogue, she also had two admonitions. Despite my good intentions, I was not in possession of moral authority on this issue. Men and women had devoted their lives to equal rights and fighting racism, and I was just now injecting myself into a tragedy as old as the country.

I asked myself, *Where had I been?* I had black colleagues and black friends and black business partners, but I was also a white, wealthy male in America—the demographic least likely to be discriminated against and, in fact, the demographic that discriminatory policies were historically designed to benefit.

Second, Mellody told me that I did not, nor could I ever, truly know what it means to be black in America. I never explicitly claimed that I did, but Mellody was offering me advice that I did not yet grasp, or heed: Empathy and emotions do not equate to knowledge or true understanding about others' circumstances. Being so new to the fight for racial justice, I had not yet put in the work to comprehend the roots and systematic ways that racism is embedded in America's everyday realities.

I took in Mellody's advice and everything I heard from people around the company. Starbucks has long been a place for healthy debate, and many people have disagreed with things I wanted to do over the years. There have been times I took the counsel of those who challenged my perspective, and times when I did not and instead followed my instincts about how to proceed. Starbucks would not be the company it grew into if I had only followed others' voices or only defaulted to my own. So as we planned Race Together, I knew there were people who felt uncomfortable with the initiative as well as those who supported it. Ultimately, it was my call how to proceed.

I had been so moved and encouraged by the open forums. They had sparked a respectful, spontaneous sharing that yielded a kind of emotional bonding. It was true and real. I envisioned that a cup inscribed with "Race Together"—followed by the reading guide days later—would have similar effects in our stores. I was wrong.

The conversation that ensued was not the one I envisioned.

The tweets came at us like fastballs:

> Not sure what Starbucks was thinking. I don't have
> time to explain 400 years of oppression to you and
> still make my train.

> Despite our difference[s] all of us—left or right, black
> or white—can agree that this Starbucks race talk idea
> is really stupid.

> The only folks happy about Starbucks baristas discuss-
> ing race with customers are the suits who run it.

> What I want to do: 1. Eat pizza 2. Pay off my loan
> debt . . . 77. Hang out with Rihanna 895. Talk about
> race at Starbucks.

> I take my coffee with as much caffeine as I can get and
> with as little political agenda as I can get.

> Will you be sending your baristas to classes on Critical
> Race Theory and Race Relations to ensure knowledge-
> ability?

Appalled Twitter users posted cascades of critical tweets. Video parodies of interactions with baristas went viral. Puns mixing coffee talk with the language of race spread like weeds. Gwen Ifill, the respected African American co-host of *PBS NewsHour,* tweeted, "Honest to God, if you start to engage me in a race conversation before I've had my morning coffee, it will not end well."

The remarks unified the public in ways I did not foresee, which was against us.

Within twenty-four hours, any control we might have presumed to have over the narrative was lost. The public response on Twitter became the news: "Starbucks' #RaceTogether Campaign Hits All the Wrong Notes, and These Twitter Reactions Prove It." "The Snarkiest Tweets about Starbucks's 'Race Together' Campaign." "The Internet Is United in Despising Starbucks' 'Race Together' Cups." The volume of the negative attention was like nothing the company had ever seen.

I was not on Twitter, but Starbucks as a brand had a strong Twitter presence. Corey duBrowa, who ran our global communications, was the company's most visible face on the social media platform, tweeting on behalf of the company under his own name. I knew Corey's background well. He'd joined Starbucks after working with Microsoft and Nike. Over the years, we'd traded stories about our upbringings. Corey had also grown up in subsidized housing, a white kid in a mostly black neighborhood south of Los Angeles. His dad taught high school in Long Beach and night school in Compton. I knew he'd expected backlash against the company and against me, but not the tsunami that crashed in.

On Monday, Corey tweeted, "One race: human." It was a lightning rod.

"Easy for you to say, mayonnaise boy," read just one of the less-offensive tweets directed at him. The responses grew vicious. Some called Corey racist. He also became a target for white supremacists. When he blocked some of the most venomous users, he attracted more. The volume and tenor of the digital attacks was so overwhelming and distracting that about midnight on Monday Corey hastily deleted his Twitter account. On Tuesday, he became the story.

"Starbucks 'Race Together' Campaign Backfires: Communications VP Deletes Twitter Account," blared a *Washington Times* headline. Corey's headshot appeared on national news, which positioned him as the executive who abandoned the conversation his company started. When Corey got back online, he received death threats, and when someone posted his home address publicly, Starbucks security determined that the threats were credible enough to warrant monitoring his house and briefing his family on safety measures.

Meanwhile, biting headlines, chastising essays, critical comments on cable news, and satirical jokes on late-night television appeared across the media spectrum, from niche blogs to national newspapers. Starbucks was called tone-deaf and patronizing. We were accused of overstepping acceptable bounds for a corporation, seizing upon a moment of national crisis to promote our brand, and preaching through our company megaphone. The company was tarred, inaccurately, for not building stores in black neighborhoods, having an all-white executive team, and "ordering" our baristas to talk about race. I was labeled a "one-percenter" who was using the company to assuage my white guilt. The reaction became the news. "The fury and confusion boiled down to a simple question: What was Starbucks thinking?" wrote *The New York Times*.

The vitriol continued throughout the week. The piling on of social media was also hurtful because it was so antithetical to our intentions. I could withstand it. Throughout my professional life, I had put myself in vulnerable public positions. The onslaught echoed the anger hurled at me when the Sonics left Seattle. The company, however, had never been under such hostile fire, even during our darkest days, and I felt terrible for our people. The smart, hardworking partners on the front lines of our business did not deserve or have the tools to deflect the public ire the program created.

None of the criticism jarred me as much as two incidents that occurred that same week in our stores. At one, a white customer refused to be served by a black barista. At another, our partners arrived to work to discover what appeared to be a bullet hole in the store window. A ball bearing had been shot through the glass. It could have killed someone. We assumed the incidents were in response to Race Together.

Putting people in harm's way was the worst possible consequence of our good intention.

By the time the Race Together discussion guides arrived in stores on Friday as planned, they got very little attention. The cup controversy drowned them out. We told our partners they could stop writing "Race Together" on cups, if they still were. In Seattle, our postmortem began.

Our internal forums had been uplifting and revelatory. But listening to personal testimonials inside the company, among partners who showed up voluntarily, was one thing. Handing an unsuspecting stranger a cup and broaching the topic of race was a completely different proposition. In retrospect, I know this seems obvious.

When we polled our store partners, many aired their displeasure, calling the effort divisive, embarrassing, and poorly explained. It's true the execution was sloppy, not properly sequenced, and too swift, no question. I have since asked myself whether the pamphlet would have landed well if the cups had not created such immediate friction. Or was introducing the issue of race the mistake in itself?

There were people who lauded the effort, urging us on: CNN's Van Jones tweeted, "Some activists won't take 'YES' for an answer. We say we want more racial dialogue. But then crucify @Starbucks 4 trying?" Others read: "Young people need to engage in these discussions & this is an awesome start!" And, "I applaud @Starbucks for attempting to start a dialogue with RaceTogether. The scale of the attempt alone is worth the praise."

The truth is that I threw Starbucks onto the third rail of society in a way that put an unfair burden on baristas and store managers. These discussions needed to be had, but not the way we had them.

I did wonder about what the viciousness of the attacks said about Americans' readiness to talk honestly and constructively about race as a nation. As staff writer Conor Friedersdorf pointed out in an essay in *The Atlantic,* "Companies found guilty of racial discrimination have attracted less heat." Race Together, he wrote, "certainly doesn't rank on any sane list of corporate misdeeds or transgressions, even if it turns out to be bad for employees, shareholders or both. . . . While Race Together should continue to be subject to critical scrutiny, the negative reaction is much more likely to do harm. It sends this message: 'No effort to grapple with race in America will go unpunished.'"

Would the combative reception Starbucks received dissuade other companies from taking on the issues surrounding race in a serious way?

"The easiest of decisions would be to lick our wounds and pack up and run," I wrote in an internal memo as the rancor died down. "But the fight for racial equality and opportunity, not just for a few, but for everyone, must continue. This is not a time to retreat, but to thoughtfully and with great discipline proceed." I didn't want us to recoil. We just needed to find a better way.

In the months and years that followed, Race Together would unleash more learning and positive activity at Starbucks as a failed endeavor than it would have if it had come off as we intended.

The history of Starbucks has been marked by singular events—some planned, some not—that forced us to consider the underlying values of the company, and to respond accordingly. Usually, a better version of us shows up. Always, we've had our critics.

When the Washington State legislature was voting on whether or not to make same-sex marriage legal, Starbucks actively lobbied on behalf of marriage equality. An organization against gay marriage called for a customer boycott of Starbucks. At our annual shareholder meeting in March 2013, after the law passed, one shareholder who disagreed with our position confronted me during the public question-and-answer session.

"Until January a year ago, our company existed without making gay marriage a core value," he said, speaking into a microphone in front of an auditorium full of shareholders, journalists, and partners. "At last year's annual meeting, I asked you if it was prudent to risk the economic interest of all the shareholders, cost the jobs of our partners, for something that would benefit the private lives of a small number of our employees." He was claiming that the boycott had hurt sales, which it had not.

When he finished speaking, rows of tense faces turned to me. I was standing onstage, listening. I did not want to disrespect him.

"I welcome your question as I did last year," I said, "because not every decision is an economic decision." I responded in the context of his false accusation that our business had suffered because we supported gay marriage.

I only needed one data point to address his specific concern: In fiscal 2012, Starbucks had performed exceptionally well. "I don't know how many things you invest in," I said, "but I would suspect not many things, companies, products, investments have returned 38 percent over the last twelve months." Supporting marriage equality was not an economic decision for me. I told him, "The lens in which we made that decision is through the lens of our people. We employ over 200,000 people in this company and we want to embrace diversity, of all kinds. If you feel, respectfully, that you can get a higher return than the 38 percent you got last year, it's a free country. You could sell your shares at Starbucks and buy shares in other companies. Thank you very much."

Starbucks thrives when it adheres to its core values. If the company doesn't follow them, it ceases to be that company.

Two years later, I felt similarly about my decision to introduce the topic of race. Doing so was not an economic decision. It embodied our values of trying to uphold human dignity by fostering civil conversations about complex topics. Even after the public battering, we would continue to address it, but in different ways.

We held more partner open forums—in Houston, Milwaukee, Baltimore, and Atlanta. They followed the same format as previous open forums. As before, anywhere from one hundred to one thousand partners showed up. Many expressed pride that we had tried to take the conversation to stores.

We also encouraged Starbucks stores to be used as places for residents and police officers to come together. The intent was to try to foster greater understanding and trust through conversations and shared perspectives. We initially worked with an established national program called Coffee with a Cop to help organize the events, which were facilitated by representatives from community groups like the YMCA, or civic leaders, or representatives from police departments, or Starbucks' own partners who volunteered to do so.

I attended my first Coffee with a Cop program at a Starbucks in Seattle, with Police Chief O'Toole. The store was packed, mostly with black members of the community, and more people were waiting in line to get in. A small group of protestors chanted "Black lives matter" outside the store. Police officers, black and white, were also in attendance. The only agenda was to let people who showed up speak and share. For two hours they did, by telling stories, providing opinions, airing complaints, and offering suggestions about how to improve relationships between residents and police. An array of topics bubbled up from the conversation:

What does effective policing look like? How do white privilege and unconscious bias affect the perception of black males? Comments veered from mass incarceration in America to inadequate schools to the lack of jobs for young people to what it's like for an officer to patrol a neighborhood where no one trusts the police. Throughout, the tone stayed respectful.

Positive feedback from people who attended these events spurred us to expand our participation in the program. By 2018, Starbucks stores around the country had hosted more than five hundred sessions.

Meanwhile, I also accepted invitations to speak about Race Together. At Spelman College, I sat on a panel titled "Can We Talk About Race?" with the school's president, Beverly Daniel Tatum, and the head of the United Negro College Fund, Michael Lomax. In 2017, I gave a speech at a meeting of the National Organization of Black Law Enforcement Executives. My intention was simply to talk about what Starbucks had been doing and what we had learned, to answer questions, and speak my truth.

And I continued to educate myself. I sought out expertise on racial justice and injustice and read more books about how white supremacy and unconscious bias have shaped society, organizations, and everyday interactions. I met with people trying to reform broken institutions. Near Seattle, I went to see former King County sheriff Susan Rahr, who showed me the reform program she'd created to train police recruits on how to defuse volatile situations without resorting to force. I also went to Alabama to meet Bryan Stevenson in person, and we talked again about his efforts to bring more fairness to America's justice system and to increase awareness of its links to the country's history of slavery.

In the summer of 2015, Starbucks sold Bryan's beautiful, revealing book, *Just Mercy,* in our U.S. stores.

I revisited the civil rights speeches and writings of Robert F. Kennedy, whose portrait I have in my office. "Each time a man stands up for an ideal, or acts to improve the lot of others, or strikes out against injustice, he sends forth a tiny ripple of hope," Kennedy famously said in a speech delivered in South Africa in 1966 to condemn apartheid as well as the discrimination in his own country. "Crossing each other from a million different centers of energy and daring, those ripples build a current that can sweep down the mightiest walls of oppression and resistance." At company meetings, I played this clip from his speech. Creating ripples was not work reserved for activists, or those who govern.

Confronting racism is not just about changing hearts and minds through conversations and interpersonal relationships. I had come to appreciate how racism manifests itself in structural ways, and must be addressed by doing concrete work to create more equity and fairness, via policies, laws, and practices. In our stores, minorities already made up about 44 percent of Starbucks' partner base. But when it came to diversity among people who worked in our headquarters, we had work to do.

In 2015, we took steps to improve our management training, mentoring, hiring, compensation, and promotions practices to address racism and unconscious bias, so that all partners were ensured fair consideration for jobs, advancement, and equal pay based on merit. In January 2017, Rosalind Brewer, the former CEO and president of Sam's Club, joined our board of directors. When she was named Starbucks president and chief operating officer, an African American woman became the second-highest-ranked leader in the company.

We already had Starbucks stores in low- and middle-income neighborhoods, but we built more, including in Jamaica, Queens; Chicago's Englewood area; and Ferguson, Missouri. One role of the stores was to employ young people from the community and offer spaces for them to receive job training.

These many initiatives grew out of the open forums and the Race Together campaign, even as we tried to find our footing on such shifting, contested ground.

Talking about race cannot heal the nation or eradicate racial injustice. But I saw it as a place to start. And we had to start somewhere. I still believe that dialogue can inch us forward.

We live in an increasingly polarized society. Few of us find ourselves talking and listening to those who are different from us. Yet Starbucks stores are places where, every day, millions of people of various races, politics, and backgrounds stand and sit side by side. Increasingly, they do so staring at phones and computers. The chances of connecting with strangers, of starting up a conversation about, say, the day's news, is dwindling, even in public "third places" designed to bring people together.

The benefits of doing so, however, remain worthwhile.

Michael Nadel, my childhood friend and protector, was not far from my mind during this entire time. After Billy and I went away to college, Michael was no longer welcome in his parents' home. He also was banned from the Bayview projects. He went to live on the streets of Greenwich Village, homeless, and over the years, Billy and I saw him periodically. Then we lost track of Michael. Eventually we heard he had moved to Florida to live with his mother after his dad died. Later, it was rumored he had passed away.

In a more recent search for traces of his life, Billy and I found old photos of Michael that people from Canarsie had posted on Facebook. The first was from June 1964. Several kids and their mothers are posing on the concrete steps outside P.S. 272, on elementary-school graduation day. Four skinny boys in ties and two girls in dresses stand front and center, proud and polished. Some have a mother's hand on their shoulder or arm. In the back of the group, peeking through taller bodies, you can see Michael's face. Not his body, just his face. He is smiling, and with his chin up and head slightly cocked you can tell he's standing on tiptoes, straining to be seen through the group.

The other photos we found were three mug shots posted by local police departments that were public record, taken between 2011 and 2013, when Michael was arrested for misdemeanor charges. Each police-station portrait captures a weary-faced, partially balding man in his sixties with bloodshot eyes, a musty beard, and parched lips, wearing what looks to be the same gray T-shirt in each photo. The nature of the charges, and the recurring T-shirt, suggest that he was living on the streets during these years. In one photo, Michael's bushy brows are furrowed, and in another his head tilts up, his mouth slightly ajar, revealing missing teeth. The man in the mug shots doesn't resemble the Michael I knew, the boy with the strength to scale eight-story buildings or defend himself against all who dared take him on. The Michael I remember was smart and brave and funny and loyal. The anger he became known for was an acquired trait.

What might have happened to that young boy, the one who strained to be seen through the group, if he'd had more love from his adoptive family and support from his school and the acceptance of his community? What might he have become if he had not been punished for the color of his skin or had to fight so hard to defend his existence?

Mellody once told me that America was born with the birth defect of slavery. "The thing about a birth defect," she said, "is that you can function, but it's always there."

I had come of age during and after the civil rights movement of the fifties and sixties, a period that transformed the country in fundamental ways and made us better, but far, far from perfect. In the decades that followed, I witnessed black Americans rise to prominence in all fields.

I also am among many Americans who foolishly perceived the election of the country's first black president as the last mile of the civil rights march. But slavery's legacies of white supremacy, institutional racism, systemic poverty, blatant discrimination, and unconscious bias still live on in our impoverished cities, our underfunded schools, our overcrowded prisons, our corporate boardrooms, and in law enforcement, the courts, and the everyday lives of black and brown families.

The faults of history cannot be undone, but if we confront them we can begin to learn, change the present, and create a better future. Discussion is a good place to start, but talking can never be enough.

In the wake of Race Together, my colleagues and I launched new initiatives inside and outside the company. The most influential move would reflect a truth that my colleague Blair Taylor voiced often as we attended the open forums together: One reason for the racial unrest that had originally sparked my attention was economic disparity.

"It's inequality," said Blair. "It's a lack of opportunity."

CHAPTER 18

Rethink the Possible

During my senior year in high school, after classes ended at 1 P.M., I would ride the L train into Manhattan and eventually get myself to 345 Seventh Avenue, between Twenty-ninth and Thirtieth Streets. That's where my job was back in 1970. I worked in a fur factory.

Before fur fell out of fashion, it was common for affluent women to drape fox stoles around their necks or walk the winter streets of New York, Chicago, and Boston in coats of sable or mink. A good portion of the expensive garments were manufactured in hundreds of mini-factories located in high-rise buildings on four square blocks of New York City's West Side known as the fur district.

It was there that I spent after-school hours in a dimly lit workroom where fox furs were primed, cut, and sewn into coats. The fox skins arrived already stripped of fat and blood, but the pelts still tainted the air with a rancid, musky odor. My job was to prepare the pelts to be cut and shaped for outerwear. I would put on my smock and as each brown, ruddy slab of skin landed on my long worktable, I would dip a large, hard-bristled wooden brush into a harsh chemical solvent and ferociously rub the skin side of each pelt until it became pliable enough to stretch. Using my bare hands, I grabbed the sides of the thick pelt and pulled until the piece lined up with the clothing pattern on my worktable. Once the wet, hairy pelt matched the size and shape of the pattern, I passed it to a cutter working at the table next to me and awaited the next skin.

Because I was paid by the pelt, I tried to rub and stretch and pass as many skins as I could in the time I had. It was not a sweatshop, but it was fatiguing labor that put blisters on my palms and made my arms break out in a red rash.

Sometimes I'd also deliver the apparel we produced. I'd push a rack of fur coats down Seventh Avenue to a wholesaler in a nearby building, or carry boxes to a UPS office and have them shipped to customers around the country.

I got the job because the company's owners were the only upper-middle-class family my parents and I knew: The Levys. They treated me well, and at the end of the day we'd drive back to Canarsie together. Two years later, I would show up on their doorstep, asking to borrow five thousand dollars for my parents.

I had other jobs when I was young—delivering the *New York Post* to apartments at Bayview, working behind the counter in a luncheonette, waiting tables—but stretching pelts at the furrier's was the toughest. It certainly instilled in me the value of hard work; the more pelts I cleaned, the more bills and coins I went home with in my pocket. Half I gave to my mother. The other half I kept for spending money. But it also taught me that there's more to work than the money you bring home. The brutal nature of the job seeded in me a desire to earn a living in a way that didn't make my skin break out in a rash.

In the summer of 2014, Sheri was in a meeting room in North Philadelphia. She could look out the window at an H&R Block and a brick building covered in graffiti. Inside the room, handwritten posters adorned the walls. "Work hard and be nice to people," one read.

It was lunchtime, and Sheri was leaning forward to make sure she heard every word that Carmen Williams, a twenty-year-old woman, was saying. Carmen was tall and lithe and carried herself with confidence. Her brown hair was sleek and straight and she wore hoop earrings. Her rolled-up sleeves revealed tattoos on her forearms.

"For me growing up, I had a different definition of normal," Carmen said. Her mother was addicted to crack cocaine, and one snowy day when Carmen was a little girl, her mom dropped Carmen and her brother off at a friend's house. They didn't have any shoes on. "My brother and me, she left us." Carmen never saw her mother again. She and her brother spent the next several years living with a verbally and emotionally abusive step-grandmother. When Carmen was thirteen, she ran away, and over the next three years she lived in more than a dozen foster homes.

Sheri was in Philadelphia with Daniel Pitasky that day to check on the job-training program that the Schultz Family Foundation was developing with YouthBuild USA. Philadelphia was one of the training sites. Founded in 1978 by a civil rights activist and visionary educator, Dorothy Stoneman, YouthBuild is a nationwide program that combines high school classes and real work experience, in which eighteen- to twenty-four-year-olds learn construction by rebuilding houses, schools, and other community spaces. The hands-on approach helps students graduate high school, land jobs, or move on to college. It also is designed to instill the necessary self-confidence to make all that possible.

Also in the room were several of YouthBuild's teachers and administrators, and more than a dozen students. People ate sandwiches from boxed lunches and sipped Snapples as they tuned into one another's stories. Now it was Carmen's turn to talk, which she did with brave honesty:

> I was sixteen years old when I dropped out of school, not because I was a bad student—I love school. But my foster home had, like, thirty cats and they sprayed my school uniform and all of my clothes. When I asked for five dollars to wash my clothes, she [my foster parent] told me she needed it for Dunkin' Donuts in the morning. I told my dean of students, and he told me uniforms cost twenty dollars and I was suspended until I returned with the

proper uniform. I couldn't afford it. That's when I was introduced to the dancing life, to make money for uniforms . . . and to support myself from being on the streets.

Instead of planning for her junior and senior years, Carmen was struggling to find a place to sleep at night. She found a job as a dancer at an adult club. Eventually, a coworker, also a dancer, told Carmen about YouthBuild. At eighteen, Carmen enrolled as a YouthBuild student and seized every opportunity the program offered. For the next two years, in addition to taking high school and community college courses, she was the logistics manager on her advanced construction team and organized community service projects. She was voted senior class president and the queen of her senior prom. She tried hard, applied herself at school, and became the salutatorian of her graduating class.

Then Starbucks found me, and became my adopted family. I was taken under the wing of other Starbucks partners, but it was more than just having a job. At first I thought, *I'm just a barista.* But it was mentoring I received. They asked about me. "How's life? How's school?" They work around my schedule, like I mattered. At first I thought I was barely good enough to be a barista. Then when my manager talked to me about being a barista trainer, I saw possibility in the future.

Carmen had graduated YouthBuild earlier that year, and in her salutatorian speech she spoke about three hats that she'd worn during her short life. As she spoke, she literally placed three hats on her head in turn. The first was a bright yellow construction hardhat, which she wore when working at YouthBuild. This hat, she said, meant the most to her, because it saved her. Next she donned a green Starbucks cap on her head, which represented the chance she was given to work with people who cared about her. The third "hat" was her prom queen tiara.

"When I was a little girl, I always wanted to be a princess. But I didn't have the innocence of a princess. I had to grow up and be a woman that I didn't want to be. The tiara was my chance to be the innocent girl that I was supposed to be." Carmen cried as she told the hat story to Sheri that day, and explained, "YouthBuild did not make me who I am. They helped bring out who I was."

By showing up at a work site at 6 A.M., laying brick, and painting walls, YouthBuild students were practicing how to be accountable and part of a team. Many were also learning what success felt like. For some, it was the first time in their lives that they were praised for achieving a goal. They were also earning money, and seeing the results of their labors in the freshly refurbished homes.

In Philadelphia, in addition to building homes, YouthBuild was testing an expanded version of the barista training program that Sheri had been involved with for years in Seattle. At Daniel's urging, the foundation was broadening the curriculum to include a wider range of skills so students would be qualified for more types of jobs, beyond making coffee. Daniel and Sheri were also trying to bring the program to other cities, and were in Philly to check on the progress of their new Customer Service Excellence Training course.

"With the people I have now, that love me and support me and care about me, and motivate me and push me when I can't push myself, I might be president," Carmen said. She laughed, wiped away tears, and sat down. At the time, Carmen was enrolled in a local college and working at Starbucks.

Sheri returned to Seattle and told me all she had heard and what she was thinking. We agreed that helping young people get a good job was one of the best ways to address problems of social and economic inequality.

"Hello, I'm Howard Schultz with the Xerox Corporation."

I said this phrase upwards of fifty times every day, Mondays through Fridays, from 1976 through 1979.

After graduating college, I didn't return to New York immediately. I had no money and wasn't quite sure what to do, so I took an hourly job at a ski lodge in Michigan to ruminate about my future. The specificity of my mother's dreams for me had dead-ended at college; neither of us knew what "next" looked like. My first stop after leaving Michigan was back to my parents' home.

At college, I had majored in communications, which was then called speech. I didn't choose it because I knew what I wanted to do when I graduated. I chose it because it came naturally to me. My college experience hadn't prepared me for a specific career. I had no mentors, no role models, and no network that showed me how my education and innate skills translated into a working life. No one volunteered to help me sort through options or explain what the options even were. And I didn't know how to ask.

In 1975, at twenty-two, I knew three things for sure: I needed to make money, I was good with people, and I did not want to live in Canarsie, at least not for long.

At first I lived with my parents while I job-hunted and saved enough money to rent an apartment with a friend. My mom and dad had moved out of Bayview and were renting one floor in a modest two-story house in Seaview Village, a development of small, connected brick dwellings. Their landlord lived in the same house. Each morning, I read newspaper want ads and applied for the jobs that seemed most in line with my outgoing nature and need for fast money: sales.

My first job was with a small company named APECO that sold office copy machines, which put it in competition with Xerox. I did well at APECO and Xerox recruited me away. Suddenly, I was working for one of the most admired corporations in America.

Xerox was the Apple of its age. Its founders literally invented an industry, mass copying, when document duplication with the press of a button was as revolutionary as the PC in the 1980s, the Internet in the 1990s, and smartphones in the early aughts. Throughout the 1960s, Xerox dominated the copier business, but by the late 1970s the company was slowly succumbing to a plague that, more often than you'd think, overtakes successful businesses: hubris. Years of fast-paced growth had created a sense of overconfidence inside Xerox, as well as a bureaucratic hierarchy of managers who had lost touch with a market being infiltrated by cheap competitors. Xerox also was not investing enough in new products to stay relevant. Its strongest asset was its highly trained, hard-charging sales force.

At twenty-three, I didn't know anything about Xerox's deeper troubles. The Xerox name still carried gravitas, and I was just thrilled to be making enough money to finally afford to move out of my parents' home.

During the first three weeks on the job, new Xerox sales hires decamped to a massive training center in Leesburg, Virginia, where we learned Xerox's proprietary sales techniques and presentation skills. It was the most formal, in-depth business training I'd ever received, and I applied myself more intensely in Leesburg than I ever did at school. My competitive nature, once reserved for sports, surfaced among coworkers who came from white-collar families and had attended Ivy League schools. We all wanted to be the best. The top performing sales people earned promotions and recognition as well as higher commissions. I, too, wanted to win. So I pushed myself to know every angle of Xerox's machines and every sales pitch we were taught. I emerged from training with a heightened confidence. At one point I was even asked to teach classes. I declined, preferring to pound the pavement.

The sales team I was assigned to didn't sell copiers, but a new kind of office computer called a word processor. For six months, new sales associates like me weren't allowed to close deals on our own. We shadowed seasoned professionals. These career salesmen—some wrinkled and quirky, others sleek and savvy—were the opposite of my father: self-propelled go-getters for whom work was financially rewarding. With their in-early, stay-late routines, they epitomized the midcentury American work ethic. They were also warriors of their trade, possessing a natural armor against rejection: you hear "no" far more often than "yes" in sales. I had a lot to learn from them.

My job was to make no fewer than fifty in-person cold calls a day. I found the names of businesses two ways. The first was by poring through the Yellow Pages, the Google of its day. Sometimes I would call a company's main number and ask to speak to the person in charge of office equipment. If no one hung up on me, I could usually set up an appointment.

More often, though, I got out of the office and went from door to office door, introducing myself to receptionists and managers who had no idea I was coming. My goal was to leave with the name of anyone who had the authority to purchase office equipment. Back at Xerox's headquarters in Midtown, I passed my leads to a full-fledged salesperson who followed up and tried to close the deal himself. I went along to watch and learn. Sometimes I shadowed my boss, Jim, who was a master salesman.

Eventually I was approved to make my own deals and earn full commissions. My assigned territory was Forty-second to Forty-eighth Streets between Fifth Avenue and the East River, a hectic turf smack in the middle of the city bustle. The territory included Grand Central Terminal, the Chrysler Building, the United Nations, and the massive New York Public Library, whose marble lions, dubbed Patience and Fortitude, eternally guarded the front doors.

Manhattan in the late 1970s was a place of high energy and high crime. The city was in transition, and the automats of my youth, with their magic walls of reappearing pie, were taking a final bow. Daylight muggings were not uncommon, and the city was filthy, with graffitied subway cars, grimy pay-phone stalls, trash that accumulated curbside, and sidewalks pimpled with cigarette butts. Times Square was not the patio for tourists it has become, but a seedy street of peep shows and prostitution.

But for all that, New York City in the late 1970s, when I was in my early twenties, was still what it's always been, an island that attracts an ambitious strain of humanity from around the world. The career I chose, sales, included top-college graduates who'd grown up in manicured suburbs and whose fathers' daily uniforms were suits and ties. But sales was also scrappier than the more predictably pedigreed fields of law and finance. Among Xerox's sales teams were folks like me who'd grown up at the far end of the tracks.

More so than in some other careers, success in sales is based on merit and individual performance. Selling gave people who might otherwise be overlooked or blocked because of gender or race more of a chance to earn economic ascent. With a potent mix of smarts, charm, and grit, someone like my boss, Jim, who was among several black professionals I encountered during my years at Xerox, had the potential to make as much as or even more than a white Ivy League graduate from Greenwich. Sales gave women and minorities a shot in the 1970s.

So in and out of office buildings we went, with business cards in our pockets and a pitch book under our arms. I'd enter a lobby, say hello to a doorman I'd already befriended, and breeze into elevators. In those days there was little to no security, so floor by floor I walked through office doors, never knowing who I would encounter on the other side. A secretary of an accounting firm having a lousy day, maybe, or an office manager of an import-export business in the mood to chat.

I visited hundreds of companies and conversed with people who spent weekdays behind desks. When I was growing up, most of the workers I encountered manned steering wheels or service counters. This new population—with their suits, ties, and new technologies—fascinated me.

My curiosity colored my sales pitches. "When was the company founded? What kind of insurance do you sell? How many factories do you have in North America? Two in Ohio? My girlfriend is from Lima!"

I was good at sales in part because I worked hard and in part because making quick connections with people came naturally. My style was to talk less than I listened, and I consistently sold more Xerox machines than many of my peers. I also caught a lucky break or two, including a huge order from a law firm that earned me a plaque back at the office and a flattering letter from a high-ranking manager. Had I stayed at Xerox longer than I did, I might have gone far.

But early on, I knew. I just knew that working at Xerox was not for me. Word processing felt impersonal. I couldn't get emotional about hardware. The regimentation of Xerox's corporate culture also penned me in. I wanted creative freedom, not scripted sales pitches. I was looking for something more entrepreneurial, even if that term wasn't in my consciousness at the time.

And as much as I pined for more financial security than my parents had, I also wanted to enjoy my job, to feel good about *how* I earned a paycheck, not just *that* I earned a paycheck. I'd grown up with a father who was bitter every day. His wasn't a working life I wanted for myself. I was after dignity and enjoyment as much as money. Such aspirations someone like my father couldn't even fathom. Liking your job? Passion? These were ridiculous luxuries for most people who raised a kid in public housing. But I wanted more than just affording a roof over my head. My success at Xerox helped me believe more was possible.

When I told my mother I was quitting Xerox, she cried. I was making one thousand dollars a month, plus very healthy commissions. Since my first job as a paper boy, dividing my pay with my parents was something we all expected. They came to rely on it. I don't think my mother was worried about losing the money if I quit. She worried about my stability. In her eyes, Xerox was a respected corporation, and I had made it inside! Why walk away from such safety and security? She was proud her son worked for such a well-regarded brand name.

My risk was a calculated one. I had another job lined up: selling for a Swedish company that no one in my family had heard of. Perstorp was setting up a U.S. division of its housewares business, Hammarplast. The chance to work for a company that sold products to consumers, not to businesses, excited me. I also was intrigued by the idea of traveling to Europe. Little did I know that working for Hammarplast would eventually lead me to Starbucks.

Despite not being passionate about Xerox, my three years there were invaluable, as the time we spend in our first jobs usually is. It put me in touch with skills I had yet to appreciate. I became a better listener and a more empathetic communicator. Door-to-door sales also primed me to shake off rejection, even respond with grace in the face of it. Moving on with optimism after defeat became habit, as did forging through self-doubt. Resilience became second nature. And because I performed far better at sales than I did at school, my success helped me to feel good about myself. I could excel in realms beyond sports. These lessons from my first job would serve me well when I really did try to become an entrepreneur, attempting to raise money from investors to fund Il Giornale a decade later.

In sales and marketing, I had found my path up and out of the projects.

As the years went by, memories of my Xerox days, or the furrier afternoons before that, became more distant. But in 2014, Sheri's efforts to get young people into their first jobs brought back to me just how confused I felt in my youth, and how clueless I'd been about a working world that was a subway ride away from Canarsie but felt a million miles from the working-class life I knew. The kids Sheri worked with reminded me that a first job is as valuable as a diploma. For some of us, even more so.

An estimated 5.6 million Americans between the ages of sixteen and twenty-four—close to one in seven young people in that cohort—were not in school or employed in 2014. They lived in small towns and inner cities. They were white and black, Latino and Native American. Some had never attended high school or had a job. Some had a year or two of high school, were still enrolled in a low-performing school they never attended, or even had a diploma but were not headed to a trade school or college and had very limited work experience. And some had dropped out of college and had no job prospects.

Even if they'd had a job before, many came from ZIP codes that aligned to federal poverty levels, and were one bad break away from living on the streets. Overall, these young people lacked chances for economic mobility, no matter how much they wanted it or tried to achieve it. They would struggle to find safe, affordable places to live and healthy, regular meals. Consequently, they were more likely to suffer homelessness and health problems, become involved in illegal activity, and rely on government assistance.

This slice of the populace had been called at-risk, disconnected, disadvantaged, poor, alienated, and underserved. More recently, however, the White House Council for Community Solutions, under President Obama, in an attempt to highlight the potential of these kids and not focus on their problems, had coined a new name: opportunity youth.

For the majority of young people who grow up in low-income and impoverished areas, rural as well as urban, it's not their will to succeed that holds them back, but lack of access to the opportunities and the right support. They face barriers that kids born in higher-income ZIP codes do not. Many do not know how to write a résumé or what's expected in a job interview. Some don't own job-appropriate clothes or don't have transportation to get to a job if they can't walk to it. And if they didn't finish high school, or if they have any kind of criminal record, many employers won't even allow them to complete an application or meet with a recruiter face-to-face. Many young folks also don't know where jobs are, or the variety of jobs that exist, or how to find them other than to seek out Help Wanted signs propped in storefront windows. And big companies aren't coming around their neighborhoods to recruit them. Their plight worsened with the Great Recession, when these young people had to compete with college graduates and experienced adults willing to take lower-paying positions.

Part of the problem is that not enough of us in corporate America see these young adults as assets. The bias is to treat them like liabilities, and to dismiss them. But if the business community doesn't extend job offers, and support them on the job, these young job seekers have no chance—and in the end, everyone suffers. When one in seven young citizens doesn't work or go to school, the economy risks losing future taxpayers and consumers. Youth unemployment is also a financial drain on communities. Measure of America, a program sponsored by the nonprofit Social Science Research Council, estimated that in 2013 the total cost of "youth disconnection"—accounting for healthcare, public assistance, incarceration—was $26.8 billion.

Sheri and Daniel worked with a national consulting firm, FSG, to conduct an analysis of the country's opportunity divide. The research included interviewing experts on the subject, and the findings confirmed that the biggest gap for opportunity youth was not having access to employment. Building pathways to jobs, which the foundation hoped to do, would require a systematic shift in how young people were trained and how businesses with jobs to fill engaged with the youth community.

As Daniel put it, Sheri and I were in a unique position to approach the youth employment problem. Sheri knew young people could make good employees and I knew companies that needed good employees, beyond Starbucks.

During this period, the foundation and Starbucks were simultaneously executing our respective efforts to serve veterans. The foundation focused on helping veterans and their families successfully transition out of the military, and Starbucks continued to hire. We all saw parallels with opportunity youth. Both populations included people with the ability and the will to do well in the workplace, but both groups also were misunderstood by the general public and overlooked by employers. The myriad government and nonprofit organizations that were developed to serve veterans and young people tended to be fragmented, which did not lead to the best outcomes for their constituents. Just as the country was failing its veterans, it was also failing millions of youth. And just as corporations were stepping up to help veterans, they needed to step up to help young men and women.

JPMorgan Chase, the global financial institution, whose CEO, Jamie Dimon, I knew and whose head of philanthropic workforce initiatives, Dr. Chauncey Lennon, Daniel knew, oversaw a veterans' hiring program called the 100,000 Jobs Mission, which was instrumental in highlighting and bringing together companies committed to hiring veterans.

One night as he was drifting off to sleep, Daniel's mind toggled between veterans and youth. Suddenly, he sat up in bed and told his wife he had an idea. He grabbed a pen from his nightstand and the closest thing he could find to write on, an empty toothpaste box. He scribbled "100,000 Opportunities Initiative," and penned out a model that addressed dual needs: increasing the supply of job-ready youth and articulating a business proposition for hiring them.

The next day he told Sheri his late-night thought: Similar to what they were developing on military installations for transitioning service members, the Schultz Family Foundation could help form a coalition that brought employers together to commit to hiring tens of thousands of young people, and perhaps create a nationwide network of businesses. The difference was that instead of going to military bases, the youth effort would have to go into communities where large percentages of disconnected young people lived.

Sheri loved it and gave Daniel the go-ahead to explore the idea.

Daniel shared it with me as well. Under the direction of Blair Taylor, Starbucks was already reaching out to young people in cities around the country, working with mayors and granting money to spur employment. Blair was already putting into practice his long-held intention for Starbucks to employ opportunity youth and be a role model for other corporations.

All of us were on the same page. A mass hiring effort could have far-reaching, measurable effects.

In the spring of 2015, a confluence of events yielded a decision to create the largest employer-led coalition to train, employ, and retain opportunity youth. We called it the 100,000 Opportunities Initiative, and it had a few pieces, including developing new recruiting mechanisms that would give young people new job skills, connect them with companies, and help them succeed on the job.

Starbucks would take the lead in reaching out to potential companies to join us. The foundation would focus on investing in and developing innovative training, hiring, and retention programs that could eventually be used in communities around the country.

Connecting corporations with opportunity youth would also require building or enhancing relationships with civic intermediaries: government-funded community groups and nonprofits, which already existed in low-income communities, as well as mayors' offices, because mayors set their cities' agendas, allocate tax dollars, and can rally attention to issues.

The next few months were a whirlwind, reminiscent of the exciting days putting together the Create Jobs campaign in 2011.

Blair led a team that began reaching out to business leaders, asking them to join our efforts and form a united coalition. Starbucks' early participation seemed to have a convening power. The list of coalition companies began to grow.

In addition to corporate members, the effort needed funding. The Schultz Family Foundation committed to providing seed money to engage outside organizations who would help execute the plan, initially the Aspen Institute's Forum for Community Solutions and FSG. Daniel and his team also reached out to local and national philanthropies that also joined, including the Rockefeller Foundation, Walmart Foundation, and the W. K. Kellogg Foundation.

In June, a small team flew to Chicago to scout the city's interest in working with the coalition. Chicago had a large population of unemployed youth—41 percent of black twenty-to-twenty-four-year-olds were out of work and out of school. Chicago's mayor, Rahm Emanuel, had vowed to help employ them. The city was also home to the nation's largest government-funded group focused on urban job creation, Chicago Cook Workforce Partnership.

Lacey All was among those who went to Chicago. A thirteen-year Starbucks partner who hailed from Louisiana and was on our social impact team, Lacey had a history of translating ideas into action. She and the team met with the local players in Chicago and pitched the coalition's intent. After several visits, she and Blair recommended that all the coalition companies gather in Chicago to announce their formation, purpose, and partnership with city officials.

As always, Vivek Varma pushed everyone to think bigger. "Let's not just talk about hiring. Let's do it!" In response, I shared an idea. We could kick off the coalition's work with a hiring fair. If we could wrangle enough employers and young people into the same space on the same day, a fair could be a galvanizing, public event that brought to life the coalition's goal: connecting youth with jobs.

The concept didn't garner much excitement, conjuring images of vanilla conference rooms with listless job seekers collecting corporate brochures and leaving résumés behind. Such a mind-numbing affair wasn't worthy of the crisis we were trying to address.

But a gung-ho, entrepreneurial spirit took hold. *Why not rethink the job fair?* we wondered. Come up with a look and feel that engaged the senses and was interactive, friendly, and fun. Create a space where people felt welcome, not unlike the atmosphere we tried to create in Starbucks stores. Why not treat young adults as customers, and give them an inspiring experience that made them feel needed and valued? Starbucks had been reimagining the coffee shop for decades. Surely we could reimagine a job fair in the same vein.

If done right—and it had to be done right, because after the Race Together campaign Starbucks did not want another high-profile debacle—a robust hiring fair could demonstrate the coalition's sincere intent to employ young people.

While the foundation and growing coalition focused on creating new pathways for young people to prepare for, find, and succeed at jobs, Starbucks took charge of the look and feel of the job fairs.

Kevin Carothers joined the team, and brainstorming kicked into higher gear. Kevin, a Montana native, had been involved in Starbucks store events since the mid-1990s, when our philanthropic focus was AIDS, arts, literacy, and the environment. He'd also orchestrated the recent open forums in Ferguson and other cities. Kevin had an infectious, upbeat energy, a precise planning style, and a fearlessness we needed.

Lacey, Kevin, and Blair led a small, tireless crew that set up shop in an office near mine. They tried to envision what a fresh-flavored job fair could look and sound like. Stickies with their ideas and to-dos papered the walls, and every day the team conferred with vendors, event producers, and people in Chicago. They booked the city's largest venue for August 13, and homegrown Chicago performers from the same neighborhoods as the youth we were targeting promised to show up and speak to attendees, for free.

The most productive thing the planning team did was try to put themselves in the shoes of young, inexperienced job seekers. Besides a résumé, what else might prepare them for work? The team consulted with Sheri, who shared what she knew about the wide-ranging needs of opportunity youth: They needed work-appropriate attire. Many didn't have a résumé and had never even interviewed for a job, let alone know how to manage money or even obtain a driver's license. Some needed safe places to live. Many had no access to computers and printers. These were barriers to employment that Sheri believed the fair could help kids overcome by making experts and resources available.

As the team planned, more companies joined the coalition and all agreed to do something most large corporations never do: hire hundreds of people on the spot, at the fair.

Two weeks before the event, we held one of several pre-fair workshops the team had arranged so young folks going to the fair could practice interviewing and put together résumés at schools and civic centers. Fewer than fifty young people showed up to the first workshop. It was worrisome. We were building the fair to accommodate thousands.

The reality of the systemic problem was revealing itself. Young people who aren't working or in school are scattered, which makes them tough to locate, reach, and help. The team was witnessing what it means not to have access.

The night of the first workshop's low turnout, a determined Lacey met with civic leaders in Chicago over deep-dish pizza. They came up with a grassroots game plan, and for the next two weeks got on their phones, reaching out to pastors at churches, encouraging them to bring their young congregants to the fair; asking radio and TV stations to run public service announcements; and inviting the media to broadcast the event's dates, and to attend.

And yet for all the deliberate planning and groundwork, we still could not predict attendance. We were throwing a huge party with a purpose for the city's youth. How many would come?

CHAPTER 19

Start Somewhere

I hobbled down a wide hallway of the convention center on my crutches—I'd torn my Achilles tendon playing basketball with Jordy and his friends six weeks earlier—and looked out the floor-to-ceiling windows to the street outside. I was stunned. It was 8 A.M. and close to a thousand people were waiting in the Chicago heat and humidity. Some were unloading from buses, dressed in their Sunday best. Sheri stood next to me overwhelmed, almost in tears.

When the doors opened at McCormick Place, the largest convention center in the country, the sea of job seekers flooded inside, poured up escalators, and streamed into the massive, fifty-foot-ceilinged space that had been created for them. Like tourists taking in Times Square, they absorbed the vibrant scene of what one news reporter called a job fair on steroids.

Dozens of brightly colored booths branded with big-company names dotted the floor, each manned by recruiters eager to chat. Smiling, red-shirted volunteers milled about as a DJ pumped music by Chicago's own Chance the Rapper into the throng. Multicolored signs directed people where to go. Along the huge room's periphery, booths of experts who knew how to manage money, find scholarships, get a GED, register to vote, apply for citizenship, or even expunge a criminal record were raring to talk. There were hundreds of laptops marked

RÉSUMÉ STATION and APPLICATIONS STATION. There was even a station for attendees to conduct mock interviews with volunteers before sitting down with actual employers.

The main event, the element of the fair that made it extraordinary, occupied almost half the floor and was concealed behind walls of black curtains. There, rows upon rows of round café tables were set up, each with bottles of water and three chairs, one for an interviewee and two for recruiters. More than two dozen companies were expected to talk to more than 1,500 prospective employees and make hundreds of job offers that day.

All told, close to 4,000 attendees would show up between 9 A.M. and 6:30 P.M. that summer day. Among them was a soft-spoken twenty-three-year-old woman named Hagar.

Hagar had left Georgia Southern University in 2012, during her sophomore year, for health reasons. She had recently moved to Chicago to live with extended family on the city's South Side, hoping to find more and better job opportunities than in rural Georgia.

Hagar had spent weeks beating the pavement, leaving her name and number with managers and sales clerks. The rejections had shaken her confidence. The only offer she got was to be a part-time cashier. She took it, but Hagar knew she was capable of doing more and earning more. When a cousin suggested she visit a community center to get some job-hunting tips, Hagar went, eager, but the counseling was geared to older adults who'd lost jobs, not young folks still looking for their first jobs.

While at the center, she saw a banner for a city program that hooked kids up with seasonal employment, so she signed up. For a month, nothing. Finally, an email arrived announcing a youth job fair to be held at the glass-encased convention center on the lake. Hagar had passed the building before. Anyone interested in the fair was encouraged to attend a workshop beforehand to fine-tune résumés and practice interviewing. Hagar went to a weekend workshop and did mock interviews with volunteers who scheduled her to meet with three companies during the fair.

When the day came, a fifteen-minute train ride delivered Hagar to the convention center. She hadn't expected it to be so big, or so crowded. Most of the attendees were black, like Hagar. At first she felt intimidated, surrounded by so many people. *Competition,* she thought. She had come alone, but others were with friends, church groups, a parent or maybe an aunt. Some wore blazers and looked professional. Others had shown up wearing sneakers with jeans and wrinkled shirts. She saw young men with bow ties and dreads and others with no ties and closely shaved heads.

Hagar's H&M blouse was tucked into a black skirt, and her hair was cropped short. She had dyed it dark after someone suggested its previous hue, green, might not make the ideal first impression. She wanted to be herself today, but she didn't want to limit her options. She was already self-conscious about her hands, which had traces of eczema.

At the registration counter, a cheerful volunteer signed her in, handed her a badge, and wished her a great day. There was time before her interviews, so rather than wait and worry—*Would they like her? Would she like them?*—she decided to calm her jitters by walking around. *I'll make it an adventure,* she told herself.

She took in the bustling scene. Young people were everywhere, pinballing from one booth to the next. Hilton. Hyatt. Target. Microsoft. Nordstrom. Lyft. Potbelly. FedEx. Walgreens. T-Mobile. More than thirty companies in all. So many options and so many business cards to collect, which could be helpful, she thought, if she didn't get a job at the companies she was interviewing with that day. She spied people at a LinkedIn booth, snapping headshots for online profiles. Hagar wasn't on LinkedIn; it intimidated her. Maybe today she'd join. By a cluster of mirrors, employees from JCPenney and Sephora were giving makeovers. *Just a little,* Hagar thought, to fill in her eyebrows, but nothing distracting. She clutched her notebook and made her way into the fray.

I tried to imagine the fair through Hagar's eyes to help understand the challenges, hopes, and anxieties of opportunity youth. It's easier to empathize with one person than 5.6 million, and the Chicago fair helped to humanize that statistic. All I had to do was walk the floor, look around, strike up conversations.

Sheri and I saw one teenage boy run over to an elderly woman in a wheelchair, declaring, "We got the job!" The grandmother let out a cry of joy, and her grandson leaned over to hug her.

At first I had been surprised that so many young men and women came with parents and grandparents. But it was a reminder of the role children play in supporting families. A job doesn't affect just one life. It alters a family. Parents who were teenagers or in their early twenties had young children in tow; one dad told a recruiter he'd brought his daughter to set a good example for her.

When a young man approached me to say hello, he lifted his T-shirt to show me where on his torso he'd been shot. He wasn't in a gang, he said, he'd just been walking home. Many of the attendees came from neighborhoods where gangs and guns were common and yet not one person I met saw himself or herself as being simply a victim—although many of them had certainly been victimized by violence, poverty, and an indifferent and sometimes hostile system. But they knew that there was more to them. They were here because they believed their lives held possibilities.

Hagar's mother had encouraged her to try to get a job with Starbucks. She told her daughter that the company covered college tuition, and the health insurance would be good for her, too. But Hagar was skeptical of working for a company in the foodservice business. She hadn't liked the jobs at restaurants she'd had back in Georgia.

Before her scheduled interview with Starbucks, Hagar approached the stand-alone Starbucks booth on the main floor. It was set up with espresso machines, and our partners were teaching fair attendees how to pour espresso shots. When one of our partners asked Hagar if she had any questions, Hagar glanced down at a page in her notebook.

"Can you tell me about different ways I can grow my career at Starbucks after starting as a barista?" The woman was impressed by Hagar's diligence, and they chatted for a while. Hagar walked away rethinking foodservice. The kind woman seemed genuinely interested in her. The two saw each other again at one of the many workshops being held that day. Hagar was listening and taking notes.

When it was time for her Starbucks interview, Hagar sat down at one of the round café tables. All around her, other applicants were fielding queries from store managers, vying for one of the job offers Starbucks would make that day. Hagar was asked about her work experiences.

"What if you found yourself in an awkward situation with a customer? How might you handle it?"

She shared the first thing that popped into her mind. At her job as a cashier at a department store, only designated salespeople who earned commissions could sell shoes to customers, so Hagar was only allowed to ring up purchases. One day, a woman walked up to the register and told Hagar she needed shoes for a funeral, but didn't know what to wear with her outfit. The woman seemed distraught and kept asking Hagar what she thought. There were no salespeople nearby. "The last thing you want to do is think about fashion when so much is on your mind," Hagar told her interviewers. So Hagar came out from behind the cash register and walked around the floor with the customer, looking at various pairs of heels and flats and suggesting styles.

Hagar was hired by Starbucks on the spot.

After she accepted, she hit the exhibit floor to find the friendly green-aproned partner she'd met earlier. "I got an offer from Starbucks!" Hagar shrieked. Our partner reached out and gave her new colleague a hug.

Four days later, Hagar showed up for her first day at a Starbucks store on Michigan Avenue. Within six months, she was promoted to a shift supervisor. In 2016, she transferred to a Starbucks community store in the Englewood neighborhood to help train other opportunity youth hires.

Several surprise performers were scheduled to speak on a stage set up in an auditorium adjacent to the fair's main floor. But when the appointed time came for everyone to transition from the fair to the forum, they wouldn't go. The attendees were so energized by the conversations they were having, the employers they were meeting, the information they were learning, and the jobs they were getting that we couldn't corral them to walk out of one room and into the next. Lacey tried announcing who was speaking—Common, Usher, will.i.am—but not even these big names peeled people away. I'd also invited Cedric King, the veteran I'd befriended at Walter Reed. He had left the hospital and was speaking around the country, inspiring audiences with his story of resilience. I wanted everyone to hear Cedric.

At first the lack of interest in the staged events was frustrating, but then we realized it was proof of the fair's success. These young people had come because they were hungry for jobs and wanted to work. Not to be entertained.

Eventually, people made their way into the auditorium. Sheri was among those who took the stage, and she congratulated the thousands of young men and women seated before her on the courage it took for them to be there. She also assured them that the companies interviewing were the fortunate ones.

"Tomorrow and the next day are just your beginning," she said. "Howard and I both believe everyone has to start somewhere." I was in the front row and could see her joy at the magnitude of what was transpiring. Twenty years earlier, she was handing out socks from the back of a van. Today, hundreds of jobs were being offered. Before our eyes, Sheri's life's work was being realized. So often, I was the one onstage, in the spotlight. This was Sheri's moment. It filled me with such pride to hear her share her wisdom and what was in her heart. She really wanted the best for these young men and women.

More than thirty companies extended six hundred offers that day, and even those who didn't leave with a job left the fair with something. A résumé, maybe, or a lead on a college scholarship. A savings plan. Advice from a recruiter. Confidence. A little inspiration.

Singer-songwriter Common, who had grown up in Chicago and just two weeks earlier had been in Hollywood to accept the Academy Award for his song "Glory," featured in the movie *Selma*, got a standing ovation when he spoke. "Today, corporations, the world, are getting to see the potential, the abilities, the gifts, the talents, the intelligence, the brilliance, that each and every one of you has."

I knew that we had to do this again.

By 2018, the 100,000 Opportunities Initiative had hosted fairs in six more cities.

In Phoenix, where one in five young people are considered "disconnected" from society, seventeen hundred attended, including a seventeen-year-old named Angel who needed a second job to help his family. He had four young siblings and a father who had been laid off. Angel accepted an offer from Starbucks.

In Los Angeles, more than six thousand young people filled the Staples Center. At least half arrived before the doors opened, forming a thick, snaking line. The breathtaking sight made the job-seeking crowd in Chicago pale in comparison. Among the attendees was a dapper young man who'd been sleeping on friends' couches for months while he looked for work. "I felt like I was needed!" he declared after getting a job offer that day.

In Seattle, Carmen Williams, whom we flew in from Philadelphia, stood onstage, told her story, and pounded her fist into her hand, saying, "There are so many resources in this room. Take advantage of it. Change your life!" That day, thirty-two companies made seven hundred offers.

There was a moment at one of the early fairs when a rumpled young man caught my eye as he drifted into a booth that Macy's had set up. The station resembled the men's clothing section of a department store. The young man's head was down as he sauntered in and came upon a table on which dozens of ties were fanned out. He looked over his shoulder, unsure of what to do, and for a long minute hovered over the colorful collection of stripes and patterns, as if assessing a puzzle.

I was about to go over to help him myself when a well-dressed volunteer approached him and said something I didn't hear. The young man picked up one of the ties, walked up to a full-length mirror, and, with his chin down and eyes on the floor, slid the silky fabric around his neck and over his T-shirt. The volunteer talked him through the ritual, the same way my dad did with me when we stood in front of a mirror, side by side, before my bar mitzvah: "Cross the wide end over the narrow end, now back under, then back over again, then pull the wide end through the loop"—*Keep the knot loose with your finger, Howard*—"and, gently now, pass the wide end down through the loop." Slowly, the young man drew the knot toward his neck to ensure it arrived unbroken. Success.

There he stood, no longer looking down but chin up, absorbed in his own reflection. In that instant, his body language changed. I watched his posture rise from crouching self-consciousness to upright confidence. I could see it! I swear he rose an inch! And then he smiled, thanked the man who'd taught him how to tie a tie, and marched back into the buzz of the main floor, ready to take on whatever challenge arose.

That moment—so brief, yet so infused with humanity—captures the outsized effects of the 100,000 Opportunities Fair and Forum on the young people who attend one of them. Dressing a kid up and giving him a free tie was not the point. Learning how to tie a tie was less about how the world would see this young man, and more about how he saw himself: as capable, and in control of how he presented himself to the world.

When such small gestures can unleash things as momentous as self-esteem, imagine the dignity that can come from getting and succeeding at a first job.

Xavier McElrath-Bey had been abused by his stepfather as a child, put in foster care, arrested for stealing a candy bar at age nine, recruited by a gang, shot in the face at age eleven, and imprisoned for thirteen years.

"When I was released, I joined the ranks of the opportunity youth," said the twenty-eight-year-old Xavier. He was telling his story to a group of business executives and local politicians at the Dallas fair. "The day I walked into a Starbucks, my life changed." The store manager had given him a chance, he said. He recalled observing his customers as he worked behind the counter. "I wanted to be one of them, a laptop-wielding professional." Xavier earned a master's degree while working part-time at Starbucks. He was currently employed in juvenile justice as the Senior Advisor and National Advocate for the Campaign for the Fair Sentencing of Youth. His job was to help reduce unreasonably lengthy sentences for young offenders. Xavier was as fine a young man as I'd ever met.

Later that day, Sheri and I walked the Dallas fair's main exhibit floor at the massive Kay Bailey Hutchison Convention Center. Located near the fair's entrance was a six-foot-tall plastic statue of the motto for the Schultz Family Foundation and the fair's Twitter hashtag, *#startsomewhere*. The bright red hashtag was almost as tall as me, and by day's end the white letters would be covered with signatures and messages from attendees and volunteers. Before we left the fair, I pulled a pen from my pocket, knelt on one knee, and wrote two sentences in the center of the hashtag:

Your station in life does not define you.
The promise of America is for all of us.

Compared to when I grew up, it's much less likely today that a young person raised in public housing, or any impoverished, low-income community in America, will move to a higher-income area. One in five millennials now live in poverty, and more members of that generation live with their parents than other generations did. They also are about half as likely to own a home as young adults were in 1975, and, based on current trends, many won't be able to retire until they are seventy-five. For the most impoverished and disconnected, the odds are worse.

Through the work I've been able to do, I've become optimistic that there is a path forward based on a few intersecting beliefs. For one, I believe that first jobs are how young people "opt in" to America. I was not the only chief executive who began a professional life selling door to door, although it's quite possible that I'm the only one who scrubbed fur hides as a teenager. What those jobs taught me was that the value of early work experiences can exceed the amount of a paycheck. Work done well—building a house, helping a customer find the perfect new shoes, earning a promotion by serving cups of coffee—imbues us with a sense of self-worth as well as a sense of purpose. With dignity. And if you're a lost young person with little proof of your potential, work can provide a window into yourself. Work also introduces us to models to which we can aspire, such as the laptop-wielding professionals Xavier wanted to emulate, or the behind-the-desk managers I encountered on my New York City sales route. A first job can make us feel part of something bigger than ourselves, and while not many first jobs pay enough to support a family or relate directly to your ideal career, they are essential first steps, the chance that every American needs.

Another belief that the 100,000 Opportunities Initiative reinforced is that the rules of social engagement for companies have changed. Corporations must do more for the people they employ and the communities they serve. And, I would argue, communities beyond their own.

Founding, owning, or leading a company in America is an extraordinary privilege. In America, we have created unparalleled circumstances for entrepreneurs to turn ideas into moneymaking endeavors and for companies to potentially achieve almost limitless growth and prosperity. But there is no guarantee that this unique aspect of American life will stand the test of time. Our economy cannot sustain itself unless pathways to self-sufficiency, not just great wealth, are open to many more people. But as it stands, too many Americans who want to pull themselves up by their bootstraps have no access to shoes. No one to teach them how to tie a tie. Not enough people imbuing them with the early fuel of self-esteem. Not enough bridges to walk across toward a better life.

I do believe that the private sector can do more of what it does for itself on behalf of the country—not in lieu of government programs, but in addition to the necessary roles government plays. Businesses can help innovate. They can help reinvent and problem-solve. They can use their resources to help citizens and consumers become more educated, skilled, informed, productive, and self-sufficient. And not in isolation or at their own expense, but in creative collaboration with governments and nonprofits. The public and private sectors are in it together.

In new kinds of public-private partnerships, we can reimagine ways to lift people up and out of poverty, and re-envision how Americans are trained and educated for employment, and how their potential is tapped by employers. In partnership, companies and governments can learn from each other. We can imbue more compassion into business and imbue public entities with the tenets of business success—accountability, innovation, fiscal responsibility—tipping all scales toward a better balance of moral purpose and high performance.

No municipality has ever brought so many national employers and support services together for so many young people and offered so many jobs so quickly as we first managed to do in Chicago. And because we duplicated the fair in other cities, the coalition of businesses, with support from private foundations, was able to scale up its success.

The fairs were a first step, but they were not the last. In each city where we held a fair, the Schultz Family Foundation continued to fund innovative efforts to help local young people become job-ready and get their first job with companies committed to hiring opportunity youth. In addition, coalition members come together regularly to share ideas about what's working. The intent is to help take the best solutions and replicate them around the country. We continue to learn.

Starbucks' own efforts to hire opportunity youth have continued, and throughout the company their attrition rates are lower than a typical partner's.

To date, the 100,000 Opportunities Coalition has exceeded its original hiring goal.

I am not suggesting that job fairs and public-private partnerships are a panacea for our country's widening economic inequalities. But programs like these do not have to be anomalies. They can be replicated, improved upon, and scaled up. Even if they transform just a handful of lives, they are worth the effort. At the very least, they provide proof that new solutions are possible.

CHAPTER 20

Share Your Blanket

I t's a hard thing, realizing that everything you thought you were going to do with your life just got flipped upside down."

That's how Tracy Spaulding described his reaction when the coal mine that his father, grandfather, brother, uncles, cousins, and neighbors worked at shut down two weeks before Christmas in 2013. With each pink slip went someone's paycheck and health insurance. For Tracy, the only future he'd ever imagined for himself after high school disappeared.

Tracy is a beefy, bearded, warm-spirited young man with a sweet smile. He was born and raised in Dunlow, West Virginia, a speck of a town in the mountains of Appalachia with barely a thousand residents. The town center is a two-pump gas station, and the mine was the town's only employer. With no alternative ways to make a living in the vicinity, some miners left for Kentucky to vie for jobs at an automobile-manufacturing plant. Others headed to North Dakota, hoping for work in the shale oil industry.

But for Tracy, Dunlow was home, his "piece of America," as he referred to it. Moving away from his mother's cooking—and from the creek where he fished for bass, and from the woods where he hunted for deer, bear, and turkey—was as unappealing to him as it was daunting. But with the mine shuttered, he would have no way to make money. This new reality was a shock, but not necessarily a surprise.

After World War II, the coal industry became the backbone of the region's economy. The black rock extracted from its mountains powered factories and lit cities during the prosperous decades that followed. But the industry had been on the wane since the 1970s. Automation continued to reduce the need for human labor, and the rise of cleaner energy sources kept lowering demand, while regulations drove up coal's prices. As the U.S. appetite for coal declined, so did demand in other countries, like China, that had once imported it but had begun to ramp up their own energy production. Despite what some politicians were promising, the tens of thousands of coal-mining jobs that had fed and clothed generations of families could not come back.

In early 2017, I knew these facts. But I didn't appreciate how these economic forces were pulling the rug out from under people like Tracy. Around this time, I read *Hillbilly Elegy: A Memoir of a Family and Culture in Crisis*. The bestselling book by J. D. Vance was introducing me and others to the hardships of families in Appalachia through the very personal lens of the author's own hardscrabble upbringing.

J.D.'s neglectful, abusive family life saddened me, but his honesty about that life, and his revelations about the love and support from his grandparents, Mamaw and Papaw, also moved me. He showed readers a childhood rife with lapses of judgment and common sense by adults who habitually shirked their responsibilities. I was reminded of my own childhood, the fighting between my mom and dad, the raucous card games, my dad's negligence with money, my mother's depth of depression. I had never shared these rough memories with more than a few people, because of the shame and pain they evoked in me. But something about J.D.'s courage in laying bare an upbringing that many people would prefer to keep private prodded me. I was ready to further explore, in a public way, episodes from my own childhood and how they influenced my priorities in business.

I was also taken with how at peace J.D. seemed with his past. On the page, he had reconciled the bad behaviors of loved ones, especially his addict mother, by trying to understand and accept their actions in the context of Appalachian culture. His assessment of the region's poverty, drug crisis, and shifting political allegiances shed light on a population that too few people outside the region understood or knew. Appalachia is part of our American family, yet the country seemed to be turning its back on these men and women when instead we needed to have *their* backs.

In short, *Hillbilly Elegy* moved me to better understand not only myself, but also my country. Like our veterans and opportunity youth, and people still fighting for racial justice, here was another substantial pocket of America that was being underserved and forgotten.

In March, I met with J.D., and we spent much of our time together talking about the nation's opioid epidemic, which was most pronounced in Appalachia.

A perfect storm of factors had contributed to this public health crisis: Workers who did manual labor jobs—often the only employment in small towns—were vulnerable to life-altering injuries that caused chronic pain, for which doctors increasingly prescribed highly addictive pain medications that were aggressively marketed by pharmaceutical companies. Many doctors used narcotic painkillers to quickly ease patients' suffering, but also to stave off lawsuits that accused doctors of failing to treat pain. In Appalachia, as in other communities, the loss of jobs due to the economic downturn and dwindling industries coincided with an explosion in despair and people claiming disabilities. The medications they sought to treat their ailments were often abused or resold through underground markets, and led to heroin use.

Overdoses had become the largest cause of accidental death in the country. J.D. told me that at a town hall he'd attended in southwest Ohio, three-fourths of the people there had raised a hand when asked if they knew someone who'd died from overdosing.

We also talked about how dependence on the coal economy had led to a dearth of entrepreneurialism in Appalachia. With mining jobs paying anywhere from $60,000 to more than $100,000 a year, there had been little call for new business ideas. J.D. had recently joined a campaign started by Steve Case, the venture capitalist and cofounder of AOL, to bring economic relief to the Rust Belt, which borders Appalachia and includes other areas of industrial decline, by seeding start-ups. J.D. and Steve were embarking on a highly publicized "Rise of the Rest" road trip to seven cities in five states in search of business ideas from local entrepreneurs to help spark economic growth.

In addition to donating one million dollars to their effort, I decided to see the region for myself. I hoped a visit would offer me a way to grasp what was happening in these rural towns and with so many Americans. As the CEO of a company with 517 stores in the region, I also felt compelled to have a better understanding of the economic upheaval and the opioid epidemic, and how it might be affecting our partners. One state was at the heart of it all, and I arranged a trip.

On an April morning before the sun was up, I left Seattle for Morgantown, a city of about thirty thousand on the eastern side of West Virginia. I traveled with a small group that included Sheri and Rajiv Chandrasekaran. On the way there, I told a story.

In the mid-1990s, I'd visited Israel with a group of business leaders. While there, we met with Rabbi Nosson Tzvi Finkel, a renowned Jewish scholar and teacher. Our group was guided into his study and waited for him to arrive. After about fifteen minutes, Rabbi Finkel finally entered the room and sat down at the head of the table. I had not known that Rabbi Finkel suffered from Parkinson's disease. His body shook so severely that it was our inclination to look away.

"Gentlemen, look at me, and look at me right now," he said as he banged the table with his hand. His speech affliction was more pronounced than his shaking body, but he spoke without a hint of self-consciousness. "Who can tell me what the lesson of the Holocaust is?" We had been jolted to attention. He called on two men, whose answers did not satisfy the rabbi.

"Gentlemen, let me tell you the essence of the human spirit." For years during World War II, he recalled, the Nazis packed millions of people into boxcars like cattle and transported them to camps where they would be put to death. People young and old stood pressed up against each other in the dark railcars with no food, no bathroom, no heat.

"After hours and hours in this inhumane corral," he said, the doors of the train were swung wide open. The light was blinding. Men were separated from women, mothers from daughters, fathers from sons, as everyone was sent off to crude bunkers to sleep.

In the bunkers, only one person for every six was given a blanket. "The person who received the blanket, when he went to bed, had to decide," said the rabbi, "'Am I going to push the blanket to the five other people who did not get one, or am I going to pull it toward myself to stay warm?'"

Rabbi Finkel, his body still shaking, looked around the table. "It was during this defining moment that we learned the power of the human spirit." Prisoners in the camps, he said, shared their blankets. The rabbi stood up and stared into our eyes. "Take your blanket. Take it back to America and push it to five other people." Then he left.

I've thought about the rabbi's directive more times than I can count. It is more complex than I originally thought. A metaphor with infinite implications, especially at a time when the gap between those of us who "have" a blanket and those who "have not" is widening. What does it mean to "share"? And what is a blanket's modern-day equivalent?

This was, in part, why Rajiv was with me.

During his two years at Starbucks, he had applied his journalistic skills to several projects, including the job fairs and a fundraising campaign Starbucks led to help hundreds of homeless families in Seattle move into safe shelters. During that period, Rajiv also began experimenting with video. With a built-in audience of millions of customers who came into our stores and used our mobile app, Starbucks was in a position to distribute content. But why just share existing books and movies? Why not create our own?

We brainstormed about meaningful stories Starbucks could tell. Our initial ideas died on the vine. Finally, one took hold, and in 2016 Rajiv and a small team, including a talented photographer and film-maker, Josh Trujillo, produced a series of short films about Americans who were solving problems in their communities. Rajiv and Josh traveled the country interviewing folks, and sometimes I joined. Eventually we amassed an eclectic cadre of people we called "Upstanders," each trying to renew, save, or revive a piece of America. In Salt Lake City, a straitlaced accountant was reducing chronic homelessness. In Baltimore, a high school student effectively campaigned to prevent a giant incinerator from being built in her community. In Florida, the owner of a car wash employed adults with autism. We also found a former inmate who opened her home to other released convicts so they had a smoother transition than she had had to life outside prison; a young entrepreneur whose app redirected restaurant food to homeless shelters; and an ex-NFL player who founded a gym for amputees. Americans were helping Americans, and we were broadcasting how.

In the fall of 2015, the first season of *Upstanders* premiered. The ten original shorts could be viewed on Starbucks' website, on our digital app, and on Facebook, all at no cost. To date, seasons 1 and 2—which are also available on Amazon's video service—have been viewed more than 150 million times.

Telling these true stories would, we hoped, not only celebrate these extraordinary citizens for their initiative and innovative spirit, but inspire more problem solving. Our intent was to use the company's platform to scale up good ideas and deeds.

In the spring of 2017, as we headed to West Virginia, the second season of *Upstanders* was in the works, and our hope was to find solutions in a state that probably needed them.

The Starbucks store on Kanawha Boulevard is located a couple of miles from West Virginia's gold-domed capitol building. The district manager and store manager greeted us when we arrived. I stepped behind the counter to say hello and pose for a few requested selfies before pulling up a chair to a cluster of café tables.

There were about fourteen partners who worked at this and other Starbucks stores in West Virginia, and I asked each to please say their name, how long they'd been a partner, and anything about their background. Some reflections rang familiar: One store manager, Ben Johnson, had been at Starbucks almost fifteen years. He met his wife, Kacey, on their first day of work. Kacey was now a nurse, and Ben said she could not have gone to nursing school without the money they cashed in from Bean Stock. The district manager told us that when a chemical spill in the state contaminated the water supply, Starbucks had to temporarily shut down one of its stores. She was proud that she was able to keep paying the partners who had no place to work until the store reopened.

Other remarks were like none I'd ever heard at a partner roundtable. Ben also told us that he coached a little league team, and of his twelve players, ten of the kids were being minded or raised by grandparents, because their parents were addicted to opioids or had died because of them. Another store manager, Stacy Collins, said her father had been a coal miner but he'd broken his back and could no longer work.

"He's addicted to pain pills," she said matter-of-factly. Stacy was peppy and pregnant, and Sheri asked her how she had avoided what can become a familial cycle of unemployment and drug abuse. "My mother is a real spitfire. She raised us to value work and family."

In the coming days, we would hear more tales of hardship and resilience.

"Today? I wouldn't even be here if my knives were sharp."

The woman who spoke pulled up her sleeves to reveal red marks on her wrists, which she'd tried to slash. Her son's father, she said, was trying to take their child away from her, and her husband wanted a divorce. She had run out of money to pay for activities to distract her from taking drugs, and, for a reason she didn't reveal, she had jumped out of a moving car. Her voice was low, tired. "Those damn knives aren't sharp enough."

The woman next to her was curled up in her chair and nursed a hacking cough. These two women were among seven patients seated along the walls in a room at the Chestnut Ridge treatment center in

Morgantown, and among more than five hundred who attended weekly sessions for people who had become addicted to painkillers and heroin and had recently begun treatment. They were also the lucky ones. Chestnut Ridge had a waiting list of more than six hundred.

Dr. Judith Feinberg was our host for the day. She was on the faculty of the West Virginia University School of Medicine, and an authority on the medical consequences of opioid addiction. Dr. Feinberg said she could give us data, but there was no more revealing way to grasp the prison of addiction than to observe those trying to break out. She allowed us to sit in on two treatment sessions that morning. This first one was for people addicted to opioids who were just beginning Chestnut Ridge's recovery program. I found it distressing to listen to their stories, but Dr. Feinberg was correct: their voices spoke to us in ways that statistics could not.

An addiction psychiatrist led the group of six women and one man. He asked the participants how they were feeling that day. The responses, including from the woman who had tried to harm herself, were heartbreaking.

Another woman, her legs shaking, said she started taking pain pills after back surgery. "My doctor fed them to me for fifteen years." She'd been in this program once before, then relapsed. Now she was back.

A younger gal told the group she was two days clean of marijuana and one day clean of alcohol. "My whole family drinks and smokes." Her dad was a coal miner.

Another woman said she was trying her best to stay clean but having trouble getting her insurance company to pay for her prescriptions. She was referring to Suboxone, the widely used medication that helps treat opioid addiction by suppressing cravings. Chestnut Ridge patients were all prescribed Suboxone and attended intensive behavioral therapy sessions. Attendance was a prerequisite for getting the medication; both were necessary to help people reclaim their lives.

Answers to the question "How are you today?" continued around the room.

"Terrible," said a middle-aged woman in a yellow sweatshirt with the word FAITH stenciled across the front. She had driven three hours to be here. Her boyfriend routinely used drugs in front of her, she said, and had been arrested the night before. The hotel room where they were staying was only paid through the following day. After that, she said, she didn't know what she would do. The younger woman who had spoken earlier offered up her house.

The lone man had been a heroin user and wanted to stay clean but kept backsliding. His brother had died two months ago. His girlfriend had just broken up with him. He didn't want to be an addict.

"I'll do whatever it takes to keep getting help," he said.

Periods of withdrawal can feel ten times worse than the flu. Each person in the room appeared so very haggard; their clothes were wrinkled with multiple days' wear. Few could sit still. Addiction had dropped them into an abyss so deep that climbing out and into recovery seemed unimaginable to me. Where do you go when you have nowhere to go? And yet they were here. They had shown up, refusing to give up on themselves. They wanted to push through.

Across the hall was proof they could do it. The second therapy group we attended included at least twenty men and women in recovery, much further along in their journey. Each began his or her testimony by stating how long they'd been clean. Everyone in that room had been free of all drugs and alcohol for at least a year. For some, it had been longer. Compared to the group across the hall, they were calm, sat still in their seats, and were neatly dressed. Shirts were tucked in. Hair was brushed. The room was not full of tension. These folks continued to show up because opioid addiction is a lifetime struggle. Like cancer, it can return. Like alcoholism, it takes a community of support to help prevent a relapse.

The difference between the two groups was striking.

After the second session, two of the women agreed to sit down with us and with Dr. Feinberg in the center's front lobby.

Sara, a young mom, must have been in her early twenties. She was wearing black leggings and kept her hands stuffed in the pockets of her zip-up sweatshirt as she told her story. She grew up in a one-stoplight town and said she discovered Percocet in high school, when her boyfriend gave her some of his father's prescription pain pills. She married and had children, but kept using. She finally tried to break the habit after Child Protective Services removed her two-year-old and three-month-old sons from her custody. She was clean now, and had them back.

I asked if she could explain why it's so hard to stop, especially when you risk losing your children. The question came from my limited experience with drug addiction. My mother and father had smoked cigarettes all their adult lives. My father died of lung cancer. I'd never smoked a cigarette, and had no interest in marijuana after trying it in college. I did drink beer when I was younger, and as an adult I enjoyed a glass or two of wine with dinner, but I had never abused alcohol.

Dr. Feinberg interjected, "People think addiction is a choice, but it's a disease." The women nodded. Opioids change your brain chemistry, she explained, forming abnormal circuits that drive compulsive behavior. Your brain believes you can't live without the drugs, even though the drugs ruin your life. Heroin and opioids are so addictive they overwhelm even the strongest parental instincts. The crisis was creating legions of foster children.

"That's where it started for me," the other woman, Jennifer, said. She wore trendy ripped jeans and a flannel button-down over a gray tee. Her long, straight hair hung almost to her waist. She was thirteen when her mother, who was an addict, sent her to school with pills to sell to classmates. She had snorted and smoked heroin for years. Now clean, Jennifer managed a restaurant and had custody of her three children. "If I didn't come here, I'd lose my job, my house, my kids."

These were astute, self-aware young women. Had I met them in another setting, I wouldn't have suspected that drugs had consumed their lives. The matter-of-fact resolve with which they recounted their dismal pasts, void of self-pity, offered clues as to just how opioids and heroin hijack the self. As with other diseases, the will to heal was not merely a matter of choice. Recovery required support from a team of doctors, mental health counselors, and caseworkers who would prescribe the right doses of medication, hold people responsible for their actions, but not saddle them with any more shame than they already felt. Said Dr. Feinberg, "Common sense has nothing to do with addiction."

Guilt, however, was common, particularly among the mothers whose babies had been exposed to addictive drugs in the womb.

In Huntington, West Virginia, across the state from Morgantown, is a nondescript brick building housing the first private, nonprofit center to exclusively treat babies with neonatal abstinence syndrome, a condition resulting from exposure to opiates in a mother's womb during pregnancy. The sign above the front door depicts a curled-up baby sleeping on a green leaf. "Lily's Place," it read. Inside, it's pink and powder blue and hushed. Pinned to a polka-dot bulletin board, ten unused disposable diapers are playfully inscribed with handwritten notes in indelible marker: *Your love and care is changing my life!!! You are making a difference!! God bless you for all you do!* It was as if the babies were talking. The young ones at Lily's Place were the tiniest victims of the opioid epidemic.

We were welcomed in by a nurse who guided us through a few short, dimly lit hallways. She permitted us to peek into pastel nurseries. Each was appointed with a rocking chair, a changing table, and maybe an animal mobile or painting. In some we could hear lullaby music. The rooms reminded me and Sheri of our grandson's bedroom, except that attached to each Lily's Place crib was a device that monitored vital signs.

Every baby here was being weaned off his or her dependence on addictive drugs.

Withdrawal symptoms for these babies included excessive crying, tremors, intestinal problems, and seizures. They also were exceptionally sensitive to stimuli, which was why Lily's Place was so quiet and muted. In their cribs or curled up on a nurse's shoulder, the swaddled little bundles appeared no different from any other newborn. The babies' internal suffering was not outwardly evident, nor could they articulate it. As she rocked a baby in her arms, Sheri was moved to tears.

Since Lily's Place opened in October 2014, more than 220 babies have spent from two to six weeks at the facility. At least half of its budget is dependent on donations and grants. It's run by a small, dedicated staff, including its full-time director, Rebecca Crowder. Rebecca exuded the friendly, zealous advocacy I'd seen in Arizona State University president Michael Crow. Despite her petite stature, she struck me as another force of nature. She was a dogged voice for those who could not speak for themselves, and she arrived at our meeting armed with empathy as well as statistics.

The high prevalence of neonatal abstinence syndrome was a new phenomenon, she told us. Most hospitals used to treat only a few cases a year. Now, babies recognized as suffering from opioid withdrawal were being born as often as every twenty-five minutes in this country. At one hospital in Huntington, which required mandatory drug testing for every mother giving birth, newborns were diagnosed with drug dependency at fifteen times the national rate, and the cost of caring for a drug-exposed newborn at a hospital was five to ten times the cost of caring for a healthy infant. At Lily's Place, however, the cost was about one-fifth the daily rate of having a newborn in intensive care.

We were led to an open area where we met two mothers whose babies had been cared for at Lily's Place. The infants had been successfully weaned from the drugs that were in their system at birth, and the mothers were in recovery. We were joined by social worker Angela Davis, who took us aside before we spoke to the mothers. She would not introduce us unless we promised to abide by her one rule.

"I have zero tolerance for judgment," she said. Most Lily's Place mothers were going through rehab, trying to get and stay clean. "The mothers already have enough guilt. They know what they've done wrong," said Angela. Rebecca reiterated Angela's point. If a parent didn't succeed, she told us, her baby couldn't succeed. These parents needed positive reinforcement.

One young mom we met held a teddy bear and a pudgy baby girl who was about four months old and had a silver bow wrapped around her wispy-haired head. Another little girl in a lacy blue top and tiny plastic sandals walked up to where I sat. I asked to hold her, and plucked her up and sat her on my lap. Both kids were smiling and so were their parents. Sheri chatted easily with the moms, asking how they were doing. Well, they said. Taking one day at a time. Staying on track. Angela congratulated them on their progress and informed us they were working hard. The reason they were here was out in the open. No hiding from the truth. And no judgment.

It would be so easy to blame these women. And yet Rebecca and Angela refused to. They were well versed in opioids' power to counter even the best human instincts. No one plans for addiction, especially a parent. Dr. Feinberg's words ran through my head: "Addiction is not a choice, it's a disease." The babies' best shot at leading healthy lives was having healthy moms.

That evening, after we left Lily's Place, Rebecca joined Rajiv and me for dinner at the city of Huntington's historic Frederick Hotel. Offices had replaced hundreds of guest rooms, but the hotel lobby retained a stately, old-world aura. We dined with five other people, all involved in fighting the opioid epidemic, which was so pronounced in Huntington. Forty million doses of opioids had flooded into the city and surrounding Cabell County from 2007 to 2012. When the government eventually cracked down on pill mills—the mom-and-pop shops that sold hordes of cheap prescription painkillers—addicts turned to heroin, which found its way to the streets via sophisticated cartels.

The city's former police chief was at the table and admitted he'd been wrong to assume, as he once did, that his city could arrest its way out of the crisis. Nor could the city blame its way out of it, said Rebecca. People who had become dependent on drugs shouldn't be demonized. "We can't prescribe our way out of it either," said a doctor. Without support and counseling, medicated recovery efforts were not effective. The state and county had enough Suboxone, but a deficit of social workers and caseworkers.

Our visit to Morgantown and Huntington had been a sobering education, providing me with a better understanding of the tragedy and complexity of the worst addiction epidemic in U.S. history. This was a man-made disaster in which a web of pharmaceutical industry leaders, doctors, lawmakers, government-appointed oversight boards, and drug dealers were all complicit. Their negligence, irresponsibility, and unfettered greed allowed pain medications and illegal drugs to pour into American communities.

Drug overdoses had killed sixty-four thousand people in 2016, more than twenty times the number murdered in the terrorist attacks of September 11, 2001, and almost as many U.S. lives as were lost in the entire Vietnam, Iraq, and Afghanistan wars combined. Yet the country was not avenging this self-inflicted assault on our own citizens with all our might.

At dinner, I heard that familiar refrain. "One way out is economic. Good jobs."

West Virginia had the lowest rate of labor participation of any state in the country. The despair and boredom unemployment breeds, and the lack of employer-provided insurance, also fed illicit drug use. Caring for the sick was half the battle. Preventing the sickness was the other.

The next day, we came face-to-face with another Appalachian ailment, high unemployment, when we drove deeper into coal country.

The shelves in the kitchen of the Under the Bridge Community Outreach Center were stocked with cans of Del Monte corn, boxes of Jell-O, and Chef Boyardee ravioli. A piece of paper taped to the wall of the homeless shelter listed rules for residents:

Rooms should be cleaned every day.
No drugs or alcohol.
Shelter dues are due on the first of the month.
Chores are to be done daily!
Get along with other residents.

Those who failed to abide by all the rules would be asked to leave.

Residents of the recently opened shelter in the depleted town of Logan, West Virginia, were out of work. They were expected to contribute to the shelter's $750-a-month rent by collecting money around town, often with a bucket and a sign.

Outside, the streets of Logan were lined with parked pickup trucks, abandoned storefronts, and wandering smokers. We had driven by an open Dollar General and a Salvation Army store. The tall, elegant streetlamps planted every ten feet and a barren family-owned furniture store were vestiges of a once-thriving coal town.

"It's just devastated, like the Great Depression," said Gregory Carper, an attorney who ran a YouthBuild group in Charleston and once lived in Logan. He'd offered to show us around. Many of those who were not already homeless were one payday away from being so. "People here don't know another way of life beyond the mountains," he said. He had arranged our visit to the shelter, as well as a small meeting with its head and members of the community.

On the second floor, we sat in a circle with half a dozen town residents.

"We're proud people, hanging by a string," said a woman who was holding a small dog.

One gentleman, Charlie Curry, worked for Appalachian Power and spoke about the pain he felt having to disconnect electricity service from families that couldn't afford it. "People have to choose whether to pay for power, food, or medication." Charlie's father had worked in the mining industry and suffered black lung and antifreeze poisoning, as well as a broken vertebra, and his employer was trying to deny him the benefits he'd been promised. This was a common theme among laid-off and retired mine workers, who were losing pensions and healthcare coverage as mining companies declared bankruptcy, which allowed them to legally shirk their obligations to employees.

The youngest man present and the most outspoken was Joey Kennedy, thirty-nine, a fifth-generation coal miner who said he'd never missed a shift and had eventually advanced into a $115,000-a-year management job. After seventeen years in the industry, Joey was unceremoniously let go with no severance. He got the news when he was returning from a business trip. Now he was a pastor at his church, and also studying to be a nurse while working the night shift as a hospital orderly. A plastic employee badge was clipped to his navy hospital scrubs. Joey and his wife barely made forty thousand dollars combined. The previous week, the bank had repossessed his pickup truck.

Joey sat next to a graying, slightly heavier version of himself. His father wore jeans and a bright yellow T-shirt, but was more subdued than his son.

My father was similar to these men in a way, but he did not go to work, as so many miners did, knowing they ran a high risk of getting severely ill or injured.

"Would you go back if you could?" I asked Joey.

"Not on your life, plus my wife would kill me." He smiled.

Finally, I asked the group what they wanted people outside Logan and West Virginia to know about their situation. Joey leaned forward as if he'd been ready to answer this question for years.

"Mr. Schultz, if I could let people know one thing. We're not idiots. We're not a bunch of dumb hillbillies. Nothing could be further from the truth. We want to work. We want opportunity. It's just been stripped away from us." Joey was angry at the industry, at government, at the system. A lot of land in West Virginia was held by out-of-state property owners who were not paying state taxes. "If they did," said Joey, "we'd have a safety blanket."

It wasn't that West Virginians expected a handout. They needed, and deserved, a bridge to a second chance.

CHAPTER 21

Gumption

On the quiet outskirts of Huntington, we parked in front of what appeared to be an abandoned factory. We walked inside the hollow shell, where fluorescent lights hung from rafters, revealing snaking pipes and dozens of square pillars that propped up the ceiling. On a wall, a washed-out sign identified the last occupant: CORBIN, LTD., GENTLEMEN'S CLOTHING MAKER.

For decades, this 100,000-square-foot factory had been filled with the hum of rows and rows of sewing machines as seamstresses pieced together pants for the garment manufacturer, whose flat-front slacks were a staple of the well-dressed man after World War II. Corbin had been founded in Brooklyn in the 1940s and moved to West Virginia in 1957, where, reportedly, it was once the largest employer in the area.

Corbin declared bankruptcy in early 2003 and the factory sat idle, collecting dust as well as trash from squatters. It was scheduled for demolition until a young West Virginian, Brandon Dennison, paid a dollar a square foot for the property in 2014. Slowly, Brandon and his team were reclaiming the space as the home for their venture, Coalfield Development Corporation.

We were here to meet Brandon. On the drive, Rajiv told me why. For all the hardships we'd been exposed to since arriving in West Virginia, we'd also encountered inspiring individuals. Angela and Rebecca at Lily's Place. The doctors and caseworkers at Chestnut Ridge. Greg, who ran the YouthBuild group in Charleston. Brandon was a healer of a different ilk, trying to serve West Virginia by injecting jobs, skilled workers, and new businesses into the fledgling economy.

His family had lived in West Virginia for six generations, and he'd grown up in the small town of Ona, the son of two college professors. Brandon had undergraduate degrees in history and political science and a master's in public affairs, and had traveled extensively around the country and the world as part of faith-based outreach and volunteer work. He could have lived anywhere. But he chose to come back home.

A trim young man in blue jeans, with a pen clipped to his breast pocket, walked across the former-factory floor to greet us. With his boyish face, he could have passed for younger than his thirty-one years. We shook hands and he began our tour, thrilled that we were here.

Coalfield Development Corporation, he explained, was a nonprofit network of five social enterprises. Each one provided a product or service West Virginians needed, including solar panels installed on roofs, fresh-grown vegetables, and custom-made wood furniture. The intention was that each enterprise would grow to be its own self-sustaining, for-profit business. For now, Coalfield Development relied on grants, government funding, and private donations to operate. Any money it made was plowed back into the business. It seemed like a lot of variety for a start-up to take on. But diversification is part of Brandon's strategy. Appalachia had become too reliant on a single industry, and he wanted to demonstrate that others could thrive.

Beyond nurturing new businesses, Brandon had a more important goal. Each enterprise existed for the purpose of providing jobs and skills training to unemployed West Virginians.

Many entrepreneurs have a "seed story," an account of the serendipitous moment their skills and interests collided into an idea. For me, that moment was discovering the espresso bars of Milan in my late twenties. Brandon told us his seed story: It was a hot July day several years ago and he was helping to repair an elderly woman's home as part of a community service project. He was in the yard, sweating from the heat, when he looked up. In the distance, through a haze shimmering above the steamy road, he saw two men with tool belts slung over their shoulders walking toward him. "Like a scene out of a movie," he said. The strangers made their way to Brandon and asked if he had work available. Brandon explained that he and his team were volunteers and had no paid jobs to offer. The men went on their way. The polite interaction lasted less than a minute, but it stuck with Brandon. For him, it represented the dilemma facing West Virginia.

"We have smart, energetic, talented people who want to work and learn and be part of something," he said. "But because the economy has become so distressed, the communities have become so depressed, there's no place for that gumption to really be applied."

Gumption. I loved this word. It described the young folks who flooded into the job fairs, the veterans I'd met on military bases. *America,* I thought, *is still an untapped reservoir of gumption.*

We turned a corner and entered a small climate-controlled room dominated by a large unfinished-wood shelving unit. On each shelf, shallow plastic trays of tiny green plants were lined up under bright white grow lights. "Microgreens," Brandon explained. One Coalfield Development enterprise, Refresh Appalachia, sells the nutrient-rich greens to local chefs.

We exited the building and wandered outside through overgrown grasses. Brandon pointed to a "practice" roof where crew members of another enterprise, Rewire Appalachia, were learning to install solar panels. Coalfield Development, he said, was the first licensed solar installer in the southern part of the state. We walked into a high-tunnel greenhouse, where long, narrow strips of planters housed kale, lettuce, spinach, carrots, tomatoes, and green peppers. West Virginia had a shortage of healthy, affordable food. These vegetables were sold at farmers' markets and to food distributors. Elsewhere, Refresh Appalachia was turning mountaintop-removal surface coalfields into sustainable farms, and teaching former miners how to grow and sell their own food.

"Hello!" I waved to a man in sunglasses and jeans working in the greenhouse. He smiled back. Coalfield Development employees are called crew members. Most would have been working in the mining industry if jobs still existed. At Coalfield, they learn multiple trades while getting a classroom education. Each crew member followed a two-and-a-half-year program that each week consisted of thirty-three hours of paid work in an enterprise, six hours of classes toward earning a GED, associate's degree, or professional certification, and three hours of life-skills training in topics like financial literacy and mental and physical health. Coalfield's training classes could also be attended, for free, by anyone interested in obtaining new skills.

Back inside, we passed a gaping hole in the floor, torn up as part of another enterprise, Reclaim Appalachia, which sells salvaged material like wood from buildings slated for destruction. In the basement, the plan was to build a theater and a space for artists.

Then we entered the woodworking shop, where sawdust sprinkled the floor and planks of oak and cherry straddled sawhorses. About half a dozen young men, some in goggles, all in jeans and sturdy work boots, operated bandsaws and lathes. Here, crew members were learning to craft desks, bookshelves, tables—all types of furniture.

Back in the factory's empty main room, Brandon had invited staff and crew members to chat with us. Six long, red-cushioned wood pews had been arranged in a rectangle. The pews were an odd sight among the rubble of industry—Brandon had bought them for a hundred dollars each at a flea market—but the idea of church benches being used in an abandoned factory that was being repurposed to revive people's livelihoods seemed oddly appropriate.

Everyone took a seat. I had many questions, and answers were graciously provided.

"Is there a bias against solar energy in the state?" Heads shook no. One of the young men explained that solar was not deemed anti-coal. At this point, the economy was so depressed all that mattered was whether you had a job.

"Has there ever been a benevolent coal company?" A few, they said. But for years, the corporations had owned the houses their employees lived in, the stores they shopped at, and the livelihoods of entire families, holding the prosperity of multiple generations in their pockets. When the companies left, everything wilted. The region had had to start from scratch. Those in the room seemed resigned to the reality that coal was not returning to West Virginia, despite the promises of some politicians. Everyone here was reinventing himself or herself by creating his or her own blankets. Using his business skills to help them imagine new futures was Brandon's way of sharing his blanket.

"We're trying to build a new story for West Virginia," said Brandon. Not by making the state into something it wasn't, but by drawing on its entrepreneurial roots—and all that gumption.

Outside, a whistling freight train thundered by with such force that I was tempted to look and make sure it wasn't going to burst through the walls.

"What if coal did come back? Would you welcome it?" Many crew members nodded yes. At first I was incredulous. According to the stories I'd heard, most coal companies showed little or no regard for the men on whose backs their money was made. Their practices were the antithesis of how I tried to steer Starbucks. Here in Appalachia, coal companies' egregious disrespect for human life, their sheer lack of responsibility, of compassion, was beyond immoral. And yet these young men said they would go back.

One of Brandon's colleagues must have sensed my confusion. "When something is such a big part of your identity and all you've known, it's hard to separate from it, even when it puts your life at risk," he said.

Their impetus to stay put is different from the restless spirit of reinvention, which comes so naturally to me. As a young man, I had been excited to move across the country to start a new life. But the men sitting with me in this obsolete clothing factory did not want to leave their hometowns. They were connected to coal. To the mountains. Leaving could extinguish that bond, and a sense of self. Relocating, even to more prosperous places, is not an option a lot of miners want. Living and dying in the places where their parents and grandparents made a living, following in their footsteps, upholding their traditions and culture, is, for some, how they define a life of dignity. Being forced to move, to become transient and disconnected, isn't just risky and intimidating, but diminishing in their eyes.

Geography and industry are intertwined with identity for many Americans. This desire to anchor, I thought, is as American as the hunger to explore. Our country's institutions—its businesses and governments—need to do a better job of giving people viable options for both: to root themselves in stable, but evolving and adaptive, communities, or venture out into the dynamic and unknown.

"I struggled to have the imagination for a different future," said a husky man in a short-sleeve navy shirt and a thin baseball cap. I'd seen him in the woodworking shop, and now he introduced himself as Tracy. He said Huntington was a big city compared to his hometown of Dunlow. It had been about three years since Tracy's family and friends had lost their mining jobs and his plans for the future had evaporated. But during his senior year of high school, Tracy had shown up to his welding class and the teacher told him a representative from a nearby company was at school that day, hiring trainees. Tracy interviewed with a rep from Coalfield Development, who invited him to become a member of the crew. He was ready, he said, to work and to learn.

Tracy was now nineteen and finishing the first of his two and a half years at Coalfield. Every day, he cut, sawed, and sanded in the woodshop until 3 P.M., then had a bite to eat and rested, before attending community college classes at 6 P.M. Higher education was never a path he expected to take.

The schoolwork could be frustrating at times, he said, and the schedule tiring. The hourly pay was also about half of what he might have earned working in a mine. And he missed home, so on Fridays he drove an hour and a half back to Dunlow.

But Tracy was not complaining. He was grateful.

This was his chance to opt into the non-coal economy.

By the summer of 2018, more than 120 people had participated in Coalfield Development's unique work-training model, more than 60 of them had completed it, and more than 600 people had taken training classes, many becoming certified in new trades. Tracy Spaulding went on to work in a steel factory, a job he wouldn't have gotten without his Coalfield experience.

Brandon blew me away, as an entrepreneur and as a person. He could have ignored the deteriorating economy in his beloved West Virginia and moved to a more prosperous place. But he refused to be a bystander. Instead, he combined compassion and capitalism to help his brethren reinvent their lives. Building Coalfield Development wasn't just about creating jobs, but about nurturing a spirit of resilience and self-reliance.

Brandon Dennison was not alone in his desire to shepherd change. When the second season of *Upstanders* debuted in the fall of 2017, he was among eleven inspiring men and women we profiled. The exposure drove more private donations to Coalfield Development, and he received calls from people who wanted to emulate his social enterprise model in other rural parts of the country. Starbucks and the Schultz Family Foundation each donated to the cause.

Something Brandon said I have not forgotten: "The story of Appalachia is central to the story of America." The same can be said, I think, about every corner of the country.

CHAPTER 22

Filial Piety

My father, my mom told me over the phone, had been diagnosed with lung cancer. Doctors expected him to live one more year. He was only sixty.

My mother's call had come as Sheri and I were loading our car. It was 1982, and we were planning to leave the next day and drive three thousand miles across the country with our golden retriever in the backseat. We'd arrive on Labor Day weekend in Seattle, where I would begin my new job as head of marketing for Starbucks.

The news shook me. After living with my parents for a while after college, I had rented a small apartment in New York City with a roommate before marrying Sheri. I didn't enjoy going home to my parents' house in Canarsie, where the mood was always heavy. My mother's depression had worsened over the years, and I still didn't talk to my father much, even when we were in the same room. But still, he was my dad. I knew what that meant.

I felt a responsibility to help care for him during what I imagined would be painful months ahead. I also felt that it was my duty to help my mother, who had come to rely on my strength. My younger brother, Michael, was away at college, and my younger sister, Ronnie, lived not far from Canarsie. I was torn. How could I leave New York now? But how could I not? I'd committed to the owners of Starbucks to be in town by early September. I needed to work, not only to help support my soon-to-be-growing family, but to help pay for my parents' housing and healthcare. Plus, I was eager to join the small coffee company. I sensed an opportunity, and I didn't want to lose it.

I went to see my father at the hospital before we took off. My mother was at my dad's bedside, visibly frightened but trying to hold it together. Standing next to him, I experienced an overwhelming mix of deep sadness and unresolved bitterness. These warring emotions, and confusion about whether to delay my move, rendered me almost speechless. This could have been an opportunity for a heart-to-heart between father and son, a moment of reckoning, of apologies, of forgiveness or expressions of love. But we had never developed a relationship where such expression was possible. So I just squeezed his hand.

"Go to Seattle," my dad said. "You and Sheri have a new life to start there."

"You must go," my mother seconded him, her face red and puffy.

My dad and I said an awkward goodbye, and I went back home to finish packing the car under a cloud of guilt and worry. At every stop along the drive to Seattle, I phoned home, not knowing if I would see or talk to my dad again.

When Rachel's mother was first admitted into the hospital with a condition doctors suspected was cancer, she did not tell her daughter right away. Rachel was living and working in Wuhan and her parents lived in Liuzhou, a city in South China, twenty hours away by train. Rachel's mother didn't want her daughter to trek home. She knew the Starbucks store Rachel managed was very busy.

Rachel is Chinese and, like many young people in her country, adopts an American name for her working life.

"Who is going to take care of my mother and father if they have health problems and I live far away?" Rachel asked me rhetorically. Her mother was sitting next to her in a lilac tweed coat, dabbing her eyes with a tissue and rubbing Rachel's back. She had recovered and traveled to Beijing today as a guest of her daughter, and to meet with me.

The two women were obviously close. Since Rachel was a baby, her mother had kept a small notebook documenting her every milestone.

It was spring 2017, and the three of us were sitting among six other Chinese partners and their parents inside a Starbucks store in a Beijing neighborhood known as 798 Art District. Up and down the streets, decommissioned military factories had been renovated into galleries and artist workspaces. Many retained their original concrete, cathedral-like interiors, creating an industrial vibe that, amid the avant-garde art scene and high-end retailers, made this a popular destination in this sprawling city of 21 million people.

I'd been traveling to China several times a year since Starbucks opened its first store here in 1999. The store we were in now was a newer one—a clean-lined, three-story structure with hand-painted murals on the walls. Sunlight streamed in through tall windows, and bits of spring pollen floated inside the room. For more than an hour, with my headset funneling real-time English translations into my ears, I listened as Rachel and her coworkers recalled health ordeals that had beset their families. They had all come to share their personal stories.

Emily's father was a farmer whose education had never gone past elementary school. When Emily was a child, he bought her books so she could learn, and Emily attended college and earned a graduate degree in law. To help pay her tuition, she took a part-time job as a Starbucks barista. After graduating, Emily turned down a university teaching position for a lower-paying, full-time job at Starbucks. Her father could not fathom why his daughter would pass up teaching to work at a coffee shop. Mr. Liu sat upright in his chair. He wore a thin gray sweater vest and stared solemnly ahead as his daughter spoke. Her coworkers were like a second family, she had explained to him, and her customers were like friends. Emily was promoted, and over time her father accepted, even supported, her choice of employer. Now, Emily said, her parents were aging and she wanted to use some of her salary to buy them medical insurance.

For most Chinese citizens, the government pays a portion of basic medical care. But coverage is uneven throughout the country, and out-of-pocket costs to treat chronic diseases or sudden illnesses can easily force a family into poverty. Although many companies in China, including Starbucks, do provide health insurance to employees, the millions of Chinese living in rural areas, folks such as Emily's parents, rely on government funds. Individual insurance policies are expensive, which is why Emily's father refused to let his daughter buy coverage for him and his wife.

The stories I heard from Emily and Rachel echoed a theme: devotion to family. The concept of *xiao,* of filial piety, is a centuries-old Confucian virtue at the center of modern Chinese culture. Belinda Wong, the chief executive officer of Starbucks China, had been tutoring me about this principle for years. "Chinese children see it as our obligation to give our parents a good life, not just financially but with love."

Belinda had also explained that the principle was being complicated as Chinese society underwent dramatic changes. Close to seven million young people were graduating from Chinese colleges each year, and many chose to live thousands of miles from where they were raised, in bigger cities with more jobs and higher pay. Making money is especially important for this generation; most are their parents' only child, and thus their sole caretakers. For many young people, earning a living is about self-sufficiency and achieving their own goals, but also about providing for their families. I could relate, if just a little.

We continued around the circle.

"I was eighteen years old when my mother got sick. I immediately went from a young girl to a woman, because I knew I must grow up to help support my family." June wore a stiff white button-down shirt with black pants. Her hair was pulled back away from her face and her lipstick was bright red. June's mother had battled cancer for more than six years. Her father, a taxi driver, had had to quit his job to help care for his wife, and had sold his car and the family home to pay her medical expenses. June's mother had passed away not long ago, and June's father had traveled ten hours to sit beside his daughter today. His grief was palpable as June told their family saga.

During my years traveling throughout China, I had come to recognize the elevated role that family plays in the culture. But it had never been as clear to me as it was on this day.

"I think my only source of happiness and joy comes from my family," said Summer, a five-year partner in black-rimmed glasses. Summer had originally joined the company for its medical insurance, she said, but over time she befriended her coworkers and, like Emily, considered them family. Summer's father seemed genuinely shocked to even be here.

"Where I am from, a small town, it is almost impossible to think about being invited to meet the big boss," he told us. "I thought it was a joke." So did his coworkers, who cautioned him not to go to Beijing to meet with the Starbucks chairman, insisting it was a scam.

This was not the first meeting of this kind. For the past three years, Starbucks China had invited hundreds of our partners' spouses, children, and parents—some of whom had never left their villages or been on a train or a plane—to Shanghai, Beijing, and Guangzhou as our guests for an annual meeting of families, which we called our Partner Family Forum.

Many parents in China do not think working in the service industry is a worthy job for their children, and we wanted to show them that Starbucks is not just a bunch of coffee shops or a heartless multinational corporation, but a place where full- and part-time workers have healthcare coverage, own stock in the company, and are given housing allowances to help pay for city living—as well as chances to learn new skills, advance their careers, volunteer in communities, and find a second family. The forums were also a way to honor our partners' parents. We wanted to celebrate the family, and to highlight reasons for parents to be proud of their kids, and our partners to be proud of their jobs.

"Thank you for trusting us with your children," I told the parents. Then, I thanked our partners for sharing such personal stories, and turned to Emily's father and asked what his dreams were for his daughter.

"I hope that she should work really hard to develop her potential," he said.

Rachel's mother chimed in: "Every day she is happy, then I am happy."

Before the group discussion ended, another partner summed it up with a universal truth, "Every mother and father has their own way of loving their children."

Despite the dire prognosis my father received in 1982, he lived five more years. As Sheri and I settled into our new home in the Pacific Northwest, I called my parents frequently and flew back to New York as often as I could. My work during those years was hectic and engrossing. I was learning so much about coffee, about retail, and about operating a small business.

It was during this period that I traveled to Milan, got my first whiff of the Italian espresso bar experience, and left Starbucks to start Il Giornale. In fact, the last time I flew my father to Seattle, in 1986, I took him to see the original Il Giornale store that was under construction in the lobby of Seattle's tallest office tower, Columbia Center. Standing in front of the half-built coffee bar, I proudly described my plans to create hundreds of places where people could come sit, visit, and be served Italian-style beverages.

I don't think my dad got it. All he saw was a store. And for him, coffee came from a can and should be brewed in a tin percolator. Why all the fuss with the fancy Italian names? His face didn't register much emotion as he listened to my big plans.

Throughout 1987, my father's lung cancer worsened. Respiratory problems made it difficult for him to breathe, and he was constantly coughing. He spent his final weeks under the watchful eyes of nurses at a medical facility that had special suites for family members. My mom had given up her job as a receptionist to stay with him, my brother was a frequent visitor, and my sister, Ronnie, was a daily presence, routinely conferring with doctors on my parents' behalf.

Just days into the new year, my mother called me in Seattle to let me know that my father would probably not survive longer than forty-eight hours. I took a flight to New York and arrived at his bedside the night before he passed away. Sitting next to him, I put my hand on his and tried to summon childhood memories of going to baseball games and tossing footballs. But painful scenes muscled in.

In that moment, I was sad for him. But maybe sadness was the wrong thing to feel for my father. He had made his choices; he probably had his reasons. Perhaps he was broken from war or financial struggles. Perhaps he had more pleasures in his life than I allowed myself to see. He was quite sociable, a big presence at gatherings. Some people feared him, but he made others laugh. I realized how little I knew this man, or what drove him. All I really knew was what I surmised: that he had never enjoyed the dignity that could come from work, or the pleasure of talking with your kids over dinner about their friends, their sports, their school—as I had known with Addison and Jordan—or the inner pride of personal accomplishment. All I really knew was the way he made me feel.

I was certainly sad for myself. I had continued to cling to a thread of hope that we could inch closer.

My father died at 5 A.M. on January 5, 1988. Once he passed away, any chance of mending our relationship died as well.

His service was held at a funeral home, crowded with family and people he and my mother knew, most from Brooklyn. Despite my dad's limitations and his temper, it was clear that many folks had enjoyed his company. Other mourners showed up to honor my mom, who had stood by him throughout his life and during his final years.

None of his children spoke at the service. Personally, I was still trying to put words to his life, and what it meant to me. Only when my cousin Alan arrived from Florida and we hugged hello did I break down. Alan was the relative with whom I was closest. He understood my complicated history with my father, and my father's volatile personality. As a kid, my cousin felt nurtured by his aunt, but he always feared his uncle.

All of us went to the cemetery. It was a bone-chilling winter day. We gathered in front of the plot reserved for his grave and shivered in the cold.

Not long after my father's death, I saw Billy, my oldest friend and Bayview neighbor. Billy had gone to school for clinical psychology and was living in Germany, teaching at a university. I was over there for business, and one evening the two of us talked for hours over steins of beer. I shared my conflicted feelings: my disdain for my father's laziness and his inability to take financial care of his family—but also my anger at his faceless employers for never showing Fred Schultz the kind of basic human decency that might have kept his self-respect from collapsing. I told Billy that I was trying to reconcile my dad's bursts of violent behavior with the kindness he showed people like Michael Nadel. I felt a responsibility to honor my father, because he was my parent, but I also wished that I'd had a childhood less filled with chaos.

Billy, who unlike me still had his Brooklyn accent, urged me to find peace. "If your dad had been successful, maybe you wouldn't have had as much drive," he told me.

I'm not sure he was right about my childhood being the source of my drive, but it definitely helped shaped what drive I had. It imprinted me with a fear of the financial insecurity that plagued my parents, a dark emotion that became the seed of something brighter.

Throughout my life, I have sought to give others a chance to be their best selves by giving them something I had needed, which was a path to escape from the shadows. Whether we are born into bad situations or manifest our own trials—or both—we all deserve opportunities to emerge from darkness into light and air. My light and air were friends and neighbors, sports and chess, college, my first job, strangers and partners who helped me start, save, and transform a business over decades. And, more than anything, my light and air is my family: Sheri, Jordan, Addison.

All these factors helped me to combat the opposing force of my father.

And yet he, too, showed me light and air.

Had my dad not given me his blessing to move to Seattle after he was diagnosed with cancer in 1982—had he and my mom asked or insisted that I stay on the East Coast—I would have done so. In freeing me to go, my dad allowed me to try to become a stronger version of myself. Both my parents, not just my mom, wanted a better life for their son.

———

One night in 2016, Chalne Xiao was in a hospital in Guangzhou, a city in southern China, watching her mother suffer painful complications from a longtime renal disorder. A doctor came into the room with a stack of paperwork in his hands and asked a tearful Chalne if she had the 30,000 Renminbi (about $4,500) to admit her mother into intensive care. Without the down payment, her mother would likely not receive treatment that might save her life. Chalne's father was at home. Earlier that year, he'd had a stroke, which had left half his body paralyzed. Chalne was already in debt from shouldering previous hospital bills and could not afford the deposit for her mom. The young woman was distraught.

"As an only child, it is my responsibility to take care of my parents when they are ill," she said. After her biological parents had abandoned Chalne, her adoptive mother and father had raised her as their own.

Chalne had been working for Starbucks for nine years and was now a store manager. The night the doctor gave her the ultimatum, she called her district manager, Edgar, who rushed to the hospital and reassured Chalne she was not alone. "He said Starbucks is my family and would always be there for me," she said. Then Edgar helped her apply for a distribution from the company's C.U.P. Fund, the money collected from partners to provide financial assistance to fellow partners in times of need.

Within the week, Chalne received 50,000 RMB from the C.U.P. Fund, and another 130,000 RMB from other partners who'd heard about her situation. For weeks, coworkers accompanied Chalne to the hospital to visit her mother. But in March 2017, a month before she and I met in Beijing, Chalne's mother passed away.

An analysis of C.U.P. Fund requests in China from 2010 through 2016, as well as an internal survey, revealed that an overwhelming number of Chinese partners, about 70 percent, were concerned with, or unable to pay for, their parents' healthcare needs. The C.U.P. Fund was one way to assist, but Belinda and her team had come up with a better idea.

Beginning in June 2017, Starbucks China would provide critical-illness medical insurance to the parents of eligible partners. Immediately, fourteen thousand Chinese partners who had been with the company for at least two years would qualify for coverage of certain medical expenses. No other multinational company in China that we knew of offered such a benefit for parents of employees, and few Chinese companies did either.

A reporter from *China Daily*, the English-language newspaper published by the Chinese government, asked why a company would spend money to help its employees' parents. I had two answers. First, not every business decision Starbucks made had an immediate or measurable economic outcome. What did I mean by this? Parental critical-illness insurance is a benefit that goes beyond what people expect from their employer, especially in China. (In the United States, aging adults are already covered by Medicare.) When our company exceeds our partners' expectations, it induces loyalty and pride, which in turn motivates them to treat their customers well and stay with the company. I also told the reporter that the parental benefit was personal for me. I mentioned the accident that had left my father in a cast and out of work with no financial support. "We all have childhood experiences that shape our lives," I said.

Belinda explained the benefit in another way: "With this new investment, we are redefining the role and responsibility of multinational companies in China." The question I'd posed publicly three years earlier—*What is the role and responsibility of a for-profit company today?*—was not meant to be asked only in America, but in all places where Starbucks had stores. Belinda had answered the question in her own way, in a country where Starbucks had originally struggled to succeed.

Starbucks' long history in China has provided me with a unique perspective on this beautiful, powerful country. I came to know the culture through thousands of conversations with Chinese citizens, by learning its history, and by meeting government officials.

Starbucks entered China in 1999, against the advice of many people who insisted the tea-drinking culture would never accept coffee, especially served in paper cups. But skeptics failed to see that as China's economic and social reforms produced more educated citizens, higher-paying jobs, an emerging middle class, and a populace increasingly connected, virtually, to each other and the world beyond the country's borders, it was also creating a niche for the larger experience Starbucks offered its customers. Urban areas like Shanghai, Shenzhen, and Guangzhou, as well as dozens of other cities with populations over one million, swelled with construction. As new residents flowed in, Starbucks' clean, comfortable environments became natural extensions of home and work for urban dwellers, especially those young people, whose apartments and offices were quite small. Just as in America, our stores became an accessible, upscale third place to meet up with people or hang out alone. But unlike in America, where the morning coffee ritual keeps our stores busiest during earlier hours, Starbucks China stores were most crowded in the afternoons and evenings.

And yet our business in China wasn't profitable for years. When we first arrived, Starbucks was just learning how to be a global enterprise. In regions like the Middle East, we licensed the right to oversee our stores to local retail experts. When it came to China, we licensed some stores' operations but controlled other stores from Seattle, which was a mistake. People at our headquarters had too much power over Chinese operations, to the point that they dictated how the telephone system was set up in our Shanghai office, and the spelling of drink names on menu boards. The whole setup was inefficient and cost us money.

When I came under pressure from investors and other people inside the company to close our China operations because they were unprofitable, I refused to bow to their short-term perspective. I knew instinctively we had to find a way to succeed in China, and so I stayed bullish on our prospects in the country. China is the world's second-largest economy, after the United States, and by 2022 more than 600 million Chinese are expected to qualify as middle class. With so many potential customers, success here would contribute to Starbucks' overall financial performance for years to come. We could get it right, if we learned from our mistakes.

In 2011, I threw myself into our Chinese operations to demonstrate to everyone how much I believed in the region and to emphasize how strategic it was to our company's success. We decentralized the management of Starbucks China and put Belinda Wong in charge. Belinda was born in Hong Kong, attended middle school and high school in the United States, and went to college in Vancouver, Canada. The day after graduating with a bachelor of commerce degree with a major in finance, she moved back to Hong Kong and began a career that would lead her to Starbucks, where she would rise to oversee a $1.2 billion business. She knew the Chinese market and had the scent of what our Chinese partners and customers wanted. Belinda also shared my values, and understood that her job was to build Starbucks into a different kind of company by achieving a balance between profitability and a social conscience in her native country. I trusted Belinda, and made sure she knew she had my full support. As she made decisions without seeking the approval of those of us in Seattle, I promised that I would have her back.

Decentralizing the management of our business in China was a seminal decision. No other business unit in the company was autonomous, and many people were uncomfortable with it. But that's what was required so we could grow in this uniquely important market. It was only possible because of the trusting relationship Belinda and I shared.

Operating as a separate business entity, basically a contained structure, freed Belinda to make big decisions. She and her team built a design studio in China to architect the country's stores. They directed our partners' volunteer activities and charitable giving to reflect the needs of Chinese communities, focusing on entrepreneurialism and the environment. They created Starbucks University, to teach partners business skills. They partnered with China's largest social network to create a program so customers could send each other Starbucks gift certificates via social media. And they offered our partners new benefits, like housing allowances and sabbaticals and critical-illness insurance for parents. Belinda also fostered—through programs and how she treated partners—the "second-family" feeling that Emily, Rachel, and others told me was one reason they stayed at the company.

And although Belinda was a compassionate soul, she did not relinquish her high expectations or shy from confrontation, especially with me. The two of us expressed our different opinions over the years in frank talks that were always informed by mutual respect.

From 2010 to 2017, Starbucks' store count in the China region increased from 406 to 3,000, while revenue rose from $128 million to $1.2 billion. By 2017, each week, more than eight million Chinese customers were visiting stores in more than 131 cities on mainland China alone. China was Starbucks' largest market outside the U.S., and our fastest-growing one. We were opening a new store in China every fifteen hours, which meant we were creating ten thousand new jobs annually.

The Chinese government had been watching our progress for years. In 2010, I was touring a new farmer support center that Starbucks was building in rural Yunnan Province to help grow coffee. While at the farm, a Chinese colleague received an unexpected email.

"Jiang Zemin is interested to meet with you in Beijing," he whispered in my ear. The former president of the People's Republic of China had spent more than a decade at the highest levels of Chinese government. He was credited with guiding China through economic reforms and opening the country to the outside world.

We rejiggered our schedule and took a 1,200-mile detour to see the former president at his private office.

We arrived at a well-guarded building on the outskirts of the city and waited, intensely curious and a tad anxious. We still didn't know why he was interested in seeing us so urgently. Finally we were led to a large hall where two stately chairs were arranged side by side, with an interpreter behind each. One chair was for me, and one was for the former Chinese president. My colleagues sat on the side of the room as I was introduced to an affable, full-faced gentlemen with large round glasses. Ex-President Jiang and I took our seats.

I noticed Jiang was holding something in his hand. Looking closely, I realized it was my first book, *Pour Your Heart Into It,* translated into Chinese. He'd read the book, he said, and then he asked me to tell him my story, right then and there, in my own words.

Taken aback, I cracked a joke. "Do you want the short version or the long version?"

"As you can see," he replied, "I'm an old, retired man and don't have much to do, so give me the long version." Others in the room laughed. I was happy to take the former president through the tale.

I disagree with Chinese governing philosophy on many fronts, especially with regard to its restricting human rights and reining in free speech. But doing business in China has not compromised how Starbucks treats its people. If our principles of inclusion, equality, and respect for human beings regardless of skin color, gender, religion, politics, or background were not embraced by thousands of our Chinese partners, and by millions of Chinese customers, we would not be successful there.

In countries outside the United States where Starbucks does business, I do not believe the company is in a position to proactively effect social and political change to the degree we might in the United States, where being an American company gives us theoretical license to try. We do not have such an expansive license in other countries. We can, however, exercise our values by how we conduct business, and share those values with leaders in other lands to show that you can be profitable and morally centered at the same time. The day after the partner parent insurance benefit was announced in China, Belinda wrote to me in an email. "We have created a storm in the insurance industry and many companies in China." Executives from other businesses were calling her staff to learn more about it. "We really are setting a great example for other companies, inspiring them to do more for their employees." Chinese media coverage emphasized Starbucks' conscience and values.

In China, I've accepted invitations to speak at other companies and universities, as well as established relationships with government officials. In Beijing in 2017, the live broadcast of a talk I gave at the Tsinghua University School of Economic Management, the country's premier business school, was watched by more than 16 million viewers. Moments such as this, and more intimate conversations like the sitdown with Jiang Zemin, are chances to tell Starbucks' story, which is one way to evoke change.

Some may think that this is not enough and that Starbucks should have done more to push change in China or get out. But just as I persevered in my decision to stay put in China when my colleagues wanted us to leave, I also would argue that remaining deeply engaged in China now is all the more important.

During my visit in April 2017, I had private meetings with other government leaders, including Wang Yang, the vice premier of the State Council, and Wang Jiarui, the vice chairman of the Chinese People's Political Consultative Conference—and we did talk about China's efforts to foster a more transparent and fair business environment for foreign companies. These leaders also asked me about Starbucks' new insurance program for parents of partners.

Earlier, in 2015, when President Xi Jinping visited Seattle, I sat with him during a meeting of U.S. business leaders. My take from these and other encounters with Chinese officials is that they appreciated the contribution that Starbucks goods and services provided their country, as well as how we did business. As a result, the Chinese government has respectfully let us run our company in their country in ways we believe are right.

I'd also established a friendship with Jack Ma, the cofounder and chairman of Alibaba Group, often referred to as the Amazon of China. Alibaba was founded the same year Starbucks opened its first store in China, in 1999, and by 2018 had become one of the most valuable companies in the world, worth more than $500 billion. Jack and I were drawn together by our entrepreneurial pasts and established a warm friendship. When Starbucks opened a magnificent new thirty-thousand-square-foot store in Shanghai, its largest and most innovative store in the world, which included a fully functioning coffee bean roastery, I asked Jack to speak at the launch party.

"Eighteen years ago, nobody imagined you could sell coffee like this in China," he said. "I told my wife, 'I don't like coffee but I like Starbucks.'"

The acceptance of Starbucks in China is indicative of why the company exists in more than seventy-seven countries. In each new market, we must earn our customers' business every day, and we do that in so many far-flung places—from the Middle East to Eastern Europe to South America—because the experience we try to create in our stores is universally appealing. As Jack Ma implied, coffee is only part of that experience. The other part is a sense of community. In each country, we try to interpret our values in a way that means something for that society.

More than pioneering a coffee-drinking culture in China, Starbucks was practicing our brand of leadership.

In the years after my father's death, my mother's health steadily declined. She developed dementia, and became more angry and detached from her family. I believe the hostility she often expressed was a manifestation of her ongoing depression. There was nothing I could do to change who she was or what she was going through, so during my adult years I tried to accept this version of my mother.

When my mother became too ill to take care of herself or to be cared for by family, a friend helped me locate an assisted living facility not far from my brother's home on the East Coast. Michael bore the brunt of the caretaking responsibility for my mother during the final and most difficult years of her life, and I've always appreciated his unique commitment to her.

Sometimes when we spoke, she became lucid and shed her vitriol. "I did the best I could," she said to me more than once.

There were times in my life when I felt my mother's best was not good enough. Could or should she have defended me, emotionally and physically, from my father?

Our relationships with our parents are usually complicated. As children, we may hold them up as idols, but as we get older we see them as the imperfect human beings we all are. As a result, we both judge and forgive our parents for their inevitable flaws, often in that order. This was certainly true for me.

Given her poor health, my mom's passing in June 2013 did not shock her family. But her funeral was starkly different from my father's. It was held on a warm, beautiful day with only a handful of family members at the gravesite, next to my father's headstone. I watched as my mother's casket was lowered into the soft ground in front of us.

I had struggled mightily writing her eulogy. As with my father, my emotions about my mother were still conflicted at the time of her death. I loved both my parents, had tried mightily to understand and respect them, and was grateful for the foundation they provided me. But as I grew up, I never felt confident that they had my back. It was only after I fell in love with Sheri that I no longer felt like I was on my own in the world. Just writing some of these words hurts, because even up until their deaths, I yearned for a different relationship with each of my parents. I like to imagine they did, too. But none of us figured out how to get there.

When the time came for me to give the eulogy at my mother's grave, I was unable to read the words I had written down. They weren't authentic to how I felt in the moment. I wanted to honor my mother. And I knew I had to be honest, with myself and with my family. Overcome with loss and anxiety, guilt and grief, I needed to say goodbye in my own way.

I folded up the paper I had in my hands and turned away from my family to face my mother. Peering into her grave, I could see her coffin, now deep in the ground. Tears and unexpected thoughts flooded out of me. I leaned over and I told my mother—and my father—that I knew they had done the best they could. And then I apologized. I said I was sorry, so very sorry, for thinking otherwise. How I wish I had said this to each of them before they died. Especially Dad. But I finally believed it. In that moment, I understood they had done their best.

Next to the hollow grave was a pile of fresh soil and a shovel. I picked up the spade, plunged it into the pile, scooped up some dirt, and dropped dark pieces of land into the gaping hole. The dirt hit my mother's casket with a definitive thump that echoed in the silent cemetery. Other family members walked up behind me. One by one, each took the shovel and repeated the Jewish tradition of participating in the burial of a loved one.

Filling a grave in this manner can be one of the most painful but also healing parts of a Jewish funeral. All I know is that each punctuating thump of ground drained me of disappointment and filled me with sorrow as I stood next to my mom and said goodbye.

CHAPTER 23

Welcoming Places

Mary Poole was sitting on the couch in her living room in Missoula, Montana, nursing her son, Jack, and scrolling through her newsfeed when her eyes locked onto a photo. A little boy wearing a red shirt, blue shorts, and brown shoes was lying facedown in smooth, wet sand, arms at his side. At first Mary thought it was a picture of a kid on vacation. Then she looked a little closer.

Alan Kurdi was a three-year-old Syrian boy whose family was trying to flee their civil-war-ravaged country when he drowned in the Mediterranean Sea. The family had been attempting to seek asylum in Greece. Alan's brother and mother also perished.

Mary cradled her son Jack in her arms and stared at the photo through the lens of a parent. She knew from her own experience that being a new mother could be emotionally trying, even when you have a safe place to live. She could not imagine what it must feel like for parents with young children to run from their homeland.

Staring at Alan, Mary felt a pang of despair. She also felt a desire to help. She donated twenty dollars to the United Nations High Commissioner for Refugees, but it felt insufficient.

Mary didn't know much about the plight, policies, or politics of the world's refugees. But she did know herself, and few things had ever moved her like the drowned little boy.

Mary wasn't alone. The tragic photograph was drawing worldwide attention to the millions of people trying to escape Syria as its civil war raged into its fifth year. Mary spoke to one of her friends, who suggested that there might be something they could do for Syrian families—even bring them to Missoula. Mary wasn't an activist. She had no background in nonprofit work, or experience fundraising and organizing volunteer efforts. She also didn't know the difference between a refugee and an immigrant or a displaced citizen. But she would learn.

When her son Jack napped, she would go online and begin to educate herself about refugees.

"Refugee," she found out, is a legal term. It defines people who are forced to flee from their countries because of war, persecution, or natural disasters. International law gives refugees the right to be protected by the country in which they seek asylum, and most refugees seek asylum in nations that border their own because they're the easiest to get to. The countries closest to the world's most dangerous conflicts—in Syria, Burma, the Democratic Republic of the Congo, Iraq, Afghanistan—tend to be poor or in the midst of their own conflicts, and the number of wealthy countries willing to accept refugees was dwindling. Under President Obama, the U.S. had capped the number of refugees it would allow into the country at 110,000 beginning in 2017, a sliver of the estimated 21 million refugees worldwide.

The photo of Alan Kurdi gave the crisis a human face. It also gave Mary a choice: she could feel sad and then go about her day, or she could do something about it.

One week after Donald Trump was sworn in as president of the United States in 2017, he signed an executive order immediately halting all refugee admissions into the country for 120 days. The order also barred all people from seven predominantly Muslim countries, including an indefinite ban on all Syrian refugees.

I took the news with a heavy heart and had concerns about its implications. The executive order was not about practicality or safety.

Many people, including me, viewed the order—in its intention, as written, and as executed—as inhumane and discriminatory. It was a blatant attempt by the president to uphold a promise he'd made during his campaign, in which he vowed to enact a "total and complete shutdown of Muslims entering the United States." Aside from its bigotry, the order's message also risked alienating our allies with predominantly Muslim populations.

As promoted by the administration, the order also perpetuated the false narrative that refugees were a threat to the safety of American citizens. The truth was that refugees are the most heavily vetted group trying to enter the United States. The security checks and already extensive vetting refugees underwent before entering the country could take years. Facts about refugees also contradict the fear-filled rhetoric: One extensive study found that nine of the ten communities that resettled the most refugees between 2006 and 2015 had become more safe. Those towns' rates of violent and property crimes actually fell. The one place that experienced more crime, in Massachusetts, was suffering from the ravages of the opioid epidemic—not from issues related to resettling refugees.

America's support for refugees may also be a moral obligation in instances when U.S. foreign policy has played a role in creating or perpetuating the humanitarian crises that result in people having to leave their homeland. To cast refugees as dangerous was not only a false argument but, in my view, un-American. To ignore our country's role in their lives' upheaval was an abdication of our nation's responsibility.

I looked up the words that famously greeted generations of European immigrants to America, from the poem "The New Colossus" by Emma Lazarus, mounted on a plaque inside the Statue of Liberty's pedestal:

Not like the brazen giant of Greek fame,
With conquering limbs astride from land to land;
Here at our sea-washed, sunset gates shall stand
A mighty woman with a torch, whose flame
Is the imprisoned lightning, and her name
Mother of Exiles. From her beacon-hand

Glows world-wide welcome; her mild eyes command
The air-bridged harbor that twin cities frame.
"Keep, ancient lands, your storied pomp!" cries she
With silent lips. "Give me your tired, your poor,
Your huddled masses yearning to breathe free,
The wretched refuse of your teeming shore.
Send these, the homeless, tempest-tossed to me,
I lift my lamp beside the golden door!"

The openness and generosity articulated in this poem has for generations spoken to America's unique strength: we are a country of immigrants, refugees, exiles, migrants, captives, and natives that became a global power. The refugee ban was its opposite: it stoked unfounded fears at home and telegraphed to the world that America was not the country we claimed to be.

In Montana, Mary Poole had been busy. Once she committed to her project of making Missoula a city that welcomed refugees, she needed to corral local support. Only then could she petition a refugee resettlement agency to open an office in Missoula. Once that process began, the agency would ask the State Department for its approval.

One of the first people she went to see was the mayor. As it turned out, the mayor's grandparents had emigrated by boat from Norway and settled in North Dakota. He believed that the American Dream wasn't reserved for people born in the United States. The good people in Missoula, he said, had an obligation to help folks in need, even if those people were outside their city.

Along the way, Mary formed a nonprofit organization named Soft Landing Missoula, which would focus on advocating for refugees and building a supportive, welcoming community where refugees could thrive. Soft Landing volunteers spent months meeting with city council members, community organizations, church groups, and officials who oversaw housing, education, and healthcare. Most agreed that helping families settle in their city was something they could do.

When her efforts made local news, Mary received calls and letters of support. But the story also attracted dissenters. Soft Landing Missoula's Facebook page got nasty posts, and the organization got calls, emails, and letters with death threats. One day, about a dozen people showed up at the courthouse to protest the settlement of refugees in Montana, which was one of only two states that did not have a refugee resettlement program. The protesters argued that refugees from Syria and other Muslim-majority nations were a threat to the country. One man called it a government-sponsored invasion.

Fear and anger did not derail Mary. Instead, she invited several of the protestors to join her for a beer at a local microbrewery. "Everyone deserves to have their voice heard," she said. After listening to their concerns, she shared facts that she had learned.

"It never became about convincing anyone to wholeheartedly agree that I was right and they were wrong," she said. "Our work is to create a welcoming community for refugees in Missoula. If we create a situation where everyone feels comfortable to welcome people whether or not they fundamentally, politically believe in resettling refugees, then we've done our job."

As they talked over beers, Mary and those who challenged her efforts discovered they had mutual interests, like kayaking, music, and the outdoors. And they, too, believed in "compassion toward neighbors," Mary learned. She did not win everyone over, but they respected each other.

The State Department eventually named Missoula a host city. The first refugees arrived in 2016, a family of six from the Democratic Republic of the Congo, an unstable country with a history of political violence and government repression. Mary recalled bringing them to a farmers' market. As they walked down the street, the mother looked around at her new surroundings. She did not yet speak English, only Swahili. "Missoula, Missoula," she said out loud.

"Home," said Mary.

The woman smiled. "Missoula home."

———

Within hours after President Trump signed the executive order initiating the so-called Muslim ban, people began protesting online, in person, in court, and in writing.

I wanted Starbucks to stand up in a way that reflected our values. The question my colleagues and I asked was how to productively express our dissent.

Starbucks did have a history of supporting refugees. The Starbucks Foundation, our charitable arm, gave financial relief for families fleeing civil conflict through its contributions to Save the Children, and two regional European charities in September 2015. More recently, as the refugee crisis in central and western Europe intensified, Starbucks also joined with the White House and a coalition of companies working to encourage their customers' support of American Red Cross efforts to aid refugees and migrants.

I consulted with Starbucks' chief operating officer, Kevin Johnson. Kevin had been a member of Starbucks' board of directors for six years before becoming our chief operating officer in 2015 and helping me lead the company. He was a person of strong character and compassion.

Together, Kevin, Vivek Varma, Virginia Tenpenny, John Kelly, who headed Starbucks' social impact efforts, and I agreed that the company needed to do something more substantial than just raise awareness or raise money. We decided to accelerate an existing effort to hire refugees in countries where they were seeking asylum or refuge, and where we had stores. There was not yet a specific plan in place, but the controversial order had captured the country's attention. This was a moment to inject a positive message into the national dialogue: when the country was shutting its doors, Starbucks was saying, "We welcome you," not just in the U.S. but around the world. As John put it, our intention was to recapture the humanity that America had shown refugees for decades, which was the opposite of what the current administration was putting forth.

On January 29, 2017, Starbucks announced it would hire ten thousand refugees around the world over the next five years.

We expected some backlash, but we did not anticipate being

accused of helping foreigners at the expense of U.S. veterans who were also struggling to find jobs. The false claim that we were ignoring servicemen and servicewomen gained traction on social media, lobbed by people unaware of the company's ongoing efforts to hire veterans. We had already employed more than 8,800 veterans and military spouses through that initiative, and expected to reach our goal of 10,000 earlier than planned.

The false accusations became news, which especially upset the servicemen and servicewomen who already worked for us. At our headquarters, partners from our Armed Forces Network came together to write a public letter to address the misinformation circulating:

> We respect honest debate and the freedom of expression. Many of us served to protect that very right, and some of our brothers and sisters died protecting it. But to those who would suggest Starbucks is not committed to hiring veterans, we are here to say: check your facts, Starbucks is already there.

That it remained so easy for social media to misrepresent the company was a little inevitable, but also our fault. Those of us at Starbucks often assumed that people outside our walls knew us as well as we knew ourselves.

The blowback was a temporary distraction. We stayed the course and our partners stepped up. Majd Baniodeh was a graduate student who had spent the past year at Starbucks researching ethical sourcing in the dairy industry for her thesis. When she heard about the refugee program, she told John Kelly she wanted to be part of it. Majd was a Palestinian who had come to the United States from her home in the West Bank at age fourteen to escape the deadly violence of the Israeli-Palestinian conflict. She arrived in Seattle as part of a U.S. State Department program created after 9/11 to promote conversations and understanding between Middle Eastern students and American families. She moved in with a Jewish family and quickly bonded with her hosts, who began referring to Majd as their daughter and sister.

Majd's biological mother is black and her father is Arab, and her husband is half Filipino and half Caucasian. In her homeland as well as in the United States, she knew how unsettling it could feel to be "different." She also had a history of accepting as well as loving people who were different from her. For Majd, helping Starbucks recruit refugees seemed a personal calling. It was her chance to make others feel welcome.

When she began overseeing Starbucks' refugee hiring efforts in the United States, the nation's political environment was contentious. Resources for refugee resettling and vetting services were also dwindling. The country had no existing system that connected corporations with refugees looking for work; most were placed at small businesses that only hired one or two, and usually for entry-level positions at warehouses, hotels, and restaurants, jobs that were often hard to fill. When Majd reached out to resettlement agencies and told them Starbucks was actively hiring, some staffers cried with joy. Not many corporations came to them. The hiring pledge sent a message: refugees are worthy of work.

Most refugees who come into the United States are highly educated. Some speak English fluently. Some must learn the language. Majd was hiring civil engineers, dentists, and lawyers to be baristas and store managers, as well as to work in our roasting plants.

By the summer of 2018, Starbucks had hired more than one thousand refugees around the world. It was well below the goal as we tried to navigate the challenges unique to refugees, but the company continues partnering with organizations to accelerate the path to employment for more people seeking a better life.

We had learned a great deal in a short time. Refugees do not tend to self-identify when applying for jobs, often out of fear or shame. But those who gain entry arrive ready to be employed. Many must pay back agencies for the cost of their one-way airplane tickets and then work to support themselves. Some will go back to school and résumé their professions. Many go on to make great contributions to American life. Albert Einstein, former secretary of state Madeleine Albright, performer Gloria Estefan, and Google cofounder Sergey Brin were all refugees; they came here from Germany in 1933, Czechoslovakia in

1948, Cuba in 1960, and Russia in 1979, respectively. Majd Baniodeh, who continues to hire refugees in the United States, arrived in 2005.

American culture and our economy benefit when people with drive and talent choose to ply their trades and grow their careers within our borders, and when people in other countries frequent our businesses and buy our products. Starbucks is but one example of a U.S.-based global company that needs to attract a diverse array of employees and customers, at home and abroad.

In 2018, President Trump further cut the number of refugees that would be allowed into the United States to 30,000 in 2019, a record low.

Hate undermines democracy, and squelches the soul of those who spew it and hear it. But hate also hurts our economy. Hate cannot be normalized.

Organizers billed their protest in Charlottesville, Virginia, as a rally to unite white nationalists. The scenes I watched showed red flags emblazoned with swastikas, lines of people carrying torches, chants of "Our blood, our soil!" "You will not replace us!" "Jews will not replace us!" I watched in horror and dismay, appalled at the vile cries of white supremacists and anti-Semites who paraded without hoods.

In Seattle, I called an open forum at Starbucks headquarters. More than six hundred people gathered in a new conference center on the third floor. Hundreds more watched the forum live on screens around the building. Standing in the middle of the room, encircled by seated and standing partners, I held up a ruddy, triangle-shaped rock the size of a fig. I asked that the stone be passed around the room.

Seventeen years ago, I told everyone, I went with a friend to Auschwitz. It was the largest concentration and extermination camp established by the German government. The day we visited was cold and gray. As we walked the grounds, we passed rows of two-story brick barracks where tens of thousands of prisoners had been forced to live in rooms so overcrowded that people had to sleep on their sides at night. We stepped over the long, snaking train tracks that had carried thousands of windowless cattle cars here, packed with people from across Europe. Here, they came to work and to die, guilty of nothing more than being Jewish, or gay, or for having different political beliefs and ethnicities than the ruling Nazi party.

We peered into the hollow rooms of former gas chambers designed for mass exterminations. We gazed up at their roofs, where chimney stacks once belched the thick dark smoke of human remains. I could not wrap my head around the inhumanity that had unfolded in the place we now stood. More than 1.1 million men, women, and children had died in Auschwitz alone. More than 6 million Jews were killed by the time the war ended and Allied Forces liberated Europe. Generations destroyed in a matter of years.

The hours we spent at Auschwitz gave me a gruesome vision of evil. *How does such systematic horror happen in our modern age?* I remember thinking. *How does it begin? How does it end?*

Just outside the camp, I bent down and reached into the mud and sand. The stone I picked up has sat on my desk ever since. It's there to remind me not of past horrors, but of the courage and the will that is possible, and required, to defeat evil.

After I shared the story of my visit and the rock with everyone, I looked around the room.

"I come to you as an American, as a Jew, as a parent, as a grandparent, as an almost forty-year partner of our company," I said. I then spoke about my profound concern about what the events in Charlottesville might mean for young children and future generations. "We are imprinting them with behaviors and conduct that are beneath the United States of America," I said.

When the stone was passed to Heidi Peiper, a mother and a thirteen-year partner who wrote for Starbucks' website, she stopped taking notes on her laptop to hold it. In her hand it felt warm.

"The rock that is going around the room is the heritage of my ancestors," I said.

I was referring to the Jewish people. My own great-grandparents had come to America decades before World War II.

My paternal great-grandfather, Max, was twenty-four when he

emigrated in 1892 from a small town called Belz, which was then part of the Austro-Hungarian empire and is now part of Ukraine, just a few miles across the border from Poland. Max was a fair-haired, gray-eyed, stout man. A tailor, he arrived with no more than ten dollars in his pocket. Three years later, his wife, Rebecca, arrived in New York Harbor with their three boys, including my grandfather Harry, who was just two years old.

On my mother's side, my great-grandfather Morris Lederman and my great-grandmother Leah were born in Russia and resettled in England, where their daughter, Esther, and sons, Woolf and Lareal, were born. The family lived in a one-room apartment in East London. Morris was a barrel maker. He came to the United States, followed by Leah and their three children, in 1919, on a ship with more than 2,800 passengers. My grandfather Woolf was a blue-eyed nine-year-old. He would grow up not far from the site of the future Bayview projects, never receiving more than an eighth-grade education.

My family came to the country during a period of mass migration of Jews, primarily from Eastern European countries. Jewish immigration has been a part of U.S. history since its earliest years. But between 1880 to 1920, America experienced an influx of Jewish people trying to escape years of oppression, segregation, and government-sponsored brutality in countries under Russian rule. During World War II, the 1,500 Jews still living in Belz—the small town from which my great-grandfather emigrated—were sent to a death camp. The chances I had relatives among those who died are high.

I didn't talk about my own family history at the open forum, but I told the partners that I'd called us together to provide a safe, loving environment to share our concerns, our feelings.

Nearly two dozen partners spoke with an honesty similar to that exhibited at the race open forums more than three years earlier. A father who had emigrated from India said that he did not know how to answer his daughter when she asked why their family chose to live in America. He wanted to give her hope, but these days he was at a loss for words.

It was a time for contemplation.

America is one of the few countries in the world that is made up of all peoples of the world. I personally believe we are exceptional not because we are a nation of immigrants, but because of *why* we have immigrants. Why do people want to come here? They come for an idea. An idea so powerful, so inherent to humanity, that it transcends time and geographic borders: the idea that all people are created equal and have a right to life, liberty, and the pursuit of happiness.

Equality for all was not the original intent of the Declaration of Independence. When the founders wrote "all men are created equal," they were excluding women, black slaves, and Native Americans. People in every generation in American history have fought to define what that declaration meant. Some to expand the definition. Others to freeze it or violently retract it. Over time and through trials, the meaning has become more capacious and inclusive. But equality for all is still an idea that has yet to be realized in practice. Every generation must keep up the fight to make those words real, to live up to a 250-year-old ideal that continues to capture imaginations because it is so universally appealing.

I am a product of immigrants. A product of my ancestors' courage, luck, and sweat. Of their mistakes, shortcomings, and failures. I am also a product of the idea of America.

I can be a bit romantic about history, but I'm also pragmatic about the present. America cannot, of course, have open borders. We need a clear, sustainable immigration policy, one that better manages the flow of people who do not pose a threat and can contribute to our economy and culture. Immigration laws can be sensible without extinguishing the *idea* that brought so many here and compels so many to stay.

"We are all walking through life with our own aspirations," I said as the open forum came to a close. "There's no country I'd rather be from, no country I'd rather go home to, than the United States of America. . . . Every one of us, and our parents and grandparents, can probably highlight a moment in the history of the country that we were deeply disappointed by. But the ideal, the aspiration and the promise of the country, despite this moment in time, is still within our grasp."

———

A few weeks before the rally in Charlottesville, I had visited Gettysburg, Pennsylvania. I'd never been to the preserved Civil War battlefield, and I had asked Professor Nancy Koehn to join me.

Nancy is a historian, author, and popular lecturer at Harvard Business School. She has used Starbucks case studies in her teaching, and so much of her research focuses on historic leaders, in particular Abraham Lincoln. Nancy, a vivid storyteller, has the rare ability to recast history in a modern-day context. Her insights remain relevant even decades after her main characters have died.

I'd known Nancy since the mid-1990s. In 2013, I invited her to speak at Starbucks' annual shareholders' meeting about the nature of leadership.

"Just tell us what you tell your students," I said.

She took the stage with her signature straight talk. "Leaders are not born in some kind of lovely, shake-and-bake kind of way, or cut from the rib of Zeus," she said. Her petite frame paced the stage. "They are made and they allow themselves to be made and they participate in their own making. . . . The path you walk is actually the best classroom you will ever find."

Experience, she said, is the clay that leaders shape into wisdom.

In Gettysburg, I wanted Nancy's wisdom by my side. As we walked, she talked about the bloody battle that took place during the sweltering summer of 1863, among the boulders and low-lying hills around us. More than forty thousand Union and Confederate soldiers, black men as well as white men, died or were wounded here.

The Battle of Gettysburg and the Civil War, Nancy posited, were microcosms of a larger conflict: a struggle between two visions of American identity. The nation was splitting apart over the issue of slavery. At the start of his presidency, Lincoln wasn't sure what to do about slavery and the almost four million African Americans held in bondage.

"Initially, he had no grand plan other than to save the union," said Nancy. After the massive loss of life in Gettysburg, it was Lincoln's brief but brilliant Gettysburg Address that helped move the country forward by reframing the Declaration of Independence as the essence of the true promise of America—that *all* men, black as well as white, are created equal:

> Four score and seven years ago our fathers brought forth on this continent, a new nation, conceived in Liberty, and dedicated to the proposition that all men are created equal.
>
> Now we are engaged in a great civil war, testing whether that nation, or any nation so conceived, and so dedicated, can long endure. . . .
>
> It is for us the living, rather, to be dedicated here to the unfinished work which they who fought here have thus far so nobly advanced. It is rather for us to be here dedicated to the great task remaining before us.

Nancy's explanation of Lincoln's address was that after even the most violent, deadly discord, societies have opportunities to self-correct. To emerge better versions of themselves.

After the hate-filled rallies in Charlottesville, I thought about what Nancy had said. The country certainly was not in civil war, but we were experiencing a period of division beyond incivility. How could we self-correct?

Speaking up was a first and necessary step. Together, Nancy and I penned an editorial for the *Financial Times*:

> We look to leaders to condemn vitriol and intolerance. . . . But not enough of our elected officials are using their voice with due force and eloquence to elevate the ideal of equality. We implore all elected officials to speak their conscience with more conviction. History shows that silence is unforgivable, for it gives bigotry license. And when meek words masquerade as moral courage, they are perceived as indifference and give the worst of human nature permission to flourish.

The bold, unapologetic racism that was on the march in Charlottesville was undeniable, as was the discriminatory nature of the president's executive order. And that same bigotry was on display in the anti-refugee posts to the Facebook page of Soft Landing Missoula.

Mary Poole was profiled in the second season of the Starbucks' *Upstanders* series in October 2017. At that time, more than thirty refugee families from the Congo, Eritrea, Iraq, and Syria were living in Missoula. More than six hundred residents had signed up to volunteer with Soft Landing—far more than the group needed.

When I went to Missoula and met with Mary, she was cradling her second child, a daughter, in her arms. She told me about an older gentleman who had been skeptical about refugees coming to Montana and had posted mean comments online. When Mary met with him a few years back, he had asked a lot of questions. How would the refugees be vetted? How would they learn English? Would they be employable? Now, the man lived next door to a Congolese family. "It was completely coincidental," said Mary. "They share food, exchange gifts. They're wonderful neighbors." When the family moved in, his wife had baked them a loaf of bread.

From her beacon-hand glows world-wide welcome . . .

Around the country, citizens like Mary were reaching out to refugees. But the Muslim travel ban, rhetoric against immigrants, and hate rallies were sending another message to the world: America was not always a very welcoming place.

CHAPTER 24

Accountable

In 1967, John McCain's Navy plane was shot down in Vietnam. The force of the ejection broke his right leg and both his arms. He was taken prisoner by the North Vietnamese and endured beatings and torture. Less than a year after McCain was captured, he received a stunning offer: he was told he was free to go home to America. The offer came soon after his father was named commander of American forces in the Pacific. The young McCain knew that others imprisoned longer than him deserved release, plus his early release would be a propaganda coup for the North Vietnamese. His jailers warned that if he stayed, he would suffer more torture and very possibly die. Still he refused his freedom.

When McCain eventually returned home, the lifelong Republican served two terms in the U.S. House of Representatives and was elected six times to the Senate. At eighty-one, in the summer of 2017, he'd been diagnosed with brain cancer, and yet he continued to live up to his nickname, Maverick, by repeatedly arguing against his lifelong Republican party when its actions collided with his personal principles. He had returned to the Capitol in July, just weeks after his diagnosis and with a scar above his left eye from brain surgery, to give a thumbs-down on a Republican bill to repeal the Affordable Care Act. In September, a frail McCain stood on the Senate floor and, for the second time, opposed the act's repeal. In a statement, McCain said he could not "in good conscience" support the Republican proposal, which had been pushed through Congress without formal, bipartisan bill-drafting procedures, and because its true effects on the American people were still unknown.

"I believe we could do better working together, Republicans and Democrats, and have not yet really tried," he said.

Not long after, on a balmy fall night, Senator McCain was in Philadelphia sitting onstage next to former vice president Joe Biden. That night, Biden, a former Democratic senator, was presenting his longtime friend and sometime political foe with the Liberty Medal to honor McCain's years of service and sacrifice for the country.

I had been invited to be among the ceremony's speakers. As much disdain as I had come to have for the political class in Washington, D.C., I viewed Senator McCain as an exception.

While I did not agree with McCain on every issue or decision he'd made in his political career, I had the utmost respect for the way he had put principle before partisanship and country before self-interest more than once.

The lights from the outdoor stage lit up the dark sky. Standing before the audience seated on the lawn of the National Constitution Center in Philadelphia, a short distance from where the Constitution of the United States had been signed in 1787, I said that speaking that evening had given me an opportunity to review Senator McCain's life. And that in doing so, I further appreciated what it meant to love something—as he loved our country—and the responsibilities that came with such love.

Behind us onstage, on a massive screen, appeared the handwritten preamble of the Constitution. *"We the people of the United States, in order to form a more perfect union . . ."*

I had reread the document prior to the ceremony. I marveled at the mix of creativity and practicality that its authors tried to achieve as they imagined how a free nation might govern itself and fulfill its founding promises of life, liberty, and the pursuit of happiness. As enduring as the Constitution has been, it remains, of course, imperfect. That is why it is constantly being amended as America grows up.

In reading the Constitution and in reviewing Senator McCain's life, I asked myself, *What does it mean to serve the country today?*

"Our Democracy remains a great experiment," I said in my speech. "All of us must see ourselves as her innovators as well as her protectors."

Six months later, less than two miles from the National Constitution Center, I was back in Philadelphia under dismaying circumstances. Something unconscionable had happened at a Starbucks, and for a moment I did not recognize the company that I loved.

On a late Thursday afternoon in April 2018, two young black men, Donte Robinson and Rashon Nelson, walked into a Starbucks in Philadelphia's Rittenhouse Square neighborhood ten minutes early for a 4:45 P.M. meeting. They were there to discuss a business idea with a friend. One of the men sat down at a table. The other walked up to the counter and asked the store manager to use the restroom. She told him that the restrooms were only available for paying customers, and she asked if he would like to order anything. He replied no and sat down with his friend. Minutes later, the manager walked over to their table and asked if she could get a drink started for them. They declined.

The store manager went to the back room and called 911.

"I have two gentlemen in my café who are refusing to make a purchase or leave," she told a 911 operator. A dispatcher radioed police that there was a "disturbance" at a Starbucks involving "a group of males refusing to leave." Within minutes eight police officers arrived, spoke to the two men seated at the table, asked them to leave, then arrested them for trespassing. Both were handcuffed and walked out of the store while customers watched in disbelief. During their unjust, unprovoked, and wrongful arrest, the two men stayed calm.

A black female customer recorded the episode and shared it with a white female customer, who posted the video online, narrating what she was witnessing. The video went viral and would eventually receive more than 11 million views, triggering a wave of outraged social media posts, often with the hashtag #BoycottStarbucks.

When I saw the video, I felt sick to my stomach. It was like watching someone I loved and trusted commit a despicable act. I desperately wanted to apologize to the two men, to their friend who arrived at the store as they were being handcuffed and led out by police, to everyone who watched the video, and to every Starbucks customer and partner.

My heart pulsed with confusion and disappointment. Like so many others who watched the video, I thought it suggested blatant discrimination by the police and Starbucks. I was desperate to know details. But I also understood that the issue at hand was bigger than the incident in the store. The video was being watched by millions. It not only had the potential to undermine the history of good works and intentions by the company and our partners, but it made me wonder how many of the black men and women watching were thinking, *That could have been me.*

After so many years of the company trying to effect positive change, the incident in Philadelphia was a blow to our soul. I ached to do something. And yet I knew the potential consequences of acting rashly, out of pure emotion. We had to take the time to respond in the right way, with compassion and educated intention. I was also limited in what I, personally, could do. I was no longer Starbucks' chief executive officer.

The first time I left the CEO job, in 2000, I returned in 2008 because the company had lost the threads that connected us to our customers.

After we emerged from the transformation, I'd often thought about succession. Starbucks' next chief had to understand our values. I wanted someone who did not perceive leadership as an entitlement, but as a privilege that had to be earned. Without these core traits at the helm, I believed Starbucks would flounder.

When I invited Kevin Johnson to dinner at my house in April 2016, I told him the time was coming for me to step aside. I asked Kevin to please consider becoming chief. Kevin had served on Starbucks' board since 2009, and been our chief operating officer for one year. He radiates a serene intelligence. People feel at ease in his presence and listen to his counsel. His passion for music was widely known, as was his penchant for noodling on the guitar.

His professional background and expertise were also crucial for Starbucks' future: during his years leading large teams at Microsoft and, later, as the CEO of Juniper Networks, Kevin had overseen complex global businesses. He also understood technology's increasing potential—behind the scenes and in front of customers—to grow companies.

After several weeks, Kevin said he was honored to accept the job.

Being the replacement for a founder comes with heightened public scrutiny and requires balancing a commitment to preserve the company's heritage with the courage to forge a new path. Kevin was aware of the inevitable pressures. But, he told me, he had come to love Starbucks and wanted to see it flourish after I left.

We transitioned slowly. The impending move was announced in December 2016, about four months prior to the official date. Our offices were next to each other, connected by a door, and we spoke several times a day, making many decisions in consultation.

Early in the morning on March 22, 2017, I started my day at Starbucks' oldest store, at Seattle's Pike Place Market. For twenty-five years, I had made a ritual of returning here on the morning of our annual shareholder meetings. I usually came alone, let myself into the front door of the store with my own key, and took a few quiet moments to run my hand over the worn wood counters and inhale the mix of sea air and roasted coffee. I never wanted to forget Starbucks' roots.

But on this day, I invited Kevin to join me. Once inside, I handed him the key to the store, and with it the key to the company. On April 3, Kevin officially became chief executive officer and assumed day-to-day oversight.

I became executive chairman. In my new role, I split my time between Starbucks' ongoing social-impact work and overseeing a new class of stores the company was opening in cities around the world. The Starbucks Reserve Roasteries are not just bigger versions of

Starbucks stores. They are the incarnation of another dream I'd had for more than a decade. In the crowded coffee market, and amid a consumer culture where more people are shopping online than in brick-and-mortar retail stores, Starbucks had to find ways to set our brand and locations apart. The Roasteries are a reimagining of how people can come together over coffee. I'd envisioned them as a wholly immersive version of the third place. "The Willy Wonka of coffee" was how I described it in a journal that I kept, and to Starbucks' lead designer, Liz Muller. A creative genius, Liz immediately grasped my vision for an elevated store experience, and why it is strategic for the brand. Ultimately, Liz is the mastermind who brought the Roasteries to life.

The first Starbucks Roastery opened in Seattle in 2014, inside a century-old building that had previously housed a car dealership. The centerpiece of the sprawling, multilevel Roastery is a fully functioning roasting operation, which includes an enormous gleaming copper silo. Rare coffee beans from farms in Ethiopia, Indonesia, Costa Rica, and other far-flung places arrive in burlap sacks. Visitors can watch as beans are expertly roasted, cooled, and transported through clear pneumatic tubes that snake from floor to ceiling. Their aromatic cargo is funneled to a packaging line to prepare them for shipment around the world, or to the espresso bar, where the beans are scooped, ground, and served. Behind the bar, baristas display the artistry of their craft by using a variety of brewing methods and sharing with customers their knowledge about the coffees' origins. The Roastery also has a tasting menu offering sample flights of coffee and a scoop bar where a variety of freshly roasted beans are available for sale by the ounce.

Like the automat of my youth, the Roasteries were designed to deliver a dose of magic. But there was no wall to hide the journey of a bean from sack to cup. It was all out in the open for everyone to see.

The second Roastery opened in Shanghai in December 2017.

In September 2018, Starbucks' story and my own came full circle. For years I had resisted the temptation to open Starbucks stores in Italy, the country where my first encounter with espresso bars seeded my dreams for Starbucks' future, as well as my own. And yet, even as we opened stores in dozens of countries, I dreamt of the time we would be ready to present Starbucks to the Italian people, and execute in a way that demonstrated due respect for the company's Italian-inspired origins while elevating coffee and design in a style that was uniquely Starbucks.

Not until I stepped inside the Roastery in Seattle did I finally know, in my heart, that the time had come to return to where it all began.

For months, I was shown dozens of potential store sites in Milan but rejected them all. We needed just the right urban locale. Finally, in 2017—in a moment as serendipitous as when I discovered my first Italian café in 1983—I was walking through Milan's city center when I looked across the street and saw the dramatic, curved façade and majestic columns of the century-old Palazzo delle Poste. It was stunning. I knew we had found the place.

The historic post office building was located in the famous Piazza Cordusio, just streets away from the iconic Duomo. Amazingly, the building was sitting idle. Within a year, Liz Muller and her team, along with local artisans, had transformed the high-ceilinged, 25,000-square-foot interior into a gleaming architectural homage to coffee, using Italian materials and design elements. At the heart of the store was a massive, fully functioning, custom Scolari coffee roaster, which was manufactured just miles outside the center of the city.

The eve of the grand opening, on September 6, was a dream come true for me. Surrounded by family, friends, and colleagues, not even the torrential rain dampened my sheer joy.

When we had first announced that Starbucks was opening in Italy, I'd said publicly we were not coming to try to educate Italians about coffee, but to share our interpretation of coffee. We were met by such skepticism. After the opening, however, Italian reviewers praised the Roastery for the originality of the experience, the expertise of our baristas, and the quality of the coffee.

Nothing in my professional life has matched the deep meaning and the ecstatic feeling of returning to Milan, especially on opening day, as I walked by the line of customers that snaked around the building and thanked people for coming. For me, it felt like a pinnacle and a homecoming. The event was most meaningful, however, because Sheri and our kids were by my side.

In the months to come, Roasteries were scheduled to open in Tokyo, New York City, and Chicago. The Manhattan location is just blocks away from where I exited the train during high school, when I came into the city to work at the furrier's and earn a few bucks. But nothing would match the meaning of returning to Milan.

The journey to that moment had exceeded my original plans in so many ways. Just as Starbucks had sought to reimagine the coffee experience, we never stopped reimagining the role that we could play in communities. Through trial, error, and individuals' triumphs, the company was providing an ever-expanding answer to the question I had first posed in 2013: *The role and responsibility of a company in society is to try to enhance communities and be a positive voice, a collaborator, a convener, a listener, an empathizer, an educator, a volunteer, a sharer, and an innovator.*

Starbucks had achieved a great deal. But success is a precarious phenomenon. It must be earned over time, and it can be lost in an instant.

After Donte Robinson and Rashon Nelson were arrested in our store, I did worry that Starbucks' past contributions would melt away in the heat of that moment. Starbucks could quickly become a company defined by one horrible act that was not reflective of our history or intentions. The company's past experiences and intentions, however, absolutely shaped how we responded to the moment.

By Saturday morning, Kevin was writing a letter to partners and customers. In it, he rightly labeled the incident reprehensible and pledged to make changes to company practices to prevent a recurrence. Starbucks stood firmly against discrimination and racial profiling, he wrote.

"You can and should expect more from us. We will learn from this and be better."

Kevin also filmed a video personally apologizing to the two young men. He was hoping to meet with them when he went to Philadelphia.

Bad weather in parts of the country made travel to Philly difficult. But by Sunday night, Kevin and Rosalind Brewer, Starbucks' chief operating officer, were holding a meeting in a downtown hotel room with Rossann Williams, the president in charge of Starbucks' retail operations in the U.S., Zabrina Jenkins, head of litigation, and Vivek. I was back in Seattle to host an open forum with our partners.

Vivek was especially aggrieved. He and I had been through so much together, and he understood the magnitude of this particular crisis. He was approaching its aftermath with his signature steady hand amid chaos. Refusing to allow the stress of the moment into his head, Vivek felt confident the company could emerge stronger.

Roz had been COO less than a year. She had first viewed the video of the arrest while sitting in a Starbucks with two young African American men whom she mentored. She watched aghast as multiple thoughts competed for her attention. Roz is a well-respected black female executive inside and outside Starbucks, and felt a special responsibility to help guide the company's response amid the growing call for accountability. Roz also thought about her son. He was twenty-three and often spent his Saturday mornings hanging out at a Starbucks in Brooklyn. Either of the men handcuffed in Philly, dressed in their sport joggers, could have been her child. She was on her way to see him at a family event. "Forget it," he texted his mom. "You have to get this fixed." Go to Philadelphia, her son urged. "Just do your best work."

Everyone wanted to act swiftly and wisely as we got to the bottom of what happened. We had to do what was right, not just be reactive, or choose the easiest and least complicated path, as tensions inside and outside the company were continuing to rise.

Early Monday morning, Kevin appeared on *Good Morning America* to answer tough questions and accept accountability as Starbucks CEO. Following the live interview, he, Roz, and Vivek met with the mayor of Philadelphia, the chief of police, and members of the city council. Officials were anxious to know how Starbucks was going help their community heal. Kevin was not defensive. They were there to listen, he said, to learn more about the city's racial divides, and be accountable for the company's own shortcomings.

Meanwhile, more than a hundred protestors had been gathering at the Starbucks store on the corner of Spruce and Eighteenth Streets. It was a loud, often chaotic scene being documented by reporters. We decided to keep the store open, rather than close it, so our leaders could talk to customers who had questions, and so people in the community could have their voices heard from the platform from which they wanted it broadcast: the store.

The staff, however, had been shaken by the aftermath of the arrests. Two other store managers and two shift supervisors from nearby locations volunteered to work at the Eighteenth and Spruce store during the protests, alongside Rossann and Camille Hymes, the regional vice president for the mid-Atlantic region.

Camille oversaw 650 stores in five states. With twelve thousand partners under her leadership, she was feeling especially protective of our people who worked in Philly, many of whom were on the front lines, in our stores, deflecting dispersed, sporadic outbursts of public ire. Carmen Williams—the young black woman who told Sheri her story of being abandoned as a girl and living on the streets before finding YouthBuild and graduating high school—was now managing her own Starbucks in Philadelphia and attending college.

In Philly, Starbucks had formal relationships with three local organizations, including YouthBuild. A lot of partners volunteered in the community to help mitigate problems like homelessness and what Camille, herself an African American, called the city's "opportunity divides." Camille saw the public indictment of Starbucks as a false reflection of the compassion that resided in so many of her colleagues' hearts.

At the store, activists from various civil rights groups crowded inside throughout the morning. At one point, a megaphone being passed from one protestor to another broadcast a tapestry of troubles that were not exclusive to Philadelphia: underfunded public schools, drugs and gang violence, biased policing, a dearth of well-paying jobs for people in poor areas, unaffordable housing, ineffective government officials. People were expressing anger at "the system," as one man told a TV reporter, not just the state of one city or the events in one store. Yet it was all of a piece, and it was unfolding in the third place.

———

Kevin and Roz met with Donte and Rashon to personally apologize on behalf of the company. They listened intently to the two men's perspectives about what happened to them in the store. Kevin asked them about their respective backgrounds, and learned that they were long-time friends as well as entrepreneurs. Everyone was interested in finding a positive, constructive path forward, for the men and for the company. That morning, Starbucks agreed with the men's lawyers to engage in mediation and, later that week, a confidential settlement was reached.

When Donte and Rashon appeared on *Good Morning America* on Thursday, anchor Robin Roberts asked what they wanted to see come out of the incident. Among their hopes was that the same situation not happen again. I'd heard the same sentiment from Starbucks partners at the open forum I cohosted earlier in the week, when I faced more than a thousand disappointed, embarrassed, confused partners who desperately wanted to feel good about how their company would respond. It was as openly critical a forum as I'd ever attended. Our people were holding us accountable for living up to our values.

One African American partner said her friends in Philadelphia had been bashing Starbucks. On the way to work that day, she had called her father, who tried to reassure her that many people understood what happened was not representative of the company. He told his daughter it would probably blow over in a week.

"Please," she said to me in front of everyone at the forum, "do not let this blow over in a week. I think we have an opportunity to do something more and different than other companies do in these situations."

Three years earlier, I had called partners together to talk about race relations in America. Now here we were, talking about it at Starbucks.

In a live interview I did with Gayle King for *CBS This Morning*, she asked if I believed what happened was a case of racial profiling.

I expected the question when I went into the interview, and wanted to answer truthfully. To do so, I leaned on insight I'd gleaned from Bryan Stevenson, the public interest attorney whose book, *Just Mercy*, Starbucks had once sold in our stores. Racial profiling exists because racism exists. It *is* a form of racism. And it cannot be abolished until we look ourselves, and our history, in the eye. So when Gayle asked me if what happened at Starbucks was a case of racial profiling, she was also asking, I believe, if racism exists among people unknowingly and unintentionally. I had to answer yes. I had learned too much about the inevitability of unconscious bias in human nature to claim we were immune to it.

"There is no doubt in my mind that the reason the police were called was because the men were African American." For that I was ashamed, and held myself personally accountable.

Starbucks is an organism that grew up around an idea—an ideal, really. Customers could come together over coffee in our stores and our company could grow, sharing its prosperity with its people and the neighborhoods it served. We wanted to do good and perform well for shareholders. "Performance-driven by humanity" is how I have long described how we needed to go about our business.

But humanity is imperfect. For all our individual and collective potential for compassion, empathy, and generosity, human beings falter. Despite their best intentions, and at times intentionally, people—and the systems they create—are radically imperfect. We are flawed. In our quest to build more perfect lives, more perfect families, more perfect companies, and more perfect unions, we fall short, make mistakes, sometimes hurt each other. Even those we love. The higher the aspiration—all people are created equal, say—the harder the fall. But also the greater the potential for growth.

"Maybe God intended for this to happen at a Starbucks."

A woman in Philadelphia made that comment on Wednesday. The two of us were seated in a large circle among dozens of members of an interfaith organization, POWER, which represented more than fifty congregations. POWER members had held peaceful sit-ins at two Starbucks stores.

POWER representatives had come to meet with Kevin, Vivek, Rossann, Camille, other Starbucks colleagues, and me in the auditorium of Mother Bethel African Methodist Episcopal Church. It was, I learned that day, the oldest church property in the United States continuously owned by African Americans.

A moving, poetic soliloquy by a local pastor began our meeting. Her smooth, rich voice filled the room with a history of racial injustice in America. It was a narrative that began with slavery and ended with the arrest of two innocent black men in a Starbucks. It was an unending story of inhumanities suffered in a country founded on the premise that black lives were not equal to white lives. It was a history of lynchings and Jim Crow laws and racial segregation and discrimination in public spaces and mass incarceration and police brutality and racial profiling and poor housing projects so isolated and repressed that their residents were willing to burn down businesses to call attention to their hopelessness.

The pastor's reflections reminded me of something else that Bryan Stevenson had said: we cannot understand the destructive nature of so many issues and policies in our country without understanding our history of racial inequality.

We went around the room introducing ourselves. I mentioned my own history growing up in Brooklyn, as well as Starbucks' misguided attempt to deal with race three years earlier.

"We did not have the moral authority to do it," I said, reflecting on Race Together and the comment that Mellody Hobson had made to me at the time. As an American, I believed I had a moral obligation to talk frankly about race, even confront it, but I did not then have the requisite knowledge, nor had the company earned public trust on the topic, to effectively and responsibly orchestrate a public dialogue. Authority must be earned. In the years since, though, through education and wider exposure, I had confronted the thicket of history, policy, and social interactions that make racial and economic inequality among the most complicated and necessary challenges for America to overcome. It was a struggle I'd been late to, but I was here now, trying to participate, understand, and learn.

For about two hours in the church auditorium, black as well as white POWER members spoke about injustices in their city, echoing the messages bellowed through bullhorns in our store. The tone of POWER members ranged from accusatory to hopeful. Listening, I felt at times defensive, given the company's history of trying to do good.

"We have always strived to build and to be a different kind of company," I said, "and what happened on Thursday is not who we are and not how we want to be." If they looked under the hood of Starbucks, I told them, I hoped they would see that we also tried to be the kind of corporate citizen that added value to society, even if our intentions were not always realized.

Toward the end of our time together, a woman across the circle from me spoke up. "Maybe God intended for this to happen at a Starbucks." Everyone seemed to pause. I tried to internalize the words as they floated across the circle. She continued. The situation could have happened at another retailer, she said, and she named a few. It could have happened at a company that was not built around the aspiration to be a different kind of employer, or a good corporate citizen, or a welcoming place.

She said that Starbucks may not have had the moral authority to talk about race with customers three years ago, but she seemed to imply that we had it now. What we also had was an opportunity. More than apologize, we could use the event to induce some positive change.

Three days earlier, on Sunday morning, I'd sent Kevin an email.

"Thinking back to 2008 when we closed all of the stores for coffee retraining. Let's close all of our stores for the afternoon for training re racial justice and conscious and unconscious bias. Let's use it as a massive teaching moment and show the country how serious we are about learning from our mistakes." This was not something to do for show, but because it was perhaps the only way to achieve what had to be done, which was to reinforce our core values and demonstrate them in how we go about our business.

I called Mellody Hobson to ask her opinion. Mellody immediately understood just how horrid the situation in Philadelphia was—for the men arrested, for black people who watched the video, and for its potential ramifications for the company. When I asked what she thought about closing thousands of stores, she paused. She was worried a mass closure would be viewed as a PR stunt. "Let me sleep on it," she said.

The next morning, Mellody called me.

"Howard, just tell me why you want to close all the stores."

"Because the company needs it," I said.

"Then do it."

CHAPTER 25

A Better Version of Us

I've never thought of the third place just as a physical environment. For me, the third place has always been a feeling. An emotion. An aspiration that all people can come together and be uplifted as a result of a sense of belonging. This is the cornerstone of our business, yes, but "belonging" is also a basic human right, which should be afforded all members of a society.

Because creating a sense of belonging is central to Starbucks' story, the company was compelled to respond to the events in Philadelphia with serious self-reflection and substance. Much more than apologize, we sought to examine bias in our own company, and also in the country, and explore ways to combat it.

These momentous topics were not ones we were equipped to address ourselves.

We were fortunate in that several respected leaders in the civil rights and black communities were among people my colleagues and I already knew.

Eric Holder, the eighty-second attorney general of the United States and a member of the board of the NAACP, advised Kevin early on not to rush to respond to public pressure for immediate answers, but to take the time to understand the details of what happened that day, and be intentional about our actions going forward.

Mellody continued to provide a wider perspective and counsel. A year prior, she had introduced me to Sherrilyn Ifill, the president and director-counsel of the NAACP Legal Defense and Educational Fund. The LDF has been a leading fighter against discriminatory policies from the civil rights era to today. In November 2017, I was honored to be a recipient of the LDF's National Equal Justice Award. Sherrilyn had called me after the Philadelphia incident and agreed to advise us. So did Heather McGhee, the president of Demos, a public policy organization dedicated to promoting economic and political equality. Heather's unique attempts to bridge the racial divide had been profiled in the second season of *Upstanders*.

Sherrilyn and Heather were interested in helping us craft a model for how businesses could deal with bias and potential discrimination— with substance and commitment to making long-term policy changes. They told us they would hold us accountable to their own standards.

When I called Bryan Stevenson, he expressed his belief that closing the stores could make a very important statement, and bias training did need to happen. Although one day of training, he rightly said, would by no means be enough.

When I got in touch with musician and civil rights activist Common, who'd spoken to job seekers at the opportunity fair in Chicago, he also agreed to lend his voice. As did actress Anna Deavere Smith.

Keith Yamashita from SYPartners called us. A business strategist, philosopher, and poet, Keith had been counseling me and Starbucks since I'd returned as CEO. He knew that providing welcoming spaces was essential to Starbucks' existence, and he volunteered SYPartners' expertise to help us craft the appropriate response.

"The company was founded on the great tradition of the coffeehouse," Keith wrote to me. "Exclusion is among the greatest threats to any third place."

When we first announced our plan to close eight thousand stores for racial bias education, Starbucks was, as Mellody had feared, accused of staging a high-profile public relations stunt.

People also remembered what had happened when Starbucks had tried to address race years earlier, with Race Together. Now, however, we were committed to approaching the issue at hand with deeper levels of sensitivity, expertise, honesty, and study.

Some people gave us the benefit of the doubt. One *Washington Post* columnist conceded that Starbucks would of course not conquer racial bias in one afternoon, but "having even the most incomplete conversation about racism in American daily life is preferable to brushing the issues aside yet again."

A team led by Vivek and one of SYPartners' top people, Jen Randle, got to work. Jen, who is African American, pushed us to be brave and honest in our approach. She and her team spent the next month in Seattle, taking over a large campaign room near my office and Kevin's.

No curriculum existed that fit our size or the nature of our business. So just as we had done with Create Jobs and the Starbucks College Achievement Plan, we had to invent something new.

The team's work sessions were self-reflective, iterative, and Socratic in their approach.

First, we asked ourselves: *Who are we today, and what kind of company do we want to be?*

So much had changed since our beginnings in 1987, when Starbucks had six stores and fewer than a hundred people. We sell more products, source more coffee, serve millions of people daily, and employ more people. Today, Starbucks customers and partners are a microcosm of America. Almost every demographic crosses our thresholds or works behind our counters, which means the increasing, inevitable diversity of the country is reflected inside Starbucks stores. We serve and employ people of all colors, backgrounds, ethnicities, economic means, religions, sexual orientations, and ages.

Every day, human joys, routines, and even traumas take place in our stores: People young and old celebrate birthdays. They visit with friends and relatives in person and online. They come in before work, between classes, and after church. They go on first dates and kiss while waiting in line. They open laptops to surf, shop, pay bills, and do homework. They read *The New York Times* and stream Fox News. They cry quietly. Laugh out loud. Get mad. They listen to hip-hop on head-phones, and to symphonies and podcasts and books. They argue about politics. They attract attention and keep to themselves. They cut business deals and rock babies. The unemployed have sat for hours at a table because they have nowhere else to be. People without homes have slept on our chairs. Those struggling with mental illness have wandered in lost. Drug users have shot up and smoked in our bath-rooms; some have died. People have robbed our registers at gunpoint, protested, and caused fellow human beings discomfort in ways seen and unseen. What happens in America happens in Starbucks.

We also asked ourselves: *How does Starbucks serve the public today?*

Starbucks partners are more than baristas and managers; they are creators and protectors of their store's environment. They do their jobs through the lens of their own life experience, and under the influence of conscious and unconscious associations we all make about others. As a business based on interacting with millions of people, Starbucks has a responsibility to help our people navigate the nuances of human interaction, which includes understanding and trying to mitigate bias.

How would we bring hundreds of thousands of partners along on the journey—quickly?

In six weeks, we would meet tens of thousands of U.S. partners in the comfort of their stores, among familiar peers, and provide tools to facilitate conversation, education, and self-reflection. One day, one bold move, was of course not enough.

So how could we ensure lasting change?

Starbucks had to shift. We had to look ourselves in the eye and ask whether we were truly achieving our intentions and realizing our core values. We had to keep trying to become a better convener, a better collaborator, a better listener and empathizer, a better educator, volunteer, sharer, and innovator—among our own people and with customers, neighbors, and communities beyond our own.

Overall, the work process reflected the tenor and lessons of Starbucks' past initiatives:

The inventive urgency of Create Jobs.

The purpose-driven camaraderie of the Come Together petition.

The moral imperative and emotional weight of the veteran- and refugee-hiring initiatives.

The collaborative spirit of the Starbucks College Achievement Plan.

The training itself was designed to be participatory, engaging, and personal, like the opportunity youth fairs and forums.

We wanted to take on racism with a steady, nuanced approach, unlike that of Race Together. The team examined the fraught intersection of human nature, neuroscience, socialized behaviors, U.S. history, laws, and individual life experiences. A lot of care was taken as to how ideas would be communicated to and absorbed by our partners, almost half of whom were people of color. We aimed to teach but not preach.

There were risks. Each store's training would be conducted without a professional facilitator; it was impossible to find and integrate some eight thousand experts so fast. The risk that the content might trigger conflict was real, but we trusted our partners. We also anticipated that the high-profile training and store closings might attract more protests. We had plans to address the worst-case scenarios.

Once again, Starbucks tried to walk a third rail in the third place.

On the afternoon of May 29, 2018, we closed thousands of stores in the United States. A sign posted on doors told customers we would see them the next day:

> *At Starbucks we are proud to be a third place—a place between home and work where everyone feels that they belong.*
>   *Today our store team is reconnecting with our mission and each other. We are sharing our ideas about how to make Starbucks even more welcoming.*

Inside, small groups of partners huddled around discussion guides and iPads. Each partner was given a blank notebook and pen. A total of 22,700 newly purchased iPads—so many that Apple had to manufacture more to fulfill our order—had been uploaded with videos that were played throughout the day, including prerecorded messages from several Starbucks leaders and outside experts.

Rossann, the head of U.S. retail operations, set the tone, urging partners to listen with respect, speak their truth, and honor the truth of others. Kevin's video set the intent: "We are here to make Starbucks a place where everyone feels welcome." Mellody was filmed sitting at a table talking with a store manager and two experts about facts and ramifications of explicit and implicit bias. Partners recalled how they'd handled challenging customer scenarios. And a short, original film we commissioned by Stanley Nelson, an award-winning black documentarian, added historic context. In seven minutes, the film *The Story of Access,* narrated by Anna Deavere Smith, provided a forthright look at the decades-long struggle for people to be given equal access and fair treatment in America's streets and parks, pools and theaters, stores and diners. The right to be respected in public spaces was at the heart of the civil rights movement, and the powerful film articulated a truth that was especially relevant for this moment: while the Civil Rights Act of 1964 outlawed discrimination in public spaces, being allowed in is not the same as feeling welcomed.

In other segments of the training, Roz outlined new store policies. "Partners," she said, "everyone who crosses the threshold is a customer," not only people who make a purchase.

But customers also have a responsibility. Upholding the integrity of the third place is an aspiration that people who come into the store can help us achieve. Customers have rights, but we would also respectfully ask them to use our spaces as intended, to act ethically, to communicate respectfully, and to be considerate of others.

For four hours, about 175,000 partners in our U.S. stores and offices in fifty states came together to think about how we all perceive people in the world, what it feels like to belong, and the history of belonging in America.

No groups protested.

The entirety of the bias training is available online, for anyone to watch. All told, closing the stores for the training cost approximately

$50 million, accounting for the development of the content, lost sales, paying our people, and more.

For the company, it was just a first step. We began creating a twelve-module curriculum that would become part of how we train new and existing partners. Kevin initiated a full review of our policies to ensure that our partners know what to do when faced with difficult decisions. All those iPads would stay in stores, and be routinely uploaded with new training materials. We also planned to hold a company-wide leadership summit to focus on inclusion and diversity.

I, too, had taken the training. It helped make me more self-aware of how I went about the interactions in my life, viewed my past, and was subject to my own unconscious biases. Among the macro insights I took away was how human dignity is eroded through the denial of access—to bathrooms, to lunch counters, to healthcare, to education, to jobs, to safe harbors.

The night before the store closings, MSNBC had broadcast a live town hall titled "Everyday Racism in America." The event was held at the Prince Theater in Philadelphia and presented as a discussion of racial bias. The show began with the viral video of the arrest in the Philadelphia Starbucks and was followed by an hour of journalists, prominent black Americans, civil rights experts, and people in the audience as well as on film sharing opinions and anecdotes.

A black couple recalled being pulled over by police as they left a house where they were vacationing; someone in the neighborhood had called the police claiming black people were stealing luggage.

A young black man was confronted by police when he was moving into a new apartment in New York City because another tenant told police someone was breaking into the building.

A black woman in the audience stood up and explained how she felt routinely ignored by sales clerks in stores, made to feel insignificant, as if her dollar was not as valuable as white customers' money.

Watching the town hall, listening to the many voices, I was reminded of Starbucks' open forums about race. *This*, I thought, *was the national dialogue I always imagined having.*

Among the MSNBC panelists was Sherrilyn Ifill, who made a resonant observation about the history of freedom in America. "It is important to ground ourselves in the reason for the lunch counter sit-ins and freedom rides," she said, referring to the civil rights movement. Freedom and equality are not just about soothing emotions and restoring dignity, "but about what it means to be a full citizen with all its benefits" and privileges. Discrimination, I understood her to be saying, hurts feelings and breaks hearts. But it's about so much more: it blocks real chances to be our best selves and live our fullest lives in a country that promises just that.

One way to describe the American Dream is as a promise—a promise of life, liberty, and the pursuit of happiness. Inherent to that pursuit, I believe, is having access to opportunities like education and good jobs, healthcare and ownership, support from family and friends, and generosity from strangers. Opportunity shows up as luck, but is also embedded into our social, governmental, and corporate constructs.

From all of my travels and the people I had met over the years, I'd been exposed to many reasons why the promise of America was so hard to fulfill for so many. For them, access to opportunities was nonexistent, or it was simply being blocked.

For veterans—the debilitating effects of warfare, broken government organizations, and uninformed, indifferent civilians hindered transitions to new careers and healthy lives.

For students—high tuition, debt, and lack of personal supports made it hard to complete college.

For opportunity youth—geographic isolation and few role models prevented them from finding first jobs and entering the workforce.

For residents of small towns like Logan and East Liverpool—abandoned industries, greedy coal companies, doctor-influenced opioid addictions, and compromised politicians created circumstances that conspired to keep hardworking people from caring for families, applying their skills, learning new ones, and earning a decent living.

For refugees—false facts, scare tactics, and stereotypes kept them from rebuilding livelihoods destroyed by war and brutality.

For people of color—the blockades to true equality were as ugly as bigotry and as invisible as unconscious bias.

Over the years, Starbucks' attempts to pave paths to opportunities for more people had far exceeded my original aspirations. And yet, in 2018, my heart was pained as I observed what was happening throughout the country. Macroeconomic trends showed an economy growing, a stock market booming. But they were not the full story. I'd been on the ground listening to people's truths, and so many continued to live in the shadows, with dignity compromised and opportunities out of reach. More and more, I was wondering if I could or should try to effect broader positive change beyond my role as a company chairman or chief executive.

There was only one way to find out.

One month after the company-wide bias training, in late June, I walked out of the company's Seattle headquarters and stepped into a sea of green. The parking lot had been emptied of cars, and about three thousand partners from stores and offices stood shoulder to shoulder in the summer sun. They had come to say goodbye. All of us were wearing green aprons.

After thirty-six years, I was leaving Starbucks.

I was going with peace. The company was in the hands of Kevin and his capable team, and my confidence was high because Kevin had embraced his role as the new guardian of Starbucks' brand and values. He is a judicious, steady, contemplative leader. These traits served him well after the Philadelphia store arrests, and he understands a truth that not many public company CEOs do: short-term financial hits are often necessary for long-term growth. That is among the foundations of the company. Kevin is the kind of leader Starbucks needed to move forward.

I was also leaving with uncertainty. I had no clear plan, just a steadfast desire to do more for the country that had given me so much. I didn't know what my future would hold. But that was true when I left Canarsie for northern Michigan, and when I moved to Seattle with

Sheri. Then as now, I felt convinced that leaving the past and embracing a different future with an open heart and mind in pursuit of greater understanding was the right thing to do.

First, however, I had to say goodbye. Standing in the front of Starbucks headquarters on that June day, my eyes watered as I took in the people I could see in front of me, and because of those I could not see. Earlier that day, Vivek told me that some three million people had worked for the company during its forty-seven-year history. Lives had been touched in ways I would never know.

"We all have Starbucks in our life journey," Kevin said to everyone gathered. "Rarely does one have the opportunity to be a part of something bigger than themselves."

When he handed me the microphone, I was in awe of the march of time.

I spoke from my heart. "In the almost fifty-year history of Starbucks, we have faced and overcome so many moments of challenges and obstacles, where people have doubted the relevancy of the company and our ability to navigate through tough times," I said. "Our resiliency is in what we know to be the equity of the brand." And the equity of the brand, I said, has always been the intimacy of the third-place experience, and the trust that we build with our customers and one another.

In the past few weeks, Starbucks' integrity had been under fire. We had risen above a tragic moment because those who loved the company and those who were disappointed by it had come together with civility and a sincere desire to be a better version of ourselves. I could not have asked for a more meaningful gift upon my exit than a collective reimagining of the third place—an idea that had seeded, saved, and shaped my own life.

It's a gray weekday when we exit the Belt Parkway, about twenty-five miles from Manhattan. The off-ramp deposits me back into Canarsie. I had returned a few times as an adult, but not for about fourteen years.

I am with two friends, and we decide to stop in the retail district for lunch. The streets are crowded with people walking, doing errands, hanging out, maybe waiting for friends. The majority of the people are black, but not everyone. It is a poorer neighborhood than it once was. We park and walk into a pizza place across the street from a mom-and-pop home-goods store and a Walgreens. I order a slice and it arrives hot and tastes fantastic. After, we walk into the small station that serves the L train. A white, blue, and red metal sign bolted to a concrete wall reads WELCOME TO CANARSIE: A CARING COMMUNITY.

I buy a MetroCard and walk through the turnstile to the platform, just to have a look around. The tracks are littered with empty glass bottles and used food cartons and dirty papers. During high school, I stood here waiting for the train to take me into Manhattan. A dented silver subway train arrives. Its doors slide open and people stream out. Above a subway car window, digital yellow letters reveal the train's current location: LAST STOP.

Back in the car, we drive to my old home in Bayview and find parking in front of a long, three-story building of muted yellow bricks. A sign out front welcomed us to P.S. 272.

I hadn't planned on visiting my old elementary school today, but now that I'm here, I'm excited. One of the front doors is propped open and we walk in slowly, immediately greeted by a security officer stationed at a desk. There is no sound of children. It's quiet. It must be summer break already, or everyone is in class. I explain to the officer that I went here "a hundred years ago."

"How many kids go here now?" About five hundred, she says, most from the projects.

"Is there a lot of crime?" Not really, she tells me, it's under control here.

I remember that the gymnasium is the door on the left.

"May I take a look at the gym?" The officer accompanies me.

It's in lousy shape. The dirty plastic floor is peeling and buckling. The basketball hoops have no nets.

"Is the principal here?" The guard points down the hallway to the administrative office. As I walk into it, several women look at me.

"Hi, I went to school here when I was a young boy. I lived in the projects. I came back here today and am a little nostalgic." I think I surprise myself with the statement. But it's true. I felt good in this school. I liked being here as a kid.

"Are you from Starbucks?" someone asks.

"Yes."

"Why didn't you say so!"

We are led into the principal's office and a woman in a black and white dress, high-heeled shoes, and long dreadlocks scoots out from behind a desk and introduces herself with an enormous grin and firm handshake. Dakota Keyes's office has the warmth of a grandmother's living room. Photographs, children's books, cards, drawings, inspirational quotes, and memorabilia compete for wall and shelf space. A closet door is covered with different versions of the word "believe" in various colors, sizes, and incarnations. It's an office cluttered with love.

"How's the school?" I ask. Members of Dakota's staff have gathered in the doorway, giddy and listening as we chat.

"We had a rough time but we're good now," she says, anxious to share. Dakota has been the principal for eleven years. When she arrived, so many kids were failing to advance that one fourth grader, who had been held back multiple times, was six feet two inches tall. Food fights occurred almost daily in the cafeteria. P.S. 272 had gotten a letter grade of F for performance by the New York City Board of Education.

"We just had to believe that we were going to get there, and then in one year we went from an F to an A," she says. Listening to her, I know the leap was no accident. This woman willed it.

Photos of kids and their art are everywhere. She says a lot of students come from single-parent homes and show up to school with emotional baggage but no pencils. "We can't get into a child's head until we get to their hearts." Sometimes she gets discouraged. "It's not the kids, not the teachers—it's the system. The system just doesn't make sense." I nod. The system needs to change.

In addition to being the principal of P.S. 272, Dakota tells us she is a doctoral student at Fordham University, studying leadership. *She's an upstander,* I think to myself.

"What's the one thing the school needs that you don't have?" I ask.

There's laughter all around, as if no one knows where to start. But Dakota has a list in her head. "I'd love a new gym. It needs to be renovated. A nice cushioned, wood floor because there was a flood." The cafeteria could also use air-conditioning, and many classroom doors are coming off their hinges. I give Dakota my personal email and phone number and promise to get it done.

Dakota's students are lucky to have her. She has their backs. Just as Michael Crow has the backs of students, and Rebecca has the backs of babies, and Brandon has the backs of West Virginia workers.

We hug goodbye.

From the school, my old apartment building, 1560 East 102nd Street, is only a short walk up a path I'd trodden thousands of times. I take my time. Half a dozen kids are playing basketball on the same concrete court where I spent so many hours trying to prove myself. Aside from their voices, it's quiet enough to hear a bird chirp. An elderly woman sits on a bench. Bayview does not strike me as a place with one of the worst crime rates in the city of New York.

As I approach my building, I can see the seventh-floor kitchen window from which my mom used to toss down sandwiches. It was also the window from which I watched her leave in an ambulance. All around are trees that have grown tall and strong in the years since I left; if they had been that big when I was a kid, we could have played skelly in the shade.

WELCOME TO BAYVIEW HOUSES. PROPERTY OF NEW YORK CITY HOUSING AUTHORITY, reads a small maroon sign at the building's entrance. I push open the heavy glass door. Inside, the walls are the same pale turquoise concrete and the elevator is still a claustrophobic box that makes a slow ascent to the seventh floor. I step out, and to my right, at the end of a narrow hallway doused in fluorescent light, is the dark red door of apartment 7G. It's just a door.

We knock but no one answers. I find the stairwell and walk up one flight to a small landing between the eighth floor and the final flight of stairs that leads to the roof. This is where I would retreat from the madness of my home, where I sat listening, and worrying, and sometimes crying—but also dreaming about Mickey Mantle, about the world beyond Canarsie.

What would I say to that little boy now? I would hug him. I would take his hand. I would tell him that he has the fortitude, the resilience—the gumption—to get through the day, the week, whatever he finds on the other side of any door. I would tell him that he is not now nor would he ever be alone. He has Billy Block and Michael Nadel and his cousin Alan. One day he will have Sheri and two wonderful children and countless loyal friends. He will be surrounded by passionate, intelligent people, and his ambitions will become theirs and theirs will become his. He will also have angels who swoop in from time to time—people who have his back and share his dreams.

I would also remind him that he has his mother and father. His parents would not always show up in the ways he wanted them to, even in the ways he needed them to, but they would do the best they could with the tools they had. In time, he would come to accept that they were imperfect, and that all he had experienced and learned from his parents would drive him to lead a life that exceeded anything he or they dared to imagine. He would live the American Dream, and he would pay it forward.

I look at the empty stairwell. Even on a cloudy day, light comes through the window.

Our Climb

Sheri and I stood on the flat sandy shores of northern France and looked out onto the dark waters of the English Channel. Along this jagged coast, at dawn on June 6, 1944, tens of thousands of Allied troops stormed through icy waters and the hail of gunfire to liberate western Europe from the grip of Nazi Germany. Among the troops were more than two hundred Army Rangers that came ashore to climb the sheer rock face of a hundred-foot cliff, with the intent of seizing control of the high ground. Not all survived the steep ascent. Those who did pulled themselves up and over the edge to arrive at a pivotal spot that President Ronald Reagan once described as the lonely, windswept point where "the air was dense with smoke and the cries of men . . ." The following spring, Nazi Germany surrendered.

D-Day has been referred to as the beginning of the end of World War II. But for thousands of young men, it was the end of their lives. Sheri and I paid our respects to many of them that day at the Normandy American Cemetery, where seemingly endless rows of pristine white headstones face west, toward home, forever afloat on a sea of manicured green grass. Just over 9,300 servicemen who died during the invasion are buried here, including forty-five sets of brothers, four women, two children of a U.S. president, and at least one father and his son.

As our guide described the blood-soaked battle that occurred more than seventy years ago, we tried to wrap our heads around the enormity of human sacrifice and loss, as well as the dire consequences that could have befallen the free world had the Allied mission failed to topple the Nazi tyranny.

It was October 2017, and I had come to Normandy to better grasp the ties that bind America's past and present, and to think about the future. We were visiting Normandy at a time in America when hate speech, racism, and the cries of white supremacists were occurring on American soil without essential condemnation, especially from the president of the United States, Donald Trump. In the chill of the salty breeze and the stillness of man-made monuments, I turned to Sheri: "What kind of country do we want our grandchildren to grow up in?" I asked as we stood among graves of those who had fought, and died, so that others might have such a choice.

I want my grandchildren to live in a country where millions of people have a chance to safely and affordably house, feed, and educate themselves and their families. I want them to live in a country where people are safe from threats and violence, within and outside our borders. Beyond that, I want them to live in a country where everyone has a fair chance to rise above their circumstances because they have access to real opportunities to learn and to work and to achieve their own definitions of success—like Carmen Williams when she found Youth-Build, and Markelle Cullom-Herbison when she got into ASU, and Xavier McElrath-Bey when he got a job at Starbucks.

Sheri and I were getting into the car to leave Normandy when I heard the voices of Americans. A woman and a man were just arriving to the cemetery. I walked over to say hello and told them we were from Seattle. The couple was from Baltimore. She was a nurse and he was a lawyer. They were vacationing in Paris, they told me.

"What made you come to Normandy?" I asked. It was about a three-hour drive.

Without missing a beat the woman answered.

"We came here to be reminded of who we once were."

Her words plunged into my heart like a dagger. *Who we once were.*

I recognized her comment's tragic assumptions, because they were once my own. But not anymore. Because of all that I have witnessed over the past few years, especially many of the experiences I have tried to capture in this book, I have come to believe that our country is not somehow less than we once were.

America has never been a perfect union, but there have always been those among us who possess the qualities that the nurse from Baltimore was searching for. Think about the courage and generosity of Leroy Petry, or Cedric King's strength and drive, or Dr. Bill Krissoff's sense of duty.

A country's character is defined by how citizens like Leroy, Cedric, and Bill live its values every day, in public and private moments.

So many of us are hungry to restore a collective sense of pride in our nation. And we have what it takes to do so. Yet many people have become numb, even accepting, to the shockingly cruel rhetoric we sometimes hear from our neighbors and leaders. But we should remember there are more Americans who speak out against intolerance than those who spew it. Just because anger and fear are louder than kindness and optimism does not mean that anger and fear must prevail, or define a new American identity. The negativity that streams through our media and social feeds is a false—or at least incomplete— narrative. Every time harsh Tweets dominate news cycles, we can remind ourselves of Mary Poole's empathy in Montana, or the compassion of Rebecca Crowder in West Virginia, or Bryan Stevenson's adamant calls for justice in our courts. Countless acts of dignity are unfolding offline, away from earshot, and they matter.

We already have what it takes to rise above divisiveness and the vitriol of a hurtful few and steer the country toward an even better "us." Not so we can be great *again,* but so we can become an even stronger, safer, more fair, prosperous, and inclusive version of ourselves.

Those who champion common-sense problem solving, and there are legions of us, are eager to keep fixing, reinventing, improving. In these pages, I tried to amplify our existing potential to eclipse dysfunction by recounting Mark Pinsky's collaborative spirit, for example, and Michael Crow's innovative bent, and Brandon Dennison's entrepreneurial gumption, and Dakota Keyes' steadfast belief in her young students, and in herself. They are reminders that the misplaced priorities of President Trump and his administration do not represent the priorities of the majority of Americans. And while there are heroes who hold office, members of both parties, Democrats and Republicans, have been complicit in the fracturing of trust that has plagued our political system for years now. In fact, I believe that the American people as a whole are better than our current political class.

As a business leader, my role has been to honor the values of Starbucks' past by giving those values new life in the present. In doing so, I have tried to educate myself, and to inspire others to find innovative ways to address pressing social problems. Through missteps and moments of achievement, I know that success is never an entitlement. The same holds true for the way of life that Americans hold so dear. Our freedom must be earned.

These days, I'm asking myself and others what it means to earn it, and to honor the sacrifices of those who came before us, be they ancestors who left homelands willingly or by force, or soldiers who served our country, voluntarily or by draft. Do we each have a duty to help new generations of Americans try to achieve their dreams? Yes, we do. How are we each obliged to fight for and grow our country now?

What are our new roles and responsibilities as citizens?

What I know in my soul is that the prejudice, inequality, and broken systems that do exist are wrong and dangerous. As Americans, they anger and shame so many of us. Personally, I can't just sit on a couch and watch the news, or run a company, while society erupts, or walk into some form of retirement and be still. On the sidelines is not where most of us want to be. We must see beyond what's in front of us. We must reimagine the promise of America. How? By using empathy to try to understand, raising our voices to condemn darkness, and casting our votes to choose the kind of leadership we want our grandchildren to grow up with. But we must also use our hard skills and resources to craft a better reality for ourselves, our neighbors and those with whom we share this land. We can protest but also plan. Search for the truth and share it broadly. Listen to others, and blend ideas. Criticize, but also create.

It's time to commit to a deeper level of shared accountability—to neighbor as well as to stranger, and to self. Americans will always have differences, because that is the nature of the republic we have created. But we owe our children a less divisive America, just as many of our parents fought for a less divided country than the one they inherited. It is time for all of us to elevate the best of ourselves.

It is time to climb, and to reclaim the high ground.

To do so we must make a choice, one that we have made before. It is a choice between renewal or decline. Our country has a history of renewal at moments when we've faced decline, but we also know that renewing our nation's honor is not a forgone conclusion. The future is not going to bend toward America because we're American. We're going to have to bend it ourselves, nudge it, move it.

At every turn, let us choose to replace meanness with kindness; pettiness with significance; hate with love; gridlock with compromise; complaints with creative solutions. As a nation, we must be tough but not at the expense of one another. So let us also champion and celebrate those with strength of character—the upstanders among us—because there are so many whose daily intentions and actions echo the heroism of the past, who strive for honesty in the present, and who are already reimagining the promise of America, and will do so for years to come.

Above all, let us choose to believe in each other because now and always—we are in this together.

ACKNOWLEDGMENTS

From the Ground Up is the most personal book I have yet to write, as well as the most consequential, given the nature and the needs of the times we are living in. I am grateful for the talent, participation, and support of so many people.

First and foremost, my wife, Sheri, and my children and their spouses—Jordan and Breanna, Addison and Tal—continue to fill my life with love, learning, and joy. Every moment is more meaningful because of each of you.

To my sister, Ronnie, and my brother, Michael: We have parallel histories, yet our life journeys are our own; thank you for honoring the journey I have chosen to share.

There is one person, above all, who deserves my profound gratitude for the pages you have read: my remarkably talented writing partner, Joanne Gordon. She was at my side during every phase of this project. She possesses the rare ability to walk in one's shoes, and she helped give me the confidence to share personal stories I had not told anyone, save for Sheri. And it was Joanne who helped figure out how to weave the stories of my past and present into one seamless narrative. I'm deeply grateful for her tireless collaboration and her true friendship.

Joanne and I especially want to express our deepest thanks to Rajiv Chandrasekaran, whose wise counsel, high standards, integrity, and unwavering commitment to helping us tell a powerful story were vital at every turn.

My longtime literary agent, Jennifer Rudolph Walsh at William-Morris Endeavor, was an early and avid champion of the story I was ready to tell.

At Random House, president Gina Centrello embraced our vision from the beginning. We were fortunate to have the talented editor Christopher Jackson as our collaborator; his candid, insightful guidance made us and the book better on every page. Thank you also to his dedicated editorial assistant, Cecilia Flores, and the design, editing, and marketing teams at Random House, who ushered the book through production.

Many people read drafts of the book, including Sheri, Alan Cohen, Alexa Albert, Faiza Saeed, Jennifer Butte-Dahl, Ian McCormick, Richard Yarmuth, Anna Kakos, and Zabrina Jenkins. There were many more, and their collective feedback has been invaluable.

Heidi Peiper and Chris Gorley were essential to ensuring that history—my own, Starbucks', and the country's—came to life with detail and accuracy.

We are also grateful for the more than one hundred individuals who were interviewed, and who generously contributed their memories and expertise.

The people at Starbucks have been my second family, and I have more respect than I can measure for the approximately three million partners who have worn the green apron over the decades, serving customers and the company. It has been my honor to serve with you. I also have been blessed to work alongside leaders with a diversity of backgrounds, ideas, and skills. The list is long, and begins with past and current members of Starbucks senior leadership teams and its board of directors, especially Mike Ullman, Mellody Hobson, Bill Bradley, Olden Lee, Jamie Shennan, and Craig Weatherup.

A very special thank you to Kevin Johnson for his friendship and dedication to the company, and to Vivek Varma for his values-based leadership and years of candid counsel.

And my deep appreciation to Nancy Kent, Tim Donlan, Gina Woods, Carol Sharp, Moana Stolz, Jaime Riley, Colleen Davis, Terry Davenport, David Glickman, and Josh Trujillo, whose contributions to Starbucks and the book have been crucial.

Through the years, many wonderful colleagues and friends have enhanced my life and work in addition to the people included in this book, and I would be remiss not to acknowledge them: Mohammed Alshaya; Plácido Arango and Ana Maria van Pallandt; Carlos Benitez; Tim Brosnan; John Carlin; Michael Corbat; Brunello Cucinelli; Nicole David; Jean-Charles and Natacha Decaux; Ric Elias; Billy Etkin; Joe and Sherry Felson; Jim Fingeroth; Steve and Patty Fleischmann; Jeff Fox; Ron Graves; Jonathan Gray; Giampaolo Grossi; Wanda Herndon; Jeffrey and Carol Hoffeld; Loren Hostek; Steve Kersch; Len and Nancy Kersch; Jason Kintzer; Nancy Koehn; Tony La Russa; Jane Lee; Dan and Stacey Levitan; Eric Liedtke; Doron and Kai Linz; June, Menchu, and Noey Lopez; Betsy and Brian Losh; Jack Ma; Luis Marin; Panos Marinopoulos; General Stanley McChrystal, retired; Matt McCutchen; Angelo Moratti; Max Mutchnick and Eric Hyman; Estuardo Porras; Rocco Princi; Jen Quotson; Jack and Nancy Rodgers; Ginni Rometty; Joe Roth; Angela Rudig; Renee Ryan; Michael Sacks; Dan and Jackie Safier; Jerry Schaft; Jim Sinegal; David Solomon; Robert Stilin; Steve Stoute; Suzanne Sullivan; Sara Taylor; Alberto Torrado; Wim Vanderspek; David Vobora; and Jake Wood.

From Joanne: I would like to thank my amazing son, Theo, for bringing his kindness, calm, wit, and wisdom into my life; my parents, David and Virginia, for inspiring my lifelong passion for learning and writing; my sister, Susan, niece, Alex, and nephew, Zachary, for their steadfast love; as well as my dearest friends—down the street and across the country—for being my second family. I also want to express my deep respect for Howard Schultz, who has trusted me with his voice and story for many years, and continues to inspire so many of us to be our best selves.

PHOTOGRAPH CREDITS

Early Years
1. Courtesy of the Schultz family
2. Brooklyn Daily Eagle Photographs, Brooklyn Public Library, Brooklyn Collection
3–8. Courtesy of the Schultz family

Onward to Seattle
1–2. Courtesy of the Schultz family
3. Courtesy of Starbucks
4–5. Courtesy of the Schultz family
6–11. Courtesy of Starbucks

Creative Civic Engagement
1. Courtesy of John Harrington/Starbucks
2–3. Courtesy of Starbucks
4. Courtesy of John Harrington/Starbucks
5. Courtesy of Joshua Jerome
6. Jeff Swensen/The New York Times/Redux
7. Courtesy of Starbucks

Honoring Heroes
8. Courtesy of Starbucks
9. Courtesy of the Schultz Family Foundation/Michel du Cille
10. Courtesy of the Department of the Army/Seventy-Fifth Ranger Regiment
11. Courtesy of Joshua Trujillo/Starbucks
12. Kevin Roche/Kevin Roche Photography
13. Courtesy of Joshua Trujillo/Starbucks

A Pathway to College
1. Courtesy of Laura Segall/Arizona State University
2. Courtesy of Markelle Cullom-Herbison
3. Courtesy of Scott Eklund/Starbucks
4. Courtesy of Ken Henderson/Arizona State University
5. Courtesy of Joshua Trujillo/Starbucks

Tough Conversations

6. Courtesy of Peter Wintersteller/Starbucks

7–8. Courtesy of Starbucks

9. Courtesy of Michael Thomas/Starbucks

10. Courtesy of Starbucks

Opportunities for All

1–5. Courtesy of Joshua Trujillo/Starbucks

In It Together

6. Courtesy of Joshua Trujillo/Starbucks

7. Courtesy of Lindsey Wasson/Starbucks

8. Courtesy of Joshua Trujillo/Starbucks

9. Courtesy of the Schultz Family Foundation

10. Courtesy of Ian McCormick

11–12. Courtesy of Joshua Trujillo/Starbucks

Upstanders

1. Courtesy of Joshua Trujillo/Starbucks

2. Courtesy of Rajiv Chandrasekaran

3. Courtesy of Joshua Trujillo/Starbucks

4. Courtesy of Starbucks

5. Courtesy of Jamie Coughlin/SideXSide Studios

6. Courtesy of Rajiv Chandrasekaran

Coffee in China

7–8. Courtesy of Starbucks

9. Courtesy of Joshua Trujillo/Starbucks

10. Courtesy of Joshua Trujillo/Starbucks

11. Courtesy of Starbucks

A More Perfect Union

1–2. Courtesy of Peter Van Beever/National Constitution Center

3–5. Courtesy of Joshua Trujillo/Starbucks

A New Chapter

6–10. Courtesy of Joshua Trujillo/Starbucks

Family

1–4. Courtesy of the Schultz family

5. Courtesy of the Schultz Family Foundation

6. Courtesy of the Schultz family

Back to the Past

7. Courtesy of Rajiv Chandrasekaran

8–9. Courtesy of Rainer Hosch/Random House

10–11. Courtesy of Rajiv Chandrasekaran

1–2. Courtesy of Rajiv Chandrasekaran

INDEX

Affordable Care Act (2010), 166, 301–2
Afghanistan, war in (2001–present), 104, 112–14, 119, 130, 139, 159, 138, 134–37
Alibaba Group, 283
All, Lacey, 232, 234, 240
American Dream, xi–xii, 100, 184, 289, 323–24, 329
American Mug & Stein, 88–89, 95–97
American Red Cross, 291
anti-Semitism, 294
 Holocaust and, 249–50, 294–95
AOL, 249
APECO, 223
Appalachia, 246–49, 251–68
 Coalfield Development Corp. in, 262–68
 opioid epidemic in, 248, 249, 252–59
 unemployment in, 259–61
 waning of coal industry in, 246–47, 265–66
Arizona State University (ASU), 170–71, 181, 332
 Schultz's commencement address at, 180, 183–85
 Starbucks College Achievement Plan and, 173–79, 182–83
Armed Forces Network (AFN), 111, 114, 116, 117, 119, 120, 292
Aspen Institute's Forum for Community Solutions, 232

Atlantic, 210–11
Auschwitz, 294–95

Baldwin, Gerald ("Jerry"), 14, 16–17, 21–22, 23, 83, 84, 86
Baniodeh, Majd, 292–93, 294
baristas, 15, 16, 25, 27, 32, 38, 41, 173
 Come Together cups and, 64–65, 71, 119, 205
 Create Jobs for USA and, 93
 Race Together cups and, 205, 207, 210
 retraining of (February 2008), 42
 scheduling work shifts for, 30
Barista Training and Education Program, 129
Bean Stock, 27–29, 30, 166, 252
Beck, Charlie, 200
Behar, Howard, 33–34, 45
Beijing, China, Schultz's visit to Starbucks in, 270–74
Bialcak, Rachael, 122–23
Biden, Joe, 302
Black Lives Matter, 191
Block, Billy, ix, 6, 11, 52, 190, 215, 275–76, 329
Bobo, Carol, 22, 23
Bourgeois, Arga, 81–82
Bowker, Gordon, 14, 17, 21–22, 23, 83, 84, 86
Bratton, William, 200
Brewer, Rosalind, 214, 309
Bridge for Girls, 145

Brotman, Adam, 77–79, 80, 196
Brown, Michael, 198
Budget Control Act of 2011, 59–60
Burrows, Cliff, 121
Bush, George W., 138
Byers, Tony, 196

caffè latte, 15
Campaign for the Fair Sentencing of Youth, 243
Carothers, Kevin, 233
Carper, Gregory, 260, 263
Carr, Chris, 191–92, 196
Case, Steve, 248
CBS This Morning, 311–12
CDFIs (Community Development Financial Institutions), 80–83, 93, 94
 see also Create Jobs for USA
Chandrasekaran, Rajiv, 196
 in Appalachia, 249, 258
 short films made by Trujillo and, 250–51
 veterans and, 138–40, 158–60
Charlottesville, Va., white nationalists' rallies in, 294, 295, 299–300
Chestnut Ridge treatment center (Morgantown, W. Va.), 252–56, 263
Chiarelli, Peter, 131–34, 135, 139, 158
Chicago, 100,000 Opportunities Fair and Forum in, 232–41, 245

Chicago Cook Workforce
  Partnership, 232
China, 277–84
  devotion to family in, 272
  insurance benefit for
    parents of partners in,
    277–78, 282, 283
  Starbucks' annual
    meeting of families in,
    270–74
  Starbucks' history in,
    278–84
  Starbucks Reserve
    Roastery opened in,
    306
China Daily, 278
Cicero, 182
Civil Rights Act of 1964,
  321
civil rights movement, 216,
  321, 323
Civil War, Battle of
  Gettysburg in, 298–99
Coalfield Development
  Corp., 262–68
coal industry, 259–61
  Vance's Hillbilly Elegy
    and, 247–48
  waning of, 246–47,
    265–66
  see also Appalachia
coffee beans:
  Arabica vs. Robusta, 14
  dark vs. light roast, 14
  Starbucks Reserve
    Roasteries and, 305–8
Coffee with a Cop program,
  212–13
college education:
  accessibility of, to
    low-income students,
    170–71
  Higher Education Act
    of 1965 and, 167–68,
    175
  new Starbucks benefit for,
    172–85; see also
    Starbucks College
    Achievement Plan
  online programs, 171,
    173–74
  rising cost of, 172
  of Starbucks partners
    before new benefit,

163–64, 166–67, 172,
  173
  student loans and,
    167–68, 172
  unaffordable for some
    during Great
    Recession, 163–64
Collins, Stacy, 252
Come Together petition
  campaign, 68–71,
  319
"Come Together," written on
  Starbucks cups, 64–65,
  71, 119, 205
Common, 240–41, 317
Community:
  importance of in Schultz's
    youth, 11–13
  in Starbucks stores, 16,
    25, 32, 33, 42, 84
  role of Starbucks in, 61,
    215–16, 309–10
  power of, 45, 190, 254,
    290
comparable store sales, or
  "comps," 38–39
Concert for Valor (National
  Mall, Washington,
  D.C., 2014), 160–62
Congolese refugees, 290,
  300
Congress, U.S., 61, 62, 110
  attempt to repeal
    Affordable Care Act
    and, 301–2
  budget crisis of 2013 and,
    63–65
  debt ceiling debacle of
    2011 and, 58–60
  government shutdown of
    2013 and, 65, 66–71
Constitution, U.S., 302–3
Craig, Allen, 92
Create Jobs for USA,
  88–100, 196, 201, 231,
  319
  donations raised by,
    93–94
  first commercial for,
    91–93
  genesis of, 76–83
  mugs imprinted with
    word INDIVISIBLE for,
    95–97

official launch of website
  for, 93
relevance and connection
  with customers
  enhanced by, 98
Starbucks investors
  critical of, 97–98, 99
Starbucks revenues
  and, 99
tag line for, 90
wristband design for,
  89–90, 93
credit rating of United
  States, 59–60
crema, 15
Cronkite, Walter, 51
Crow, Michael, 170–72,
  173, 174, 175, 180, 182,
  183, 184, 328, 334
Crowder, Rebecca, 257, 258,
  262–63, 328, 333
crowdfunding, 78–80
Cullom-Herbison, Markelle,
  163–64, 176–78,
  181–82, 332
Culver, John, 105
C.U.P. Fund, 277
Curry, Charlie, 260
Customer Service
  Excellence Training
  course, 222

Dahl, Kenneth, 130, 157
Dallas, 100,000
  Opportunities Fair and
  Forum in, 242–43
Davis, Angela, 257, 258,
  262–63
death benefits for soldiers,
  denied during 2013
  government
  shutdown, 67
debt ceiling debacle (2011),
  58–60
Declaration of
  Independence, 297,
  298–99
Defense Department, U.S.,
  112
  Gates's leadership of,
    109–11
Demos, 317
Dennison, Brandon,
  262–68, 328, 334

dignity,
  in America, xi, 76, 137, 323,
  and the human condition, 45, 76, 99, 185, 212, 266, 322, 324, 333
  and Starbucks, 76, 84
  of work, derived from employment, x, 7, 76, 151, 227, 242, 244, 275
Dimon, Jamie, 160, 230
"Discuss" television campaign, 202
Dixon, Mary, 180–81
Donald, Jim, 34–35
draft:
  lottery of 1972 and, 101–4, 107
  volunteer vs. conscripted army and, 140, 334
duBrowa, Corey, 208–9
Duprey, Cynthia, 87, 94

East Liverpool, Ohio, 88–89, 94–97
Eco-Baby Day Care, 94
Election Day (2008), free coffee for voters in, 60
Emanuel, Rahm, 232
Emily (Chinese Starbucks partner), 271–72, 273, 280
entrepreneurs, 59
  challenges faced by, 23, 83, 86–87
  innovation and, 29–30
  loans for, 78, 79, 81; see also Create Jobs for USA
  managers of Starbucks stores as, 43
  see also small businesses
equality:
  in America, xii, 211, 297, 299, 317, 323, 324
  JFK's campaign speech and, 50, 71
  Lincoln's Gettysburg Address and, 298–99
  in marriage, 211–12
  at Starbucks, 282
  original intent of Declaration of Independence and, 297

Equal Justice Initiative, 199
espresso bars in Milan, Schultz's first experiences in, 13–14, 15–16, 23, 38, 263, 274

Feinberg, Judith, 253, 254, 255, 258
Ferguson, Mo.:
  Brown shooting and subsequent riots in, 198, 200
  Schultz's visit to, 201
Financial Times, 299
Finkel, Rabbi Nosson Tzvi, 249–50
Fisher, Arnold, 133
For Love of Country (Schultz and Chandrasekaran), 158–60, 196
  Veterans Day concert and (2014), 160–62
forums, see open forums
Fox News, 61
Frappuccino® blended beverage, 32
Friedersdorf, Conor, 210–11
FSG, 229, 232

Garner, Eric, 191
Gates, Bill and Melinda, Foundation, 129
Gates, Robert, 109–11, 114, 118, 119, 122, 124, 129, 133, 134, 157
Gates, William H., Sr., 85–86, 100, 150
Get in the mud mantra, 43
Gettysburg Address (Lincoln), 298–99
Giffords, Gabrielle, 157
Giornale, Il, 21–26, 31, 33, 274
  became Starbucks Corporation, 26
  money raising for, 21–25, 83–86
  original mission statement for, 25, 26, 34, 147
  staff hired for, 25, 26
  Starbucks Coffee Company bought by, 26, 83–86
Gonzales, Miguel, 87, 94

Good Morning America, 309, 311
Gorelick, Harold, 24
Great Recession, 229
  college unaffordable for some during, 163–64
  effect on families, 163–64
  Schultz's efforts at job creation during, 76–83; see also Create Jobs for USA
  unemployment in, 75–76
Greenburg, Scott, 85
Griffey, Ken, Jr., 91
Griffin, Jimmy, 87, 94

Hagar (Chicago job fair attendee), 236–37, 238–39
Hammarplast, 227
Hanley, Dervala, 173–74
Hausenware, 94–95
Hawkins, Patrick C., 67
HBO, Veterans Day 2014 concert broadcast by, 160–62
healthcare benefits, 30, 66, 67, 166
  Affordable Care Act and, 166, 301–2
  for parents of Chinese partners, 277–78, 282, 283
  for part-time Starbucks employees, 26–27
  for terminally ill workers, 27
  Wall Street's short-term perspective on, 47–48
Higgins, Daniel, 113
Higher Education Act (1965), 167–68, 175
Hillbilly Elegy (Vance), 247–48
Hines, Rodney, 80–81, 201
Hobson, Mellody, 205–6, 216, 313, 314–15, 317, 321
Holder, Eric, 316
Holocaust, 249–50, 294–95
Honighausen, Ulrich, 94–95, 97, 100
Horn & Hardart Automat, 89

Houston, Hurricane Ike in (2008), 81–82
Hudson, Jennifer, 160
Huntoon, David H., Jr., 105, 107
Hurricane Ike (2008), 81–82
Hurricane Katrina (2005), 44–45, 201
Hymes, Camille, 310, 313

Ifill, Gwen, 207–8
Ifill, Sherrilyn, 317, 322–23
immigration:
  of Schultz's ancestors, 295–96
  Starbucks open forum on, 294–97
  see also refugees
innovation, 29–30, 38, 245
Iraq War (2003–2011), 104, 115, 139, 159
  rationale for, 138
  survival of soldiers severely wounded in, 134–35
Israel, Schultz's visit to, 249–50
Italy:
  espresso bars in, 13–14, 15–16, 23, 38, 263, 274
  Starbucks Reserve Roastery opened in, 306–8

Jaffe, Joanne, 200
James, Mick, 117–19, 120
Japan, Starbucks stores in, 32–33
Jenkins, Zabrina, 309
Jiang Zemin, 281–82
job creation, 61, 76–83, 88–100
  in Appalachia, 262–68
  see also Create Jobs for USA
  at Starbucks, 325
jobs programs for young Americans, see 100,000 Opportunities Initiative; opportunity youth; YouthBuild USA

Johannesburg, South Africa, opening of first Starbucks stores in, 184
Johnson, Ben and Kacey, 252
Johnson, Kevin, 291, 304–5, 308–9, 311, 313, 316, 317, 321, 324, 325
Johnson, Lyndon B., 102, 167–68
Joint Base Lewis-McChord (Wash.), 157
  Schultz's meeting with military veterans at, 130–31
  Starbucks district managers' tour of, 121–22
Jones, Van, 210
JPMorgan Chase, 160, 230
June (Chinese Starbucks partner), 272
Just Mercy (Stevenson), 199–200, 214, 312

Kaiser Family Foundation, 139
Kamikazi, Liliane, 142–45
Kellogg, W. K., Foundation, 232
Kelly, John A. C., 66–67, 68, 70, 133, 291
Kelly, Mark, 157
Kennedy, Jackie, 51
Kennedy, Joey, 260–61
Kennedy, John F., 55, 214
  assassination of, 50–51, 52, 133
  campaign speech of, 49–50, 71
Kennedy, Robert F., 102
Kenny G., 24
Kent, Nancy, 109
Kerrigan, Jim, 27
Kersch, Harry (father-in-law), 18, 20–21, 24, 100
Kersch, Rae (mother-in-law), 18, 20–21
KeyArena, Seattle, 153, 156
Keyes, Dakota, 327–28, 334
Kickstarter, 78

King, Cedric, 135–37, 159, 161, 240, 333
King, Gayle, 311–12
Koehn, Nancy, 298–99
Kraning, Kenny, 29
Krissoff, Bill, 159, 161, 333
Krissoff, Nathan, 159
Kurdi, Alan, 286–87

Lazarus, Emma, 288–89
Lederman, Lillian ("Nana"; grandmother), card games run by, 3–7
Lederman, Morris and Leah (great-grandparents), 296
Lederman, Woolf ("Poppy"; grandfather), 5, 296
Lennon, Chauncey, 230
Levitt, Arthur, 109
Liberty Medal, 302
Lily's Place, Huntington, W. Va., 256–58, 263
Lincoln, Abraham, 99, 298–99
Lomax, Michael, 213
Los Angeles, 100,000 Opportunities Fair and Forum in, 241
Los Angeles Police Department (LAPD), 200

Ma, Jack, 283, 284
Mahoney, Luke and Catarina, 86–87, 94
Mantle, Mickey, 36–37, 329
Margolis, Ron, 22, 23
marriage equality, 211–12
Martin, Trayvon, 191
McCain, John, 133, 301–3
McClellan, Clyde, 95–97
McElrath-Bey, Xavier, 242–43, 244, 332
McGhee, Heather, 317
Measure of America, 229
Medal of Honor, 111, 112, 114, 161
Melville, Herman, 14
merchant mind-set, 89
Merrill Lynch, 80
microfinancing, 78, 80
  see also CDFIs

Milan, Italy:
    Schultz's first visit to
        espresso bars in,
        13–14, 15–16, 23, 38,
        263, 274
    Starbucks Reserve
        Roastery opened in,
        306–8
military bases, Starbucks
    stores on or near, 117,
    119, 120, 123
military service, 100–124
    civilian-military divide
        and, 139–40
    conscription vs.
        volunteering and, 140
    Gates's insights into,
        109–11
    Petry's experiences in
        Afghanistan and,
        111–14
    of Schultz's father, 104,
        140–41
    Schultz's Walter Reed
        visit and, 132–38
    Schultz's West Point visit
        and, 104–9
    Starbucks' free brewed
        coffee and, 117, 119,
        120
    suicide rates and, 131–32,
        139–40
    Vietnam draft lottery and,
        100–104
military spouses, Starbucks'
    hiring commitment
    and, 119, 120, 122–23,
    292
military veterans, 129–40,
    157–58, 230, 323
    book featuring stories of,
        158–60
    Chandrasekaran's series
        of articles on, 138–40
    Foundation's first
        long-term strategic plan
        for, 157–58
    high influx of, into
        civilian society (2013),
        118–19
    PTSD and TBI among,
        119, 132, 158
    skills brought to
        workplace by, 118

Starbucks' hiring
    commitment and,
    116–24, 132, 139, 292,
    320
transition of, from active
    duty to nonmilitary life,
    130–31, 139–40
Veterans Day 2014
    concert in honor of,
    160–62
at Walter Reed National
    Military Medical
    Center, 132–38
Missoula, Mont., refugee
    resettlement in,
    286–87, 289–90,
    300
Moby-Dick (Melville), 14
Mockingbird, 127
money matters, 147–52
    impact of not having
        money and, 151–52
    Schultz's childhood
        experiences of
        financial insecurity
        and, 7–8, 22–23,
        147–50, 151, 167, 276,
        278
Moody's Analytics, 90
Moreno, Jennifer M., 67
Morgan Stanley, 77
MSNBC, 322–23
Muller, Liz, 306, 307

NAACP Legal Defense and
    Educational Fund
    (LDF), 317
Nadel, Michael, 189–90,
    215–16, 276, 329
National Organization of
    Black Law
    Enforcement
    Executives, 213
Nelson, Rashon, 303–4,
    308, 311
Nelson, Stanley, 321
neonatal abstinence
    syndrome, 256–57
"New Colossus, The"
    (Lazarus), 288–89
New Orleans:
    four-day leadership
        conference for store
        managers in, 43–47

impact of Hurricane
    Katrina in, 44–45, 201
New York Police
    Department (NYPD),
    200
New York Post, 219
New York Times, 62, 209
New York Yankees, 36–37
Next Chapter Books (Barre,
    Vt.), 94
Nixon, Richard M., 102
Nocera, Joe, 62
Normandy landing, Schultz's
    visit to site of, 331–33
Northern Michigan
    University (NMU),
    165–66, 167–69, 223
Novak, Frank, 165, 166

Obama, Barack, 58, 59, 61,
    62, 192, 228, 287
Obama, Michelle, 161
Oklahoma City Thunder,
    155–56
Olsen, Dave, 33
100,000 Jobs Mission, 230
100,000 Opportunities
    Initiative, 230–45,
    320
    in Chicago, 232–41, 245
    civic intermediaries in,
        231
    coalition of business
        leaders in, 231–32
    effects of, 241–42
    in Dallas, 242–43
    funding for, 232
    in Los Angeles, 241
    new kinds of public-
        private partnerships
        and, 244–45
    in Phoenix, 241
    in Seattle, 241–42
One Mind for Research,
    132, 158
online education programs,
    171, 173–74
Onward (Schultz), 41, 143,
    181
open forums, 33–34
    on immigration, 294–97
    on race relations, 192–99,
        202–3, 207, 210, 212,
        215, 322

opioid addiction, 248, 249,
      252–59, 288
   of babies exposed to drugs
      in womb, 256–57
   Chestnut Ridge treatment
      center and, 252–56,
      263
   deaths caused by, 248,
      259
   as man-made disaster,
      258
   Suboxone in treatment of,
      253, 258
Opportunity Finance
      Network (OFN),
      81–83, 90, 97
opportunity youth, 228–45,
      320, 323
   coining of name for, 229
   first jobs for, 230–45;
      see also 100,000
      Opportunities Initiative
   job training program for,
      219–22; see also
      YouthBuild USA
   obstacles faced by, 228,
      229, 243
   Starbucks' hiring of,
      238–39, 245
Oprah Chai Tea, 145, 157
Oswald, Lee Harvey, 52
O'Toole, Kathleen,
      200–201, 213

Patterson, Cody J., 67
Peiper, Heidi, 295
Pell Grants, 175
Perstorp, 227
Peters, Joseph M., 67
petition campaign, to end
      2013 shutdown of
      federal government
      (Come Together),
      68–71, 319
Petry, Leroy, 111–14, 117,
      159, 161, 333
Philadelphia, 303–4,
      308–23
Phoenix, 100,000
      Opportunities Fair and
      Forum in, 241
Pike Place Market (Seattle),
      Starbucks store in,
      305

Pinsky, Mark, 81–83, 90,
      93, 97, 100, 334
Pitasky, Daniel, 129
   veterans issues and,
      130–31, 133, 135, 157,
      158
   youth employment and,
      220, 222, 229, 230–31,
      232
PlayNetwork, 77
Plepler, Richard, 160
police:
   Coffee with a Cop
      program and, 212–13
   and Eric Garner death,
      191
   and Michael Brown
      death, 198
   and community relations,
      198–201
   Schultz's meetings with
      local law enforcement
      officials, 200–201,
      213–14
Poole, Mary, 286–87,
      289–90, 300, 333
Porcarelli, Rob, 114, 116–19,
      120
post-traumatic stress
      disorder (PTSD), 119,
      132, 158
post-9/11 wars, 104, 161
   health declines among
      military personnel in,
      139
   survival of soldiers
      severely wounded in,
      134–35
   see also Afghanistan, war
      in; Iraq War; military
      veterans
Pour Your Heart Into It
      (Schultz), 26, 281
Powell-Pointer, Saunjah,
      195, 196
POWER, 312–14
Prentice, Arnie, 24–25
presidential election of
      2012, 99
Progress Fund, 97
Promise of America, 243,
      335
   achieving the, 323, 334
   defined, 71, 172, 299

Schultz as beneficiary
      of, 62
"Promised Land, The"
      (Springsteen), 162
P.S. 272 (Canarsie), 215–16,
      326–28
"pulling" shots of
      espresso, 15

race relations, 189–217,
      308–23, 324
   black leadership voices
      and, 192
   Black Lives Matter and,
      191
   black men killed by police
      and, 191, 198, 199–200
   Coffee with a Cop
      program and, 212–13
   "Discuss" campaign and,
      202
   generational divide among
      African Americans
      and, 191–92
   new Starbucks training
      curriculum and, 322
   open forums on, 192–99,
      202–3, 207, 210, 212,
      215, 322
   Philadelphia store arrests
      and, 303–4, 308–23
   profiling and, 199, 308,
      311–12
   Schultz's childhood
      mixed-race friend and,
      189–90, 215–16
   slavery's legacies and,
      216–17, 313
   Starbucks' compendium
      on, 196
   Starbucks management
      and, 214
   Starbucks stores in low-
      and middle-income
      neighborhoods and, 215
   store closing for bias
      training and, 314–15,
      317–23
   white nationalist rallies in
      Charlottesville and,
      294, 295, 299–300
Race Together campaign,
      204–11, 215, 233, 313,
      318, 320

combative reception of,
207–9, 210–11

cup controversy and, 205,
207, 210

discussion guide for,
204–5, 210

Hobson's views on, 205–6

postmortems on, 210–11,
213

Rachel (Chinese Starbucks
partner), 270–71, 272,
273, 280

Rahr, Susan, 213–14

Randle, Jen, 318

Reagan, Ronald, 133, 331

Reclaim Appalachia, 265

Refresh Appalachia, 264

refugees, 286–300, 323

America's moral obligation
to, 288

false narrative about
threat posed by, 288

Lazarus's "The New
Colossus" and, 288–89

photograph of drowned
Syrian boy and,
286–87

resettled in Missoula,
286–87, 289–90, 300

Starbucks' hiring
commitment and,
291–94, 320

Starbucks' open forum on
immigration and,
294–97

Trump's policies on,
287–88, 289, 291, 294,
300

remote workforce, 32

Rewire Appalachia, 264

"Rise of the Rest" road trip,
249

Roberts, Robin, 311

Robinson, Donte, 303–4,
308, 311

Robinson, Lucas, 112–13

Rockefeller Foundation,
232

Rodgers, Jack, 24–25

Romney, George, 169

Romney, Mitt, 169

Roosevelt, Theodore, 105

Rwandan genocide (1994),
142–45

Ryan, Matt, 172–73, 175,
196

St. Louis, open forum on
race relations in,
198–99, 203

same-sex marriage, 211–12

Save the Children, 291

Schultz, Addison ("Addy")
(daughter), 56–57, 151,
275, 329

Schultz, Breanna (daughter-
in-law), 151

Schultz, Elaine (mom), ix, x,
7, 8, 10, 12, 14–15,
19–20, 28, 55, 56, 100,
189, 219, 227, 255,
269–70, 276, 328

death of, 284–85

depression suffered by,
52–54, 269, 284

husband's death and, 274,
275

JFK's assassination and,
50–51, 52

JFK's campaign speech
and, 49–50, 71

money problems and,
7–8, 22–23, 147–50,
151, 167, 276

Nana's card games and,
3–7

son's college education
and, 164, 165, 166, 169,
223

Vietnam draft lottery
and, 101, 102, 103,
104

Schultz, Fred (father), ix, x,
7, 11, 14, 28, 50, 51, 53,
54, 55, 56, 76, 103,
152, 165, 166, 189, 223,
284, 285

baseball loved by,
36–37, 92

chess disliked by, 40

death and funeral of,
150

injured on the job, 8–9,
278

lung cancer and death of,
255, 269–70, 274–76

military service of, 104,
140–41

money problems and,
7–8, 22–23, 147–50,
151, 167, 276, 278

Nana's card games and, 3,
4, 5, 6, 7

son's college education
and, 165, 166, 169

work life of, xi, 7, 8–9,
21, 26, 75, 227, 276,
278

Schultz, Harry
(grandfather), 296

Schultz, Howard:

bar mitzvah of, 148–49

as baseball fan, 36–37,
91–92

as chess player, 39–40

childhood of, ix–x, xii,
3–13, 49–55, 125–26,
128, 147–50, 189–90,
325–29

college education of,
164–66, 167–69, 223

death first experienced by,
51–52

early work experiences of,
218–19, 222–28,
243–44

as entrepreneur, 21–31,
56, 84, 227–28

feelings of powerlessness
experienced by, 54–55

financial insecurity
experienced by, 7–8,
22–23, 147–50, 151,
167, 276, 278

first forays into political
activism, 60–72

as fur factory worker,
218–19, 228

immigration of ancestors
of, 295–96

parenting and values of,
150–51

playground games and, 9,
10–12

student loans of, 167–68

sudden wealth of, 150–51

team sports and, 12–13,
164–66

as Xerox salesman,
222–28

see also Starbucks Corp.;
specific topics

Schultz, Jordan (son), 24, 105, 151, 199, 235, 275, 329
as sports fan and journalist, 91–92
Schultz, Max (great-grandfather), 295–96
Schultz, Michael (brother), ix, 3, 6, 7, 8, 148, 269, 274, 284
Schultz, Ronnie (sister), ix, 3, 6, 7, 269, 274
Schultz, Sheri Kersch (wife), 18–20, 21, 22, 25, 53, 57, 84, 86, 92, 100, 105, 107, 133, 143, 249, 269, 274, 285, 308, 329, 331, 332
first jobs for young people and, 228–34, 235, 238, 240, 243; see also 100,000 Opportunities Initiative
husband's first meeting with, 18–19
job training for young people and, 219–22; see also YouthBuild USA
learning about opioid addiction and, 252, 256, 257–58
marriage of, 20
parenting and values of, 150–51
personality of, 19
pregnancy and childbearing of, 21, 23
veterans and, 129–30, 157–58
volunteering with at-risk youth, 126–30, 151
Schultz Family Foundation, 127–30, 268
establishment, early days, and leadership of, 127–28
first executive director hired by, 129
first jobs for opportunity youth and, 228–34; see also 100,000 Opportunities Initiative
job training for young people and, 219–22;

see also YouthBuild USA
motto for, 243
refugees and, 291
veterans and, 129–30, 157–58, 160, 230
Scotland, Robyn, 87, 94
Seaside Brewing, 94
Seattle, 100,000 Opportunities Fair and Forum in, 241–42
Seattle Mariners, 152
Seattle Police Department (SPD), 200–201
Seattle SuperSonics, 152–56
fans as stakeholders in, 154, 155, 156
new arena for, 153–54, 155
relocated to Oklahoma City, 155–56
Schultz's sale of stake in, 154–56
September 11, 2001, attacks, 104, 115, 131, 137, 138
shutdown of federal government (2013), 65, 66–71
Come Together petition and, 68–71, 319
Siegl, Zev, 14
skelly, 10–11
slavery:
legacies of, 216–17, 313
Lincoln's Gettysburg Address and, 298–99
small businesses, 77–83
challenges faced by, 86–87
entrepreneurs' seed stories and, 263–64
loans for, 77–78, 80–83, 88–100; see also Create Jobs for USA
as source of new jobs, 77–78, 79
Smith, Anna Deavere, 317, 321
Smith, Orin, 34, 154
Social Science Research Council, 229
Soft Landing Missoula, 289–90, 300

solar panels, in Appalachia, 263, 264, 265
South Africa:
opening of first Starbucks stores in, 184
RFK's condemnation of apartheid in, 214
Spaulding, Tracy, 246–47, 267
Spelman College, 213
Spielberg, Steven, 161
Sports Illustrated, 153–54
Springsteen, Bruce, 160, 162
Standard & Poor's, 59–60
Starbucks Coffee Company, 24, 269–70
acquired by Il Giornale, 26, 83–86
early days of, as coffee roaster and retailer, 14–15, 16–17
espresso bar idea and, 16–17, 21, 38
Il Giornale renamed as, 26
mission of, 25–26, 30, 60, 76, 117, 193
Starbucks College Achievement Plan (SCAP), 170–85, 320
advisors assigned to students in, 177–78
ASU chosen as educational partner for, 173–74, 175
contest for graduating partners in, 179–80
Cullom-Herbison's story and, 163–64, 176–78, 181–82
economic benefits for Starbucks of, 175–76, 182
genesis of, 170–76
improvements made to, 178–79, 182–83
incentivizing students to finish in, 176, 177
as model for other corporations, 183
online programs as best fit for, 173–74
partners' college education before,

163–64, 166–67, 172, 173
Pathway to Admission curriculum for, 182
Valdez's story and, 178–80
for veterans, 182
waiting period for tuition reimbursement in, 177, 178–79
Starbucks Corp.:
boycotts of, 115, 211–12, 304
brainstorming summit at (2008), 41–42
customer experience as focus of, 27, 31–32, 41, 46
decline and transformation of (2007–2011), 24, 38–39, 41–48, 61
global expansion of, 32–33, 34, 35, 147, 283–84, 306–8
growth and success of, 31–33, 35
healthcare benefits for full- and part-time workers at, 26–27, 30, 47–48, 66, 67
investment vs. expense, 98
pressure to eliminate, 47–48, 67, 166
hiring commitment of, for military veterans and military spouses, 116–24, 132, 139, 292, 320
hiring commitment of, for opportunity youth, 238–39, 245
hiring commitment of, for refugees, 291–94, 320
initial public offering of, 150
inspiration for, xi
interior decor of stores, 41, 42
jobs created by, 77, 325
Johnson named CEO of, 304–5

loans made to coffee farmers by, 78
new products introduced by, 32, 42, 99, 145
new senior executives working in stores, 172–73
original mission statement for Il Giornale and, 25, 26, 34, 147
political activism of, 60–61, 63, 64–72
Schultz's 2008 return as CEO of, 39, 40, 41, 304
Schultz's 2017 departure from, 324–25
Seattle headquarters of, 65
shareholder meeting of (2014), 145–47
social responsibility as mission of, 34, 147
as social spaces, 31
stock options for all workers at (Bean Stock), 27–29, 30, 166, 252
as "third place," xi, 203, 279, 306, 316–17, 320–21, 325
Twitter presence of, 208–9
values of, 26, 29–31, 34, 41–42, 44, 60–61, 146–47, 211, 212
variations of beverages and, 31
see also specific topics
Starbucks Foundation, 83, 93, 291
Starbucks Reserve Roasteries, 305–8
opened in Italy, 306–8
#startsomewhere, 243
State Department, U.S., 289, 290, 292
Statue of Liberty, 288–89
Stern, David, 155
Stevenson, Bryan, 199–200, 214, 312, 313, 333
stock options at Starbucks (Bean Stock), 27–29, 30, 166, 252

Stoneman, Dorothy, 220
store managers:
as entrepreneurs, 43
four-day leadership conference for, 43–47
strategic role of, 41, 45
student loans, 172
Schultz's college education financed by, 167–68
of Starbucks partners, 167
Suboxone, 253, 258
Summer (Chinese Starbucks partner), 273
Sunshine's Health Food Store and Vegetarian Deli, Houston, 81–82
Swanson, Sarah, 29
SYPartners, 41, 317, 318
Syrian refugees, 286–87, 290

Tarr, Curtis, 101
Tatum, Beverly Daniel, 213
Tau Kappa Epsilon, 168
tax cuts, expiration of (2013), 63–65
Taylor, Blair, 196, 217, 231–32, 233
Tenpenny, Virginia, 96–97, 117–19, 291
"Transformational Agenda," 41–42
traumatic brain injuries (TBI), 132, 158
Treehouse, 127
Trujillo, Josh, 250–51
Trump, Donald, 332, 334
refugee policies of, 287–88, 289, 291, 294, 300
Twitter, 192, 207–9

Under the Bridge Community Outreach Center, 259
unemployment:
in Appalachia, 259–61
in East Liverpool, Ohio, 88–89, 94–97
impact of, 75–76
of opportunity youth, 228–34

unemployment (*cont'd*):
  Schultz's efforts to do
    something about,
    76–83
  see also job creation
Upstanders, 251, 268, 300,
  317
USA Today, 204
Usher, 240

Valdez, Beth, 178–80
Values, 25
  accountable for, 311
  actions that reflect,
    68–69, 195, 212, 284,
    291, 314 (see *healthcare
    benefits, Bean Stock,
    store closings*)
  in America, 333
  early imprinting of, 3,
    25, 84
  examples and importance
    of, 19, 25, 319
  as integral to business,
    26, 30, 44, 67, 82, 212,
    282
  parenting and, 151
Vance, J. D., 247–49
Varma, Vivek, 66–67,
  76–77, 78–80, 147,
  291, 325
  100,000 Opportunities
    Initiative and, 232
  race relations and, 196,
    309, 313, 318
  veterans and, 116, 133,
    135, 138–40, 158
veterans, *see* military
  veterans

Veterans Day:
  concert on National Mall
    on (2014), 160–62
  free brewed coffee for
    veterans or active-duty
    military personnel on,
    117, 119
Vietnam War, 105, 140, 301
  draft lottery during,
    101–4, 107
  Schultz's respect for men
    who fought in, 102–3

Walmart Foundation, 232
Walter Reed National
  Military Medical
  Center, Bethesda, Md.,
  132–38, 240
Wang Jiarui, 283
Wang Yang, 283
Warshaw, Ted, 122
Washington Post, The,
  138–39, 158, 159, 208,
  318
wealth inequality, 151–52
Weatherup, Craig, 170
West Point, U.S. Military
  Academy at:
  diversity of cadets at, 108
  history of, 105–6
  Schultz's visit and
    discussion with cadets
    at, 104–9
White House Council for
  Community Solutions,
  228–29
white nationalists, 332
  Charlottesville rallies of,
    294, 295, 299–300

will.i.am, 240
Williams, Carmen, 219–22,
  241, 310, 332
Williams, Rossann, 309,
  310, 311, 313, 321
Winfrey, Oprah, 144, 145,
  157, 161
Wong, Belinda, 272, 277,
  278, 280–81
Woods, Gina, 90, 93–94,
  143, 196
World Series of 2011, 91–93
  Create Jobs commercial
    aired during, 91,
    92–93
World War II, 104, 105,
  140–41, 161
  Holocaust and, 249–50,
    294–95
  Normandy and Schultz
    visit, 331–33

Xerox Corp., Schultz's sales
  job at, 222–28
Xiao, Chalne, 277
Xi Jinping, 283

Yamashita, Keith, 317
Yankee Stadium, Schultz
  and his father at,
  36–37
young people, *see*
  opportunity youth
YouthBuild USA, 128, 129,
  219–22, 260, 263, 310,
  332
YouthCare, 126–27, 129

Zhang, Nia, 80, 90

ABOUT THE AUTHORS

HOWARD SCHULTZ is the former chairman and chief executive officer of Starbucks Coffee Company. He grew up in Brooklyn public housing and was the first in his family to graduate college. After founding a small café business, he bought Starbucks, which grew from eleven stores to more than 28,000 under his leadership. In 2018, Starbucks ranked fifth on Fortune's list of World's Most Admired Companies. Schultz and his wife, Sheri, co-lead the Schultz Family Foundation. His other books include *Pour Your Heart Into It: How Starbucks Built a Company One Cup at a Time*; *Onward: How Starbucks Fought for Its Life without Losing Its Soul*; and *For Love of Country: What Our Veterans Can Teach Us About Citizenship, Heroism, and Sacrifice*. Schultz has been recognized for his passion to strengthen communities, and is the recipient of the Robert F. Kennedy Human Rights Ripple of Hope Award, the Horatio Alger Award, and the Rev. Theodore M. Hesburgh, C.S.C. Award for Ethics in Business from the University of Notre Dame. He and Sheri live in Seattle and have two children.

JOANNE GORDON has spent more than twenty-five years writing about work, business, and leadership. She has authored and collaborated on eight previous books, including *Onward,* with Howard Schultz, in 2011. A former writer for *Forbes,* Joanne also holds a master's degree from the Medill School of Journalism at Northwestern University.